The *Annual Review of Adult Learning and Literacy* is an important part of the Dissemination Initiative of the National Center for the Study of Adult Learning and Literacy (NCSALL). NCSALL is a collaborative effort between the Harvard Graduate School of Education and World Education, a nonprofit organization based in Boston. NCSALL's partners include The Center for Literacy Studies at The University of Tennessee, Rutgers University in New Jersey, and Portland State University in Oregon. NCSALL is funded by the Educational Research and Development Centers Program, Award Number R309B60002, as administered by the U.S. Department of Education's Office of Educational Research and Innovation through its National Institute for Postsecondary Education, Libraries, and Lifelong Learning.

NCSALL is pursuing a program of basic and applied research that is meant to improve programs that provide educational services for adults who have low literacy skills, who do not speak English, or who do not have a high school diploma. Ongoing studies include research in the areas of learner motivation, teaching and learning, staff development, and accountability.

The contents of the *Annual Review* do not necessarily represent the positions or policies of the U.S. Department of Education, nor are they endorsed by the federal government.

Annual Review of Adult Learning and Literacy

Volume 3

John Comings, Barbara Garner,
Cristine Smith, Editors

Annual Review of Adult Learning and Literacy

Volume 3

A Project of

The National Center for the Study of
Adult Learning and Literacy

JOSSEY-BASS
A Wiley Company
www.josseybass.com

Published by

 JOSSEY-BASS
A Wiley Company
989 Market Street
San Francisco, CA 94103-1741

www.josseybass.com

The material in this publication is based on work sponsored wholly or in part by the Office of Educational Research and Improvement, U.S. Department of Education, under contract number R309B60002. Its contents do not necessarily reflect the views of the department or any other agency of the U.S. government.

Jossey-Bass books and products are available through most bookstores. To contact Jossey-Bass directly, call (888) 378-2537, fax to (800) 605-2665, or visit our website at www.josseybass.com.

Substantial discounts on bulk quantities of Jossey-Bass books are available to corporations, professional associations, and other organizations. For details and discount information, contact the special sales department at Jossey-Bass.

ISBN 0-7879-6062-4   ISSN 1527-3970

FIRST EDITION
HB Printing   10 9 8 7 6 5 4 3 2 1

The Jossey-Bass

Higher and Adult Education Series

Contents

⟶ Tables, Figures, and Exhibits

Tables

Figure

Exhibits

⎯⎯ Foreword

"So many books, so little time." This phrase comes to mind whenever I'm confronted with the wide range of things to read in the library, a bookstore, or even on the bookshelves in my home. When will I ever have the time to read all the wonderful books I hear about and see around me?

As an instructor in an adult basic skills development program, I find myself voicing a similar refrain—"So many learner goals, so many instructional ideas, so many program requirements . . . yet so little time, money, space, equipment, and other resources." How can instructors reconcile the desire to meet learner needs and program goals with the challenges we face: limited funding, part-time instructors, and conflicting programmatic concerns? Is it the role of adult basic education to prepare people for the workforce, to give them access to a right they were denied (universal education), or to give them equal access to that very valuable commodity, information? Sometimes instructors' views clash with the philosophies of their programs; sometimes program philosophies clash with the mandates of program funders.

As in mathematics, these problems can be "worked" in several different ways: by trial and error; guess and check; working backward; solving an easier, related problem; eliminating wrong answers; making a systematic list; or looking for a pattern. Do these methods work? They work with math word problems, but the programmatic challenges we face as adult educators center on complex human concerns, not discrete, impersonal word problems. As instructors, we can't afford the cost of failure that attends trial and error or guess and check. Learners arrive in our programs fragile, anxious, and in need. How can we focus on the most effective instructional strategies? How can we select the most appropriate means of professional development? How can we encourage learners to take ownership of their education?

Again, there are no easy answers. I have always found the best sources of guidance to be the experience and wisdom of my peers and quality research. The term *quality research* raises questions. Where can it be found? How can I be sure that the information is valid and reliable? If I'm going to spend the limited time I have as a reader, I want to make sure that what I'm reading is the best.

This is where the *Annual Review of Adult Learning and Literacy* comes in. It's a one-stop source for the best, most current information on research, policy, and practice in adult literacy and learning. As an instructor, I value the information and analysis each volume provides on issues that I confront daily in the classroom. I need to be more knowledgeable about learning disabilities and how they may affect my students' performance. I need to have confidence that assessments of classroom activities are reliable measures of learner progress. I want the latest, research-based information on how adult learners achieve numeracy. This third volume of the *Review* contains this information and more, written by respected leaders in the field. Its contents will help me become a more effective instructor and will direct me to other valuable sources of information.

So many books, so little time? You have the solution in hand: read *this* book.

SUSAN K. COWLES

~~~ Preface

The National Center for the Study of Adult Learning and Literacy and Jossey-Bass are pleased to publish this third volume of the *Annual Review of Adult Learning and Literacy.* The *Review* serves as the journal of record for the field of adult learning and literacy. The audience for the *Review* includes the policymakers, scholars, and practitioners who are dedicated to improving the quality of practice in adult basic education (ABE), adult English for speakers of other languages (ESOL), and adult secondary education (ASE) programs.

The *Review* always begins with an overview of the significant developments in the field of ABE during the year (in this case, 2000). It concludes with a bibliography on a broad topic of current interest to the field (here, family literacy). The *Review* often presents a description of the adult literacy system of another country, but this was not possible for this volume. The country case studies will resume in Volume Four. This volume also continues several topical strands. Volumes One and Two contained chapters on reading instruction and writing instruction; this volume contains a chapter on numeracy instruction. Volume One contained a chapter on ESOL assessment, and this year the *Review* contains a chapter on ABE assessment.

In the foreword, Susan Cowles, an ABE teacher from Oregon, talks about teachers' need for research that helps them improve their practice. Since teachers in our field have so little time to access current information about topics on which to base good practice, she advocates the *Annual Review* as a reliable source.

In Chapter One, Lennox McLendon, executive director of the National Adult Education Professional Development Consortium, captures the major policy and implementation activities of the year 2000. He describes the response of the ABE field to two important events: the first was the first full year of federal funding under the Workforce Investment Act. At state and local levels, the implementation of policies that focus on outcomes was and remains a challenge. The second event was the publication of *From the Margins to the Mainstream: An Action Agenda for Literacy,* which grew out of the National Literacy Summit held in early 2000. Whether the *Agenda* proves to be an impetus for action will be reported on in next year's *Review.*

When the *Review* was established, the editors wanted it to be a place where the history of the field of ABE in the United States was recorded, but the first volume begins with coverage of the year 1998. Dr. Thomas Sticht fills in the missing centuries from Colonial America to the present in Chapter Two. Sticht identifies the beginning of federal government involvement as a literacy program for soldiers waiting out the winter at Valley Forge. Sticht uses four themes to describe the history of ABE: the role of the military; the shift of image from a self-improvement program to one of charitable education; the demands of education as a result of immigration; and a debate on whether the system should be focused on providing a liberal education or on developing human resources. This chapter surveys adult literacy in terms of the federal government's involvement. In future *Review* volumes, we hope to have chapters that look specifically at the history of adult literacy supported by other funding sources and to go deeper into some aspects of the history, such as how adult literacy has played a role in minority communities.

In Chapter Three, Mary Ann Corley and Juliana Taymans review the literature on adults with learning disabilities. They first explore the definition of *learning disability* and the prevalence of learning disabilities in the population served by the adult education and literacy system. The authors then describe the literature on adults with learning disabilities and discuss the components of effective service delivery to adults with learning disabilities. They conclude with a call for researchers, policymakers, and practitioners to pay much greater attention to learning disabilities as a barrier to success for many of the students who come to adult literacy programs.

As a follow-up to the chapter on ESOL assessment in Volume One, John Kruidenier examines ABE assessment in Chapter Four. Kruidenier begins by providing an overview of the literacy skills that ABE assessments are measuring and the tools that are used to make those measurements. He then discusses the many reasons why assessments take place. Most of the chapter is focused on a detailed description and critique of the tools now available for assessing reading and writing skills in adults, concluding with an analysis of the current status of assessment in ABE and what should be done to improve assessment.

Chapter Five is the third in a series of articles that focus on instruction. Reading was addressed in Volume One, writing in Volume Two. This volume includes a chapter on numeracy. Dave Tout and Mary Jane Schmitt begin by exploring the many terms used to describe the learning of mathematics by adults, explaining why *numeracy*—making meaning with numbers and mathematical processes—is the term they chose for their overview. They then describe adult numeracy education in the United States, numeracy in the K–12 system, and adult numeracy in several other countries, with an emphasis on trends, best practices, and research. They conclude with a call to give more attention to numeracy in adult literacy programs and to provide more resources to improve practice and pursue research.

In Chapter Six, John Sabatini, Lynda Ginsburg, and Mary Russell explore recent efforts to professionalize the field of ABE through teacher certification. This chapter begins with working definitions of the terms *professionalization* and *certification* and by highlighting the value they hold for the field of ABE. It then describes K–12 and ABE experiences with certification. Case studies from Massachusetts and Texas allow the reader to see how a certification system might work. The chapter concludes with a discussion of the obstacles to change and the ways that new policies, changes in practice, and further research can support teacher certification that leads to a more professional workforce for the field.

In Chapter Seven, Vivian Gadsden reviews current areas of interest in the growing field of family literacy. She provides a brief history of the development of the field, articulates its many varied dimensions, and brings the reader up-to-date on issues of most concern and interest to researchers and practitioners, including parent-child literacy, emergent literacy, and means of assessment and evaluation. She follows up with a bibliography of publications that provide more information on each of the areas of interest she identifies in the chapter.

As the *Review* goes to press, a new administration in Washington, D.C., has yet to identify adult literacy as a national priority, but shows some signs of interest. The new Secretary of Education, Ronald Paige, was a supporter of family literacy in his previous position as superintendent of schools in Houston, Texas, and his public statements include a call to raise the visibility of adult and family literacy within the Department of Education. The field can learn from history. During the twentieth century, attention was paid to the field of adult learning and literacy when literacy skills were needed to address a national problem. At times when large numbers of immigrants entered the country, during the two World Wars, and during the War on Poverty of the 1960s, adult learning and literacy were seen as part of the solution to these problems. In the beginning of the twenty-first century, the country needs a better-educated workforce, parents who can help their children succeed in a more demanding school system, and informed citizens who can make our political system work better. The *Review* can be a valuable source of information for those who will help the field make a case for how it can address these national issues.

JOHN COMINGS
BARBARA GARNER
CRISTINE SMITH
EDITORS

~~~ The Editors

John Comings is the director of the National Center for the Study of Adult Learning and Literacy (NCSALL) at the Harvard Graduate School of Education. Before coming to Harvard, he spent twelve years as vice president of World Education. Comings worked on adult education programs in Nepal for six years and in Indonesia for two years and has helped design and evaluate adult education programs in several countries in Asia, Africa, and the Caribbean. In the United States, he has served as the director of the State Literacy Resource Center in Massachusetts, assisted in the design of instructor training programs, and directed projects that focused on improving the teaching of both math and health in adult education programs. His research and writing has focused on the impact of adult literacy programs on reading ability and life changes such as health and family planning practices, the program factors that lead to that impact, and the issue of persistence in learning in the United States and developing countries.

Barbara Garner is director of publications for NCSALL and a senior program officer at World Education. Having held many different positions in the field of adult basic education, including teacher, staff developer, program administrator, and curriculum writer, she currently edits the NCSALL publication *Focus on Basics*.

Cristine Smith is NCSALL coordinator and a senior program officer at World Education. Smith coordinates NCSALL's dissemination initiative, is directing a four-year study on adult basic education staff development under NCSALL, and is the national coordinator for Practitioner Dissemination and Research Network run by NCSALL. She has worked on staff development issues in the field of adult literacy for twelve years.

───✻─── The Contributors

Mary Ann Corley is a principal research analyst with the American Institutes for Research in Washington, D.C., where she serves as director of the California Adult Literacy Professional Development Project. She is also founding director of the National Center for Literacy and Social Justice. As director of the National Adult Literacy and Learning Disabilities Center from 1996 to 1999, Corley led the research, development, and training on Bridges to Practice, a nationally disseminated training module for literacy providers serving adults with learning disabilities. She is an author of the Web site of the National Center for Learning Disabilities (http://www.ld.org). Former jobs include Maryland GED (general education development) administrator and adult basic education supervisor for Baltimore County Public Schools. In 1988, the Baltimore County Program she directed was named Outstanding Adult Education Program by the U.S. Secretary of Education. She has authored articles, textbooks, and professional development materials on adult literacy, with emphasis on GED preparation, workplace literacy, and learning disabilities. She serves on the board of directors of the American Association for Adult and Continuing Education, the National Association for Adults with Special Learning Needs, and the Professional Advisory Board of the National Center for Learning Disabilities.

Susan K. Cowles teaches classes in the adult basic skills development department at Linn-Benton Community College, Corvallis, Oregon. She directs the Science and Numeracy Special Collection of online resources (http://literacynet.org/sciencelincs) for the National Institute for Literacy (NIFL), and she is a founding member and past president of the Adult Numeracy Network. She conducts professional development trainings at the state, regional, and national levels, with an emphasis on topics in numeracy, technology, and the use of science as a context in which to teach basic skills. Her publications include the

NIFL Fellowship Report, *Teaching and Learning with Internet-Based Resources*, "Technology Melts Classroom Walls" in *Focus on Basics*, "Using Internet-Based Resources in Math Instruction" in *Adult Learning*, and "Science for All Americans" in *U.S. Joint Global Ocean Flux Study News*. In recognition of her work, Cowles has been selected by the National Science Foundation as a participant in the program Teachers Experiencing Antarctica and the Arctic. In January 2002, she will join a scientific research team at Palmer Station, Antarctica, for a six-week expedition studying aspects of the Antarctic coastal ecosystem (see http://tea.rice.edu).

Vivian L. Gadsden is associate professor and director of the National Center on Fathers and Families in the Graduate School of Education at the University of Pennsylvania. Formerly associate director of the National Center on Adult Literacy at Penn and project director for the families and literacy strand, Gadsden focuses her research on intergenerational family development and literacy and the implications of parent-child literacy for schooling and learning across the life-course. A significant area of her work explores the learning and literacy needs of low-income, minority fathers and examines the issues of race, poverty, and gender in home, school, and social contexts. She is working on a longitudinal, intergenerational study of literacy in African American and Puerto Rican families, focusing on the transfer of knowledge and beliefs from mothers and fathers to children; a project on the development of young, urban fathers; and a project on father-child and mother-child literacy and the uses of technology among low-income children. She has published numerous journal articles and book chapters on issues related to families, learning, race, and culture and is coeditor (with Daniel Wagner) of *Literacy Among African American Youth: Issues in Learning, Teaching, and Schooling.*

Lynda Ginsburg is a senior educational researcher at the National Center on Adult Literacy at the University of Pennsylvania, where she focuses on adult numeracy research and instruction, educational technology, and assessment and evaluation. She directs the adult literacy components of the U.S. Department of Education's NorthCentral and SouthEast Regional Technology Consortia and was the developer and executive producer for *Captured Wisdom*, a multimedia CD-ROM set highlighting effective practices of integrating technology into adult literacy instruction. She is also the external evaluator for Pennsylvania State University's Pennsylvania Workforce Investment Network project to help adult basic education providers serve employers and incumbent workers. She recently coauthored "Learning Online: Extending the Meaning of Community," available online at http://www.literacyonline.org. She is also the author of articles on adult education and tutoring in the *Encyclopedia of Mathematics Education* (2001). Ginsburg is president of the Adult Numeracy Network, is a technical adviser for the Equipped for the Future Assessment Framework Consortium, and sits on the advisory board for National Institute for Literacy's Literacy Information and Communication System Numeracy and Science Special Collection.

John Kruidenier is an education consultant based in Bryn Mawr, Pennsylvania, specializing in literacy and technology issues. Recent projects include work on a summary of adult basic education reading instruction research for the National Institute for Literacy. He has worked as a researcher at the Harvard Graduate School of Education, the IBM T. J. Watson Research Center, and the University of Pennsylvania. In addition to private practice, his teaching experience includes work at the high school level as a learning disabilities specialist and at the adult level as an instructor at the Harvard Reading Laboratory for Adults. He is the author of several papers and conference presentations on adult literacy, the literacy development of students with learning disabilities, literacy instruction, the uses of educational technology, text processing, and literacy courseware.

Lennox L. McLendon is the executive director of the National Adult Education Professional Development Consortium, the policy and professional development arm of the Adult Education State Directors. His more than thirty years of experience in the field of adult literacy include teaching adult basic education (ABE), adult high school, English for speakers of other languages, and preparation for the certificate of general educational development (GED). He spent twelve years as a state director of adult education and represented state directors for nine years on the National Coalition for Literacy, serving two years as chair. He is on the faculty of the ABE graduate program at Virginia Commonwealth University in Richmond. His recent publications include *State Adult Education Management and Leadership Functions: A Self-Assessment for Adult Education State Directors* and a book coauthored with Kathi Polis titled *The Adult Education State Director's*

Going to Scale Guide for Planning, Implementing, and Evaluating State Program Improvement Initiatives.

Mary Russell is a senior educational researcher at the National Center on Adult Literacy at the University of Pennsylvania. She is the project manager of the English Literacy/Civics professional development project, a Web-based system that will address the professional development needs of the nation's teachers of English for speakers of other languages (ESOL) for adults. She is a cofacilitator for the Professional Development Kit team and project. She also manages Project CONNECT, which is developing distance learning materials to allow ESOL learners unlimited opportunities to access instruction through the Web. She has done research and program evaluation in areas related to classroom practice and professional development. Her most recent publications are "Learning Online: Extending the Meaning of Community," which is available online at http://www.literacyonline.org; "Understanding Assumptions About Teaching Writing to Adults," *Focus on Basics,* January 2000; and *Teaching by Design: New Models of Professional Development for Teachers,* forthcoming. She is a founding member of the Adult Literacy Professional Development Association and is secretary of the American Educational Research Association Special Interest Group on Adult Literacy and Adult Education.

John P. Sabatini is a senior educational researcher at the National Center on Adult Literacy (NCAL) at the University of Pennsylvania. He has conducted research, development, and evaluation in educational technology, cognitive psychology, reading acquisition and disabilities, and assessment. He is a designer of online assessment and instruction products in the LiteracyLink Star Schools project. He also designs and conducts research and formative evaluation for other NCAL research and development projects, including LiteracyLink, the Professional Development Kit project, Project CONNECT, and the English as a Second Language/CivicsLink. He is chair of the Research Committee of the National Coalition of Literacy and technical and research adviser to the Equipped for the Future Assessment Framework Consortium, the General Education Development (GED) Testing Service, the National Education Goals Panel, and the National Assessments of Adult Literacy. He is also a member of the NIFL/NCSALL Reading Research Work Group. He collaborated with Richard L. Venezky on the *Study of Adult Reading Acquisition* and is coediting with him a themed issue on adult reading and disabilities for the Scientific Society for Study of Reading. A recent publication is "Teacher Perspectives on the Adult Education Profession: National Survey Findings About an Emerging Profession," which is available online at http://www.literacyonline.org.

Mary Jane Schmitt is codirector of the National Science Foundation-funded Extending Mathematical Power (EMPower) Project at TERC in Cambridge, Massachusetts. The goal of EMPower is to extend mathematics reform to adults and out-of-school youth by building on standards-based K–12 math curricula. She also serves as coprincipal investigator for the Parent Involvement Project at the Massachusetts Department of Education, where she previously served on the project staff of the Statewide Systemic Initiative known as PALMS (Partnerships Advancing the Learning of Mathematics and Science). She has led the development of the ABE Math Standards Project and the National Institute for Literacy-funded Adult Numeracy Network *Framework for Adult Numeracy Standards.* She cochaired the first national Conference on Adult Mathematical Literacy (1994) and cofounded the Adult Numeracy Network (1995). She has served on the board of directors of Adults Learning Mathematics: A Research Forum and is a member of the Adult Literacy and Lifeskills Survey numeracy team.

Thomas G. Sticht is an international consultant in adult basic education. From 1983 to 1999 he was president and senior scientist of Applied Behavioral and Cognitive Sciences, Inc. He has taught at Harvard University and the University of British Columbia and is a recipient of the International Reading Association's Albert J. Harris Award for research on learning disabilities, a member of the Reading Hall of Fame, and UNESCO's International Literacy Prize Jury. He served on the National Governors Association's Advisory Group for National Education Goal 6 (adult literacy), the California Workforce Literacy Task Force, the National Commission on Working Women, the National Commission on Testing and Public Policy, and the Secretary of Labor's Commission on Achieving Necessary Skills (SCANS). In 1997, the *Reading Research Quarterly* reported that his research on adult literacy was one of the thirteen most influential lines of research on literacy in the last thirty years.

Juliana M. Taymans is a professor of special education at George Washington University in Washington, D.C. She is lead faculty member for the transition special education program and is active in teacher preparation. Currently, she serves as special education adviser for an urban partnership program between George Washington University and the District of Columbia Public Schools. She is a trainer and consultant in adult education for individuals with learning disabilities and attention deficit disorder. She is coauthor of *Unlocking Potential: A Post Secondary Guide for Individuals with LD and AD/HD* (2001).

Dave Tout started out as a secondary school mathematics and science teacher, and has specialized in numeracy and basic math in adult basic education since 1978, working within a range of programs in technical and further education colleges, universities, community education, adult multicultural education, and industry in Australia. He has had wide experience not only in teaching and training but also in working at state and national levels in research, assessment, curriculum and materials development, management, and policy development. He has been involved as a writer on most of Australia's significant adult numeracy curriculum and assessment tools and has helped to produce a range of teaching and training materials, including *Measuring Up: An Interactive Multimedia Computer Resource for Numeracy Learners, I Can Do That, Numeracy on the Line,* and *Adult Numeracy Teaching: Making Meaning in Mathematics.* He is the regional manager of and a numeracy consultant for Language Australia: The National Languages and Literacy Institute of Australia.

Annual Review of Adult Learning and Literacy

Volume 3

CHAPTER ONE

The Year 2000 in Review

Lennox L. McLendon

———

I f the year 1999 was dominated by the intense efforts
of the federal government to establish guidelines for compliance with
the Workforce Investment Act (WIA) of 1998, the year 2000 was dominated by the field's efforts to implement plans to meet those guidelines. In addition to engaging in this time- and labor-intensive work,
the field witnessed four significant events that influenced adult basic
education (ABE) across the country: a national summit to develop an
action agenda for the field; developments in federal appropriations,
including the emergence of English literacy and civics funding in state
grants; rekindling of discourse among the parties involved in national
research and evaluation projects; and changes in leadership at the national level. This chapter provides an overview of these events.

CONTINUING IMPLEMENTATION OF
THE WORKFORCE INVESTMENT ACT

The year 2000 marked the second year of WIA implementation, and
federal and state adult educators continued to grapple with their new
roles. Under previous federal legislation requirements, practitioners

at the state and local levels had been responsible for following a some-times complex set of national regulations. The WIA limited federal regulation and, in its place, asked states and local practitioners to set performance standards, to collect and report data on the extent to which students meet the standards, and to improve the quality of pro-gram services. In addition to the performance standards established to comply with the WIA, the two major literacy volunteer networks, Literacy Volunteers of America and Laubach Literacy Action, accred-ited the first local programs during 2000 using their own performance standards.

Initially, the field reacted positively to the initiative, but state di-rectors quickly learned that it can be much easier—if less rewarding—to enforce someone else's regulations than to create your own plan and follow it. Many found themselves reading back over the ideals pro-posed in their state plans and contemplating the harsh realities of putting them into operation, especially given that 89 percent of their teachers are part-time, that they depend on thousands of volunteers to provide significant services, and that many of the directors them-selves also provide vocational education, supervise federal programs, and perform other duties on top of their ABE responsibilities. In ad-dition to the challenge of training staff to comply with the rigors of the new system, there is the inherent challenge of keeping track of a student population that is often transient and of whom 40 percent are considered to be limited English proficient (LEP). Social Security numbers allow for data matching with employment systems, but many LEP students don't have Social Security numbers. Survey follow-up with undereducated native-born and LEP students has met with lim-ited success. Though many adult educators nationwide still support the intentions of the WIA, they remain challenged to provide the data Congress needs to confirm that adult basic education is having an im-pact on students' postenrollment employment and postsecondary par-ticipation nationally.

Another WIA implementation task facing state and local adult ed-ucators was the establishment of standards for the three performance indicators in the law: literacy level advancement; postprogram activi-ties in job training, job advancement, and postsecondary education; and secondary credentials (high school diploma or certificate of Gen-eral Educational Development [GED]). Standards came to be defined based on the student's intent for enrollment. For example, students who enrolled in order to get a job fell into the cohort intending to achieve that goal. This process included having each student claim a clear goal upon enrollment and following up on that student after the program to determine if the goal had been achieved. Neither the goal-setting process nor the follow-up procedures had been in place prior to passage of the WIA, and state and local programs committed themselves to developing the procedures and training practitioners to provide the data, analyze the performance reports, and make program adjustments at state and local levels to improve the quality of the services—quite a feat for the first year of operation.

The challenge of meeting the provisions of the WIA was further complicated by the high turnover rate in state director positions. During 1999 and 2000, nearly half of the state director positions were vacated and refilled. Thus, in 2000, half of the directors were relatively new to the job. As a result, they were faced with learning their new assignments while preparing the local programs for a difficult transition from regulatory to performance-driven systems. Did the WIA create this turnover? Or was it a coincidence? Was it easier to move on to another job than to design and implement a performance-based system? Will the influx of new directors benefit or limit the transition to the WIA system? These questions can be answered only in time to come.

NATIONAL LITERACY SUMMIT

In 1989, Forrest P. Chisman of the Southport Institute for Policy Analysis and Associates published the document *Jump Start: The Federal Role in Adult Literacy,* which was to serve as a road map for advancing the ABE field. Much activity then resulted in a refocused National Literacy Act of 1991, a document that by its nature was limited to the national level. The act had a limited impact on state and local governments, which had no such plan for themselves.

A decade later, a new road map was needed, and this time the agenda was to activate the field at the national, state, and local levels. The National Institute for Literacy engaged a group of national partners supported by planning grants from Time-Warner and the Lila Wallace Foundation to take on this task. The planning partners included the Division of Adult Education and Literacy of the U.S. Department of Education (DAEL/DOE), the National Adult Education Professional Development Consortium (NAEPDC), the National Center for the Study of Adult Learning and Literacy (NCSALL), the National Coalition for Literacy (NCL), and the Commission on Adult

Basic Education (CoABE). Their goal was to engage practitioners from all sectors of the profession in the development of an action agenda for ABE. With this agenda in hand, the diverse field would be able to speak with one voice and move forward.

In February 2000, 150 ABE practitioners and partners met in Washington, D.C., to craft a draft agenda. The resulting document was disseminated across the country, stimulating a host of local, state, and regional get-togethers to refine the agenda. These responses were integrated into one document, *From the Margins to the Mainstream: An Action Agenda for Literacy* (National Institute for Literacy, 2000), which was published in summer 2000 and launched at a congressional event in September. The event featured presentations by former U.S. Democratic senator Paul Simon of Illinois, Reps. William Goodling (R-Pennsylvania) and Tom Sawyer (D-Ohio), and a panel of partners Web-cast from the House Chamber across the country. The national action agenda, focusing on three themes—resources, access, and quality—was distributed across the country with group discussion guides (Nash & Smith, 2000) as a call to action for state and local groups to embrace the agenda and develop action steps to move it forward. The agenda focused on three major areas—resources, access, and quality—and a number of strategies were discussed to address the needs associated with each. The goal was to prompt every local, state, and national ABE and literacy organization to adopt one or a number of these strategies as a part of their year's work. Together the field would then advance the profession toward increased resources, greater access, and improved quality of service.

In the fall, the Division of Adult Education and Literacy of the U.S. Department of Education and the National Institute for Literacy took the lead in providing funds for the National Coalition for Literacy to hire staff members to support national, state, and local engagement in advancing that agenda. Contrary to the Jump Start experience, the goal is to engage practitioners at the local and state levels as well as at the national level, supporting hundreds of organizations in identifying action agenda items they will commit to advancing.

Adult basic education is a rich conglomeration of public and private organizations and agencies at the national, state, local, and community levels. Because of that diversity, the field has suffered from disjointed vision and advocacy. It is hoped that the action agenda will help the field speak with one voice to move itself forward.

APPROPRIATIONS

The National Coalition for Literacy has set a federal ABE appropriations goal of $1 billion. During 2000, progress was made toward that goal. Congress debated through October, past the presidential election in November, and, finally, in December approved the fiscal year (FY) 2001 funding. A surge of $90 million brought the state grants for ABE and literacy past the half-billion-dollar mark to $540 million. A large part of that surge was contributed by the $70 million for English Literacy/Civics (EL/Civics) Education. The final FY 2001 appropriations are listed in Table 1.1.

One of the big winners in the appropriations process, as indicated in the table, was Even Start. Congressman Goodling began the process with the introduction of HR 3222, Literacy Involves Families Together (LIFT), a family literacy bill. Typical of Congress's orientation in fall 2000, LIFT merged bills of similar ilk to produce more comprehensive legislation. Many of the LIFT components were included in new language for FY 2001, which included renaming the Even Start program as the "William F. Goodling Even Start Family Literacy Program," after its founder. Not only was funding increased by $100 million, it was approved for another five years.

A second winner in the appropriations process was the EL/Civics Initiative funds, which more than doubled from $25.5 million in FY

ABE and Literacy Program	Final FY 2001 Appropriation (Dollars in Millions)	FY 2000 Appropriation (Dollars in Millions)
State grants for adult education and literacy	540	450
National leadership activities	14	14
National Institute for Literacy	6.5	6
Prison literacy	5	5
Incarcerated youth offenders	17	14
Reading Excellence Act	286	260
Even Start	250	150
Community technology centers	65	32.5

Table 1.1. Fiscal Year 2001 Appropriations.

2000 to $70 million for FY 2001 as a part of the State Grants for Adult Education and Literacy. Thus most of the $90 million increase in state grants came from this designation.

Contrary to the WIA climate, in which it was thought desirable to avoid federal set-asides and let the states decide how to target funds, a movement emerged in the Clinton administration to address English literacy needs throughout the country. In FY 1999, the U.S. Department of Education Division of Adult Education and Literacy managed a national discretionary grant program for EL/Civics services for the provision of "integrated English literacy and civics education services to immigrants and other limited English proficient populations." The National Coalition for Literacy took the lead in getting the FY 2000 funds—$25.5 million—assigned to the state grants. To avoid small grants, a minimum grant was established and, as a result, thirteen small states did not receive funds.

During summer 2000, discussions began regarding the provisions for EL/Civics in FY 2001. An ad hoc coalition of a dozen or so interest groups—including representatives from several Asian and Spanish-speaking organizations as well as the NCL, the Center on Applied Linguistics, and NAEPDC—met to discuss the expansion of EL/Civics funds and services. They felt that funds should go directly to community-based organizations rather than through the state grants. The resulting position papers and discussions solidified the support for the EL/Civics efforts.

As support for expansion of EL/Civics grew, the ABE state directors, who supported the congressional preference to continue channeling funds through state grants, proposed three principles to guide the discussion:

• Ensure that EL/Civics funding is an additional allocation to states and not supported from limited existing state grants.

• Avoid small grants to ensure that each grant is sufficient to have an impact on the state and will make it worthwhile for the state to run a competitive solicitation process.

• Ensure that no state receives an FY 2001 grant below its FY 2000 level.

As the year 2000 came to a close, the 2001 budget was approved, increasing funding for EL/Civics to $70 million, including provisions for each state to receive a minimum grant of $60,000.

DISCOURSE BETWEEN RESEARCH AND EVALUATION PROJECTS

One item of consensus in the field is the limited funding for ABE research and evaluation projects. Furthermore, concern prevails regarding the coordination and collaboration among the few projects that are funded from the DOE National Programs, the Planning and Evaluation Service (PES), and the Office of Educational Research and Improvement (OERI), as well as the National Institute for Literacy projects. To rectify this long-standing concern, OERI hosted a colloquium of the currently funded projects, including the following:

• Evaluation of Effective Adult Basic Education Programs and Practices, Judith A. Alamprese, Abt Associates

• "What Works" Study for Adult ESL Literacy Students, Larry Condelli, American Institutes for Research

• Pilot Study of the Crossroads Café Program, Annette M. Zehler, Development Associates

• The Adult Literacy Classroom as a Social System, Hal Beder, NCSALL-Rutgers University

• National Evaluation of the Even Start Family Literacy Program, Robert St. Pierre, Abt Associates

• Adult Learner Persistence Study, John Comings, NCSALL

• Adult Reading Components Study (ARCS), John Strucker, NCSALL

• Longitudinal Study of Adult Learning, Steve Reder, NCSALL

Two state directors, a representative from the national volunteer community, as well as the executive director of the NAEPDC also attended. The resulting frank discussions provided opportunities for project staff members to compare issues and findings, for state directors to hear about the progress of each project, and for researchers to better prepare their findings for dissemination through the state directors and to the field. OERI intends to continue the sessions to ensure that the evaluation and research projects inform each other and build on each other's work as well as to give representatives from the field an opportunity to inform researchers as to how to best prepare their products for use in the field.

DEPARTURE OF KEY PLAYERS

It would be hard to overstate the contribution that Rep. Goodling has made to education in the United States. A former public school teacher and principal as well as the founder of Even Start, Goodling served twenty-six years in the House. As chair of the House Education and Workforce Committee, Goodling was an ardent supporter of family literacy and adult basic education. His focus on "quality not quantity" and "products not process" is reflected in the Workforce Investment Act's delegation of decision making and accountability to the states. In recognition of his devotion to education, Congress established the William Goodling Institute for Research in Family Literacy at Penn State University. The mission of the institute is to carry on his tradition of documenting the impact of family literacy programs. The Goodling Institute is a partner with the National Center for Family Literacy and the National Institute for Literacy.

Goodling was a champion for the cause of adult literacy in the House of Representatives, just as Senators James Jeffords (I-Vermont) and Edward Kennedy (D-Massachusetts) have been in the Senate. In Congress, the term *champion* refers to a member who believes in and works for a given cause, who proposes supplemental funding for the cause when money is available, and who fights for it when funds are jeopardized. Goodling will be hard to replace.

With the change in administration at the end of 2000, the field saw the departure of another key supporter, Dr. Patricia "Trish" McNeal, as assistant secretary of the Office of Vocational and Adult Education. McNeal was the most accessible assistant secretary in decades. She was present at many discussions with state and local practitioners at critical times during her administration. She challenged the field to move forward and moved mountains to give states support for their work in adult literacy. She was a model for public servants at all levels.

Another important era came to an end in the leadership of the Adult Education State Directors. A decade ago, this group established the National Adult Education Professional Development Consortium to provide for the policy and professional development needs of state directors and their staff members. Judy Koloski, formerly state director of ABE in Maryland and executive director of the American Association of Adult and Continuing Education, became the first NAEPDC executive director. She provided a single point of contact on ABE issues for Congress and the White House and provided significant national leadership for nearly a decade. She retired in 1999.

SUMMARY

In the year 2000, adult educators at the national, state, and local levels got down to the practical details of developing a new working relationship, with the federal office now having significantly less regulatory authority and the states having significantly more responsibility for their practices. The year 2001 holds much potential. The degree to which state and local adult educators adopt the action agenda in *Margins to the Mainstream* will determine not only the depth and breadth of the advancement of the field but also the unanimity of its voice. Adult basic education is a rich conglomeration of public and private organizations and agencies at the state, national, and community levels. Without a common focus, this diverse field's vision and advocacy can become disjointed. The action agenda holds out the promise for the field to speak in a concerted voice that could well have a positive impact on the appropriations process in the coming year, increasing the possibility that the National Coalition on Literacy's $1 billion goal will become a reality. The field could benefit from the OERI's ongoing support for national research and evaluation collaboration. The limited research funds are served well by that leadership. A challenge in 2001 is the search for a new champion in the House Education and Workforce Committee. On the Senate side, Sens. Jeffords and Kennedy remain committed to adult literacy issues. However, the void in the House will limit the success of policy work on the Hill.

The year 2000 has established a number of opportunities and a few hurdles. Under the banner of *Margins to the Mainstream* and the leadership of the National Coalition, ABE's multiple layers and levels have the unique opportunity to focus on promoting mutual interests and resolving organizational differences. The degree to which the field continues to advance will be a reflection of the degree to which that focused effort occurs.

References

Chisman, F. (1989, January). *Jump start: The federal role in adult literacy.* Southport, CT: Southport Institute for Policy Analysis.

Nash, A., & Smith, C. (2000). *Summit action agenda: Group discussion and planning meeting guide.* Cambridge, MA: National Center for the Study of Adult Learning and Literacy.

National Institute for Literacy. (2000). *From the margins to the mainstream: An action agenda for literacy.* Washington, DC: Author.

CHAPTER TWO

The Rise of the Adult Education and Literacy System in the United States: 1600–2000

Thomas G. Sticht

In the last decade of the twentieth century nearly 40 million people enrolled in the programs of the U.S. Adult Education and Literacy System (AELS)[1] (Sticht, 1998). What is even more remarkable than the sheer number of enrollees is the fact that these adults were for the most part members of the very population identified in numerous studies and reports as being unlikely to seek such education (Quigley, 1997, pp. 191–217; Beder, 1991, pp. 67–99).

Studies of participation in adult education generally note that when it comes to education, the "rich get richer," meaning that those people with the most education are the ones who seek out more education (Kim & Creighton, 2000). But of the more than 31 million enrollees in the AELS from 1992 through 1999, 7.9 million were the working poor, more than 3.3 million were welfare recipients, 9.3 million were unemployed, and 2.2 million were incarcerated (U.S. Department of Education, 2000). More than two-thirds of the 15 million enrollees during 1992–1996 had not completed twelve years of education or received a high school diploma, and more than 3.4 million were immigrants (U.S. Department of Education, 1998).[2]

With roots stretching back some four hundred years to the religious instruction, vocational apprenticeships, and common schools of the original thirteen colonies and to the first federal involvement in adult literacy education during the Revolutionary War, the AELS experienced a huge growth spurt just some thirty-six years ago with the passage of the Economic Opportunity Act of 1964. This act, which provided federal laws and funding for adult basic education (ABE), was followed by the Adult Education Act of 1966, which moved ABE from the poverty programs of the Economic Opportunity Act to the education programs of the U.S. Department of Education (DOE) (Rose, 1991, pp. 14–18).

Today the AELS is an adult education delivery system funded in part by federal monies appropriated by the U.S. Congress and in larger part by the states and localities. In 1998, the DOE estimated that of some four thousand federal grant recipients, 59 percent were local education agencies (public schools), 15 percent were postsecondary institutions (mainly community colleges), 14 percent were community-based organizations, 4 percent were correctional institutions, and 8 percent were "others" (including libraries, literacy councils, private industry councils, and sheltered workshops) (U.S. Department of Education, 1998).

This chapter provides a broad-brush history of the emergence of the present-day AELS in the United States over the last four hundred years.[3] Exhibit 2.1 provides some historical signposts for keeping track of the four-century span of the chapter. The first column presents important dates associated with the historical events listed in the second column, which are those events traditionally given as critical in general, popularized histories of the United States (such as Davis, 1995). Finally, the third column presents some—but far from all—of the significant events, institutions, and people in the history of the rise of the AELS.

In the discussion that follows, the progression from Colonial to contemporary times follows a path from general to specific, reflecting the emerging nature of the AELS. That is, the earlier history of adult education is characterized by a broad array of educational activities engaged in by adults with a wide range of educational and socioeconomic backgrounds. Over the decades, it becomes possible to discern people, organizations, and events having a more direct influence on the eventual formulation and passage of the Adult Basic Education Section of the Economic Opportunity Act of 1964 and the subsequent

Date	Historical Event	AELS Development
Seventeenth & Eighteenth Centuries		
1607–1732	Original thirteen colonies established over 125 years: Virginia, 1607; Massachusetts, 1620; New York, 1626; Maryland, 1633; Rhode Island and Connecticut, 1636; Delaware and New Hampshire, 1638; North Carolina, 1653; South Carolina, 1663; New Jersey, 1664; Pennsylvania, 1682; Georgia, 1732	Nonformal adult learning in homes, churches, taverns, stores, town meetings; formal education in apprenticeships and by commercial teachers of writing and other skills. Founding of colleges, public (common) schools, private libraries, and other institutional foundations of the present AELS.
1775–1783	American Revolution	Washington at Valley Forge initiates first federal government adult literacy education activity and directs U.S. Army chaplains to teach basic skills to enlisted troops.
1776	Declaration of Independence, July 4	
1783	Treaty of Paris ends Revolutionary War	
1789	George Washington becomes first President of the United States	U.S. Navy employs schoolmasters and teachers in 1799.
Nineteenth Century		
1812–1815	War of 1812 with England	Navy regulations of 1802 direct chaplains to teach writing and arithmetic to sailors.
1846–1848	Mexican War; United States spans the East Coast to the West Coast; "Manifest Destiny"	Public school system begins to emerge; evening schools for adults; growth of institutions for the "diffusion of knowledge" (libraries, women's literary clubs).
1861–1865	Civil War	National Education Association formed in 1857.
1865–1877	Reconstruction	Freedman's Bureau established for educating former slaves.
		Jane Addams founds Hull-House for immigrant education in 1889.

Twentieth Century

	Cora Wilson Stewart starts Moonlight Schools in 1911, stimulates state and national illiteracy campaigns.
1914–1918	World War I	U.S. military develops group tests of intelligence for literates and illiterates.
	American Association for Adult Education formed in 1924.
1929–1941	Great Depression and the New Deal	The Civilian Conservation Corps and Works Progress Administration programs of the New Deal fund adult literacy education at the federal level.
1941–1945	World War II	U.S. Army trains illiterates and creates GED tests during World War II.
1950–1975	Korean War; Vietnam War	Laubach Literacy International founded in 1955. Literacy Volunteers of America founded in 1962.
1964–2000	The Great Society and the War on Poverty	Economic Opportunity Act of 1964; Adult Education Act of 1966 formalizes federal and state roles in the AELS.

Exhibit 2.1. Signposts in the Development of the Adult Education and Literacy System in the Context of U.S. History.

passing of the Adult Education Act of 1966, which provided the federal organizing framework for the present AELS.

During my research for this review, four themes emerged that reveal critical social forces involved in the formation of the AELS: the role of the U.S. military, the movement for self-improvement and charitable activities, immigration, and the movement for a liberal education that makes "good citizens" versus human resources development for economic productivity.

1. *The U.S. military.* From the Revolutionary War to contemporary times, the U.S. military has played a foundational role in the development of the AELS, providing literacy instruction to hundreds of thousands of young adults and securing information on the language and literacy abilities of adults that has stimulated political action on behalf of adult literacy education.

2. *A shift from self-improvement to charitable education.* From the middle of the nineteenth century to the middle of the twentieth century, adult education went from being regarded primarily as a middle-class activity for self-improvement in the wake of a flood of new scientific and technical knowledge to being regarded as a charitable activity for the benefit of the undereducated and mostly lower economic classes.

3. *Immigration.* A continuous, albeit uneven, stream of immigrants has brought millions of adults into the nation. Beginning in the late nineteenth century and continuing to the end of the twentieth century, immigration has created a persistent need for a system of adult education that can provide instruction in the English language and knowledge of American culture.

4. *Liberal education versus human resources development.* Related to the second and third themes, particularly during the second half of the twentieth century, has been the conflict between those individuals and organizations favoring a national adult education system focused on broad, liberal education for all adults and those favoring a "human resources development" point of view, seeking education for the least well-educated adults to enable them to contribute to the economic productivity of the nation.

In addition to these four themes, two topics, concerning the definitions of *adulthood* and *literacy,* are especially salient across time in the area of adult literacy education. The history of adult education is complicated by changing ideas about who is considered an adult. In Colonial times, according to Long (1975), girls and boys aged fourteen years were likely to be considered adults. Using U.S. Census Bureau definitions of adulthood and literacy, Soltow and Stevens (1981, p. 5) reported that in 1840, 1850, and 1860 census enumerators were interested in the literacy skills of "adults" twenty years or older, while in 1870 "adults" were ten years or older. Cook (1977) reported that from 1900 through 1940, persons aged ten years or older were used to calculate illiteracy statistics for the U.S. Census. From 1950 through 1970, "illiteracy" or "functional illiteracy" was estimated for those aged fourteen years or older and was based on the highest number of school grades completed.

The definition of *adulthood* in government regulations regarding adult literacy education has changed only a little over the last half-century. Under the Economic Opportunity Act of 1964, ABE was to be provided for those eighteen years or older. In 1970, amendments to the Adult Education Act dropped the definition of an adult to age sixteen or older (Rose, 1991, p. 19). This age of sixteen or older has persisted to the present as the definition of adults qualified for programs funded under Title II of the Workforce Investment Act of 1998. Currently, the number of adults qualifying for adult education is based on U.S. Census data giving the number of adults sixteen years or older, out of school, who have not completed twelve years of education.

In most studies of the history of literacy in the early United States, the term *literacy* has been more or less understood as the ability to read or write. Studies of the prevalence of literacy among adults during Colonial and Revolutionary times have used indicators such as signatures on wills, marriage licenses, military records, or other legal documents to infer the prevalence of literacy (Long, 1975; Lockridge, 1974; Gubb, 1990).

During the 1800s, U.S. Census enumerators asked respondents about the number of adults unable to read or write, and in 1870 they asked, "Can you read and can you write?" (Soltow & Stevens, 1981). From 1900 to 1930, the Census asked people whether they could read or write in their native language (reading was always considered the less difficult of the two literacy skills, and those taught to read were often not taught to write) (Long, 1975). After 1930 questions about literacy were dropped and people were instead asked to give the highest grade in school they had completed (Cook, 1977). At different times during this thirty-year period adults with less than three, four, five, or eight years of education were considered "functionally illiterate," a higher standard of literacy than that indicated by signatures or the simple ability to read or write (Cook, 1977).

In addition to changing definitions of literacy, it should be noted that there has been a shift across time in how people who are not literate are addressed. In the earlier years of the growing nation and up through the mid-1980s, it was common to talk about "illiterates" or "functional illiterates," and organizations gave themselves names like National Illiteracy Crusade and Commission on Illiteracy (Nelms, 1997). But in the last decade of the twentieth century, the community of literacy workers has been more likely to talk about literacy and degrees of literacy than about illiteracy and to address the development of literacy rather than the "stamping out of illiteracy" (Sticht, 1984). In this chapter I retain the common usage for the time period under discussion.

THE COLONIAL PERIOD AND EARLY
NATIONAL PERIODS: 1600–1799

Adult education during the Colonial and early National periods included apprenticeships for young adults aged fourteen and older as well as a number of opportunities for learning reading, writing, mathematics, and a variety of trades and crafts in commercial schools (Long, 1975; Cremin, 1970; Knowles, 1962).

The foundations for our present-day public school system were laid early in the Colonial period. A Massachusetts law of 1647 provided "(1) That every town having fifty householders should at once appoint a teacher of reading and writing, and provide for his wages in such manner as the town might determine; and (2) That every town having one hundred householders must provide a grammar school to fit youths for the university, under a penalty of 5 pounds for failure to do so" (Knowles, 1977, p. 6). This basic arrangement for a common school set the stage for the subsequent emergence of the tax-supported school system that provides for the largest number of programs in the contemporary AELS.

Present-day public libraries had their origins in the private collections of well-to-do colonists. Some of these collections were donated to towns for general use by their citizens and some parish libraries were available to the public. However, the largest impact on library use came from the organization of "subscription libraries" established by a voluntary association of individuals who contributed to a general fund for the purchase of books made available to association members. The first such library was established in 1731 by Benjamin Franklin, who later established the Junto, a club whose members studied and discussed intellectual concerns such as morals, politics, and natural philosophy (science and technology) as a form of self-improvement (Knowles, 1977, pp. 7–11; Kett, 1994). These early library and discussion groups provided a foundation for the later emergence of public libraries as well as institutions such as the Lyceums of the nineteenth century. Early on, these institutions played active roles in the liberal education of adults for the purpose of self-improvement. Later, they also began to provide basic literacy instruction for many of the least literate adults in what became referred to as "second chance" or "remedial" education rather than "self-improvement."

Though the education of children in reading and writing was first expected of parents and later of common schools, the teaching of reading and writing to adults was generally left to enterprising tutors and various commercial, proprietary schools that taught vocational as well as basic literacy skills. Tutors advertised in Colonial newspapers, often noting that they taught children during the day and adults in the evening. Between 1733 and 1774, more than four hundred such advertisements were published in the *South Carolina Gazette,* and many similar notices appeared in newspapers in Virginia, North Carolina, and Georgia (Gordon & Gordon, 1990, p. 252). Between 1765 and 1767, one William Elphinistan advertised for students in the *New York Mercury,* offering to teach "persons of both sexes, from 12 years of age and upwards, who never wrote before, to write a good legible hand, in 7 weeks one hour per day, at home or abroad" (p. 246).

While there is scant evidence regarding the extent to which adults learned to read and write during this time, Galenson (1979) used occupational records for samples of native-born colonialists and found that minors were less literate than older workers, which suggested to him that adults engaged in some literacy learning. By comparing the signatures of girls and widows on legal documents, Main (1991) estimated that in the period 1673 to 1694, 13 percent of girls signed documents of guardianship, while 32 percent of women signed documents of deeds (p. 585, Table 4). In another study estimating literacy learning in adulthood, Main presents data comparing the signing of guardianship papers by children with the signing of deeds by adults born in the same time period. About 45 percent of girls born between 1700 and 1745 signed letters of guardianship, while 60 percent of women born during those years signed deeds (p. 582). These studies led Main to suggest that some females learned to write as adults during and directly following the Colonial period and National periods.

If the ability to write one's name (rather than just making a mark on a document) is evidence of literacy, then, excluding American Indians and African Americans, there was near universal literacy, in excess of 80–90 percent, for both men and women by the end of the eighteenth century (Perlmann & Shirley, 1991). Of course, all such studies of literacy during these early years of the nation depend on samples of adults who do not represent the entire adult population of the colonies and so are contentious on the basis of sampling bias. For instance, Herndon (1996) presents data from documents of "transients" (nonpropertied persons) showing that, just as in contemporary times, literacy rates for New England's poor, including whites, American Indians, and African Americans, were considerably lower than the rates estimated on the basis of property document signatures. Kaestle (1991a) provides a critique of literacy estimates that rely on the signing of documents such as military records and deeds.

One of the more significant events in adult literacy education during the later eighteenth century was the first commitment of government resources for teaching literacy skills to troops of the Continental Army. In 1777, General George Washington asked the Continental Congress to provide funds for a small traveling press that could be used to write about the war (Houle, Burr, Hamilton, & Yale, 1947). While this request was tabled and eventually forgotten (p. 13), General Washington's desire to communicate with his troops in writing led him to direct chaplains to teach the soldiers at Valley Forge basic literacy skills (Weinert, 1979).

By the end of the eighteenth century, the Navy employed schoolmasters and teachers to teach reading and writing to seamen (Langley, 1967). Navy regulations published in 1802 included among the chaplain's duties the following requirement: "He shall perform the duty of a school-master; and to that end he shall instruct the midshipmen and volunteers, in writing, arithmetic, and navigation, and in whatsoever may contribute to render them proficients" (Burr, 1939, p. 111). As these and later examples illustrate, from the very beginnings of the United States of America, the military has played a key role in the emergence and development of the AELS. The military continued to contribute to the AELS by educating former slaves who served in the Union Army during the Civil War.

THE ANTEBELLUM, CIVIL WAR, AND RECONSTRUCTION PERIODS: 1800–1899

Kaestle (1991a) observed that "One of the 'causes' of higher literacy rates, in a sense, is higher literacy rates. For example, as more people become literate, the amount of fiction circulating commercially will increase and newspapers will become cheaper; in a society where more reading material is available, there is more motivation for people to learn to read and to use their skills. If schools turn out more highly literate people, this will, in turn, affect the job structure, which can affect the future demands placed on schools. Thus one of the effects of literacy at the societal level is that it fosters more literacy" (pp. 28–29).

The rapid assent of literacy in the United States might well be traced to the influence of the writings of those who advocated for freedom from British rule and the creation of a new democratic republic. For instance, Thomas Paine's tract *Common Sense* went through repeated printings totaling more than 100,000; by 1810 more than 360 newspapers were circulating in the new nation (Knowles, 1977, pp. 13–14). In the twenty years after 1830, five times as many books were published than in the preceding sixty (Kaestle, 1991b, p. 54). Truly, the nineteenth century became the prime example of how more literacy begets still more literacy.

The explosion of knowledge being released in volume upon volume of fiction, scientific, and technological writings begged for dissemination to a wider audience than those who could afford to possess books, and numerous adult education activities were taking place. To make books more readily available, following on Benjamin Franklin's idea of a "subscription" membership library, fee-based libraries such as the Mechanics' Apprentices Library of Boston were created, followed by the eventual rise of tax-supported public libraries in the New England states and the eventual formation of the American Library Association in 1876 (Knowles, 1977, pp. 15, 19–20).

As noted earlier, popular demand for knowledge spawned the Lyceum movement, a national network of local study groups that numbered more than three thousand by 1835. The aim of group members was self-improvement through learning and mutual teaching. One of the movement's most significant effects was to mobilize public opinion in favor of tax-supported public schools. Another was to serve as a model for adult study and learning. This later encouraged the formation of the Chautauqua Institution in western New York, which grew to sponsor education programs across the nation and led in 1878 to the "first integrated core program of adult education organized in this country on a national scale" (Knowles, 1977, p. 37).

Perhaps the most important occurrence in the nineteenth century for the future of the Adult Education and Literacy System was the rise of the national system of state-supported schools. Overcoming resistance from private schools, conservative taxpayers, church schools, and other vested interests, those in favor of publicly supported schools saw them established in most northern states by 1850. Following the Civil War, by 1880, each of the thirty-eight states then in the Union had free public schools, including both elementary and high schools, and a chief educational officer.

With the growth of the public school system came parallel growth in evening schools for youth and adults in both elementary and high schools. For the most part, these evening schools served young people who could not attend school during the day, and their curriculum was the same as that followed in the daytime. Still, these evening schools laid the foundation for today's adult education programs in the public schools (Knowles, 1977, p. 30).

A large number of voluntary associations formed during the nineteenth century contributed to the rise of the AELS. Among many others were the Young Men's Christian Association (founded in 1851), the Young Women's Christian Association (1855), the National Teachers Association (1857), the American Library Association (1876), and the General Federation of Women's Clubs (1890). All promoted educational activities for youth and adults, including literacy education for adults (Knowles, 1977, chapters 2, 3; Gere, 1997).

In 1870, the National Teacher's Association amalgamated with the American Normal School Association and National Association of School Superintendents to become the National Education Association (NEA) (Wesley, 1957), which was to play a major role in the emergence of the AELS in the first half of the twentieth century.

Education of African Americans

In the Antebellum period, the education of African American slaves was generally forbidden by various state laws. For instance, acts passed by the General Assembly of North Carolina in 1830 made it a crime punishable by thirty-nine lashes to teach "slaves to read and write, the use of figures excepted" (Jacobs, 1861/1987, p. 270). Nonetheless, many adult slaves were taught to read and write by abolitionist whites or other slaves. Some learned from their masters or by overhearing tutors working with their masters' children or by other surreptitious means (Woodson, 1919/1968).

During the Civil War, the Union Army provided many educational opportunities for former slaves (Cornish, 1952). Blassingame (1965) provides numerous examples of educational activities engaged in by officers of the Union Army, including the work of one General Banks: "General Banks sought to eradicate the widespread illiteracy among the 18,585 Negro troops serving in the Department of the Gulf by appointing several members of the American Missionary Association as lieutenants in some of the colored regiments. Banks appointed these men for the sole purpose of teaching the Negro soldiers. Later, Banks realized that he could not procure enough teachers for the Negro soldiers. As a result, on November 30, 1864, Banks modified his system by ordering the chaplain in each regiment to teach the colored soldiers" (pp. 156–157).

After the Civil War, the U.S. Congress created the Bureau of Refugees, Freedmen, and Abandoned Lands as the primary agency for reconstruction. This agency was placed under the jurisdiction of the War Department and was popularly known as the Freedmen's Bureau (Stubblefield & Keane, 1994, pp. 164–166). The Freedmen's Bureau provided education for freed slaves, engaging teachers who were primarily from voluntary organizations, such as the American Missionary Association. Collectively, these organizations became known as Freedmen's Aid Societies. Between 1862 and 1872, fifty-one antislavery societies, involving some 2,500 teachers and more than 2,000 schools, were conducting education for freedmen (pp. 164–165). Citing fiscal burdens, the U.S. Congress disbanded the Freedmen's Bureau in 1872.

Immigrant Education in Settlement Houses

In the middle of the nineteenth century, J. W. Hudson published his *History of Adult Education* (Hudson, 1851/1969). According to Houle (1992), Hudson was apparently the first to use the term *adult education,* which he regarded as the organized and institutional provision of learning opportunities, principally for "the lower classes of the community" (p. v). Excluding the many service organizations providing education for former slaves, most of the adult education activities that arose during the nineteenth century were not intended to help the "lower classes" but as means of self-improvement for the somewhat educated "middle classes," as mentioned earlier. These organizations included the many women's literary clubs that surfaced as an integral part of the growth of the women's movements for suffrage, temperance, and general equality as citizens of the growing democracy.

An exception to these middle-class self-improvement efforts was the importation of the idea of settlements or neighborhood centers from London, where Toynbee Hall center was founded in 1884. In 1886, Stanton Coit founded the Neighborhood Guild (later called University Settlement) in New York City, and in 1889 the most famous of the settlement houses, Hull-House, was founded in Chicago by Jane Addams and Ellen Gates Starr (Knowles, 1977, p. 65; Addams, 1910, 1930). Hull-House was founded to help immigrants adjust to American life. At the end of the nineteenth century, hundreds of thousands of immigrants were coming to America, most of them poor and undereducated, and some four hundred settlement houses had sprung up, inspired by the work of Jane Addams and Hull-House. The settlement houses provided basic education, including reading, writing, and English-language training. Many provided health care that the hundreds of thousands of immigrants, most of them crowded into urban tenement slums, could not find elsewhere (Davis, 1995, pp. 229–230). The work of these settlement and neighborhood centers was instrumental in stimulating the federal government's Americanization movement in the first half of the twentieth century, and they were the forerunners of the community-based groups that make up 14 percent of the AELS today (U.S. Department of Education, 1998).

THE RISE OF THE ADULT EDUCATION AND LITERACY SYSTEM: 1900–2000

With the Civil War in the fading distance and a general prosperity throughout the nation, the turn of the twentieth century saw a plethora of institutions and organizations engaged in one way or another in adult education. Knowles (1977) catalogs the following institutions that emerged in the late 1800s and early 1900s to advance what he called "the adult education movement in the United States": business and industry, colleges and universities, cooperative extension services, foundations, government agencies (including the military), voluntary health and welfare agencies, independent and residential centers, labor unions, libraries, mass communications media (newspapers, books, magazines), museums and art institutes, proprietary schools, public schools, religious institutions, and voluntary associations.

Within this rich assemblage of adult education institutions, all of which have contributed to the rise of the AELS to a greater or lesser degree, some institutions and individuals stand out. Among the institutions are the U.S. military, the National Education Association, and the Carnegie and Ford Foundations. While the military's contribution to the emergence of the AELS primarily concerned the invention of the technology of mass standardized testing (Sticht & Armstrong, 1994), the National Education Association and the Carnegie and Ford Foundations helped to establish the profession of adult education by forming associations for educating and training professionals in the field of adult education, conducting research in and disseminating information about adult education, and providing guidance and advocacy for shaping adult education policies at the federal and state level (Knowles, 1962, 1977; Stubblefield & Keane, 1994).

Among the many individuals who helped the AELS emerge, one, Cora Wilson Stewart, played a major role in focusing attention on the problems facing illiterate and semiliterate adults (Nelms, 1997). She created programs of instruction for adult literacy education, mobilized tens of thousands of volunteers as teachers and tutors for adult literacy programs, and advocated strongly for public support of educational opportunities for adult literacy learners. More is said about Stewart and her work later.

Throughout the twentieth century and up to the present, a tension has existed between those advocating for the professionalization of adult education as a broad, liberal, general educational enterprise for adults of all social classes and educational levels and those advocating for adult literacy education for the least educated and most needy citizens or those foreign-born who have immigrated to the United States in search of a better life (Rose, 1991; Stubblefield & Keane, 1994). The large institutional educational providers, mainly the tax-supported public school systems in the states, have typically favored adult education in the broadest sense, while those community-based organizations that rely heavily on charitable contributions and volunteers to accomplish their work typically favor service to the least educated and most needy adults.

To a considerable extent, the history of the rise of the AELS in the latter half of the twentieth century is the history of the struggle between and the mutual accommodation of these two philosophies of adult education that made possible the passage of the Adult Education Act of 1966. This struggle is traced in a summary fashion in subsequent sections. First, however, there is an overview of the military activities in World War I and World War II that influenced the thinking of adult educators in each philosophical camp.

The Role of the U.S. Military in the Rise of the AELS

As noted earlier, during the eighteenth century, the Continental Army set the precedent for federal provision of adult literacy education when chaplains tutored the troops fighting the Revolutionary War. In the nineteenth century, during the Civil War, the Union Army provided African Americans and other soldiers with literacy education, and, following the war, during Reconstruction, the War Department took initial responsibility for the Freedmen's Bureau and the education of former slaves.

But it was in the twentieth century that the military had its greatest influence on adult education. In 1917, during World War I, the U.S. Army sponsored the development of the first group-administered, standardized tests of "intelligence" for literates, illiterates or low literates, and non-English-speaking recruits (Yerkes, 1921). This had the immediate effect at the time of providing "objective" evidence that large numbers of native-born young adults were not literate and that large numbers of immigrants were neither literate nor functional in the English language. This information fueled the cause of advocates of adult education, who could claim that large numbers of adults were in need of literacy education and that large numbers of immigrants needed education to help them become "Americanized."

On one hand, the World War I experience with "intelligence" testing convinced some people that large numbers of adults, both native- and foreign-born, were mentally incapable of benefiting from adult education (Stubblefield & Keane, 1994, p. 187). On the other, in what has been a second major influence of the military on adult education, it has repeatedly demonstrated that thousands of adults considered "uneducable" could indeed acquire at least basic literacy skills within fairly brief periods of instruction lasting from six to twelve weeks. In World War I, literacy education for both native- and foreign-born young adults was accomplished in so-called Development Battalions.

Nearly twenty-five thousand illiterate and non-English-speaking troops had received such training by February 1919 (p. 182).

The military's testing efforts developed the technology, and the propensity to use the technology, of standardized testing to determine for large groups of people exactly who would get what sort of educational or occupational opportunity. This had a major effect during World War II, when, in 1942, the tests of General Educational Development (GED) were developed to give military service members a chance to use their experience in the military to qualify for a high school education equivalency certificate (Baldwin, 1995; Rose, 1990). For tens of thousands of members of the armed services who had cut short their high school education to serve the nation during World War II, obtaining the equivalent of a high school education made it possible for them to get jobs and to use the GI Bill to pursue further vocational training or a college education. Many of the GIs who did go on to college became the first in their families to earn a university degree (Olson, 1974). Today the GED is widely used in both the United States and Canada to certify high school equivalency. In the United States, the AELS devotes an increasing portion of its resources to helping adults acquire a credential that has its technical origins in the "intelligence" tests of World War I and served the vocational and educational needs of the troops during and after World War II.

As indicated later, the results of the military's standardized tests of "mental ability" initially developed in 1917 would play another pivotal role in shaping the AELS almost half a century later, in the early 1960s, as part of a new "war," this time fought not on foreign soil but at home, the domestic program called the War on Poverty.

The Adult Education Professionalization Movement

The drafting and eventual passage of the Adult Education Act of 1966 was largely the result of two major, interactive strands in the movement for adult literacy. One worked toward the goal of professionalizing and expanding adult education, the other toward that of helping the least well-educated native- and foreign-born adults to acquire basic literacy and language skills.

The professionalization movement started in the early 1920s and aimed at forging a professional field of adult education from the disparate activities of educators in the many institutions identified by

Knowles (1977). The work of these various institutions captured the attention of the Carnegie Corporation of New York in the early 1920s. The Carnegie Corporation was founded by Andrew Carnegie in 1911 to promote the diffusion of knowledge among the population. One of his major contributions toward this end was to donate millions of dollars to help develop and support public libraries (Learned, 1924). Based on this interest in diffusing knowledge, it was natural for the Carnegie Corporation to become interested in the broader array of institutions that could help people acquire the knowledge they needed to more effectively manage their lives (Rose, 1989).

In 1924 the Carnegie Corporation Board of Trustees directed the new president of the corporation, Frederick P. Keppel, to initiate a program of activities that would move the many efforts in adult education forward. Keppel had been an assistant secretary of war in World War I, and he knew about the wartime programs of education for soldiers and other activities in adult education (Keppel, 1926/1968). He was devoted to the role of broad, liberal education for adults, and, working from the recommendations of an advisory council of adult educators and the results of several studies and regional conferences, in 1926 he committed Carnegie Corporation funding to the administrative support of a new adult education organization, the American Association for Adult Education (AAAE) (Rose, 1989; Stubblefield & Keane, 1994, pp. 187, 192–193; Knowles, 1977, pp. 190–192).

A major function of the AAAE was to screen applications from adult educators who were applying for funds from the Carnegie Corporation. The association also conducted research, experimental projects, and other such activities that would advance adult education. It published the *Journal of Adult Education* to disseminate information about adult education and to promote the use of the term *adult education*, hoping to bring coherence to the field by giving it a name (Stubblefield & Keane, 1994, p. 193).

From 1926 to 1941 the Carnegie Corporation provided administrative support for the AAAE; additional funding came largely from membership dues. Membership was limited to individuals and organizations having "a direct and usually professional interest in adult education" (Knowles, 1977, p. 197). In 1941 the Carnegie Corporation ended its support of the AAAE, and from 1941 to 1951 the AAAE relied mainly on membership dues. These dues were inadequate to support the AAAE, and, in 1951, based on the recommendation of a Joint Commission for the Study of Adult Education consisting of members from five organizations that practiced adult education, the AAAE approached the Department of Adult Education of the National Education Association (NEA) to discuss the formation of a new association.

The NEA, which originated in the mid-1800s, had become the major organization representing teachers and administrators working in the nation's expanding tax-supported public school system. It was a primary force for the professionalization of teaching and a strong advocate for public education. Early on in its history, the NEA recognized the problems of illiteracy for both foreign- and native-born Americans and, through its Department of Adult Education, played a major role in the subsequent movement to advance adult education as a mainstream component of education in the United States. In 1951, when approached by the AAAE to discuss their mutual interests in adult education, the Department of Adult Education, now called the Division of Adult Education Service, was separated from the NEA and its membership merged with that of the AAAE to form the Adult Education Association of the United States of America (AEA/USA) as the major association for promoting the professionalization of adult education.

The Americanization Movement

In the latter part of the nineteenth century there was a growing concern among civic groups and state and federal policymakers about the large influx of illiterate immigrants into the country. In 1910, the U.S. Census indicated that 7.7 percent of adults—more than 5 million people—were illiterate and that almost 30 percent of these individuals were foreign-born. In 1917, after the results of the military's standardized tests had confirmed that large numbers of both native- and foreign-born Americans were not literate in any language, the government passed a law that prohibited immigrants from entering the country if they were sixteen years old or older and could not read in any language (Cook, 1977, pp. 11, 13).

For the millions of illiterate foreign-born who were already in the country, the idea arose to "Americanize" them in immigrant education programs. Between 1915 and 1919, the Federal Bureau of Education gave extensive professional aid to groups interested in providing Americanization education (Cook, 1977, p. 19). Many of these programs were provided by public schools in evening classes, and many of the teachers and administrators of these schools were members of the National Education Association. In 1920, the NEA formed a Department of Immigrant Education to provide professional members working in the Americanization movement with assistance. As the movement for adult education began to spread, the NEA in 1924 changed the name of the Department of Immigrant Education to the Department of Adult Education and broadened its mandate beyond concern for immigrant education to include adult education in general (Knowles, 1977, pp. 173–174).

At first, membership in the NEA's Department of Adult Education was limited to public school educators and served to advance their work. In 1927, it redefined its membership to include "all those educators who instruct adults from beginning English classes to evening high school and general evening classes in special subjects, all under public auspices" (Knowles, 1977, p. 210). With this new, expanded definition, the NEA Department of Adult Education became more competitive with the AAAE for the membership of adult educators working "under public auspices," whether in public schools, libraries, museums, or other settings.

By 1945, the NEA Department of Adult Education had become the Division of Adult Education Service, a staff advisory office of the NEA. Then, as indicated earlier, to put an end to the competitiveness between it and the AAAE and to more effectively represent the totality of adult education, in 1951 the NEA Division of Adult Education Service was dissolved and its membership merged with that of the AAAE.

Cora Wilson Stewart and the Illiteracy Movement

In the first third of the twentieth century, Cora Wilson Stewart stands out as an exemplar of what one person can do to advance a cause. Stewart's cause was the eradication of adult illiteracy, and she began to work for it in her home state of Kentucky. In 1911, while she was superintendent of public schools in Rowan County, she started a program to eliminate adult illiteracy. This program, according to Cook (1977), "might well be classified as the official beginning of literacy education in the United States" (p. 13).

The schools operated only on moonlit nights so people could find their way to and from school safely, hence the name *Moonlight Schools*. The schools were staffed by volunteer teachers from the day schools for children. Stewart was convinced that adults should not use the same materials as children to learn to read, so she developed for adult students the *Rowan County Messenger,* a newspaper with short sentences and lots of word repetition. In teaching writing, she concentrated first on teaching adults to write their own names, believing that this was a vital way to develop what we would today call self-esteem.

The success of the Moonlight Schools, coupled with Stewart's apparently superior public speaking and presentation skills, helped to spread the success of the Rowan County experiment to numerous counties in Kentucky, and, in 1914, the governor of the state established an illiteracy commission, the first such commission in the United States (Cook, 1977, p. 14).

Nelms (1997) reports that Stewart's strong advocacy for adult literacy education took her in 1918 to the annual convention of the NEA, where her speech so impressed Mary C. L. Bradford, then president of the NEA, that Bradford quickly established an NEA Committee on Illiteracy and issued a proclamation calling for the Americanization of immigrants and the teaching of literacy to native-born illiterates. Stewart was invited to chair the committee, which she did until 1925.

From 1916 to 1926, Stewart carried out numerous activities on behalf of the education of illiterates. Not only did she chair the NEA Committee on Illiteracy for seven years, she also led a crusade in Kentucky to eliminate illiteracy, developed *The Soldier's First Book* to teach military recruits to read during World War I, conducted dozens of illiteracy conferences throughout the United States, chaired from 1919 to 1925 the Illiteracy Division she had convinced the General Federation of Women's Clubs to form, chaired the Illiteracy Section of the World Conference of Education Associations five times, spoke about adult illiteracy issues before the Democratic National Convention in 1920, and initiated the National Illiteracy Crusade in 1926 (Nelms, 1997).

Throughout these years when the adult education movement was forming and Americanization was the primary goal emphasized by the federal and many state governments, Stewart continued to focus on native-born illiterates. She denounced the NEA's naming of a Department of Immigration because she feared it would overshadow work with native-born illiterates. Later, she denounced the replacement of the Department of Immigration with the Department of Adult Education because she thought that the emerging field of adult education was too broad and "middle class" and did not focus on the educational needs of the least literate and most economically needy. These concerns led her in 1925 to resign as chair of the NEA Committee on Illiteracy, and in 1926 she struck out on her own to advocate for programs for adult illiterates by forming the National Illiteracy Crusade, with the goal of wiping out illiteracy by 1930.

But the economic collapse following the stock market collapse of 1929 and the start of the Great Depression got in the way of these efforts. Though Stewart was instrumental in getting President Herbert Hoover to appoint the National Advisory Committee on Illiteracy in 1929, by 1933, funding ran out, and the committee concluded its work. After that, Stewart's work centered mostly on the National Illiteracy Crusade. By the time of World War II, national interest in the cause had faded, and Stewart turned her energies away from adult illiteracy issues to the activities of the Oxford Group, a religious organization advocating a particular form of spiritual life within the Christian faith. She died in 1958 at the age of eighty-three.

The Human Resources Conservation Movement

During the Great Depression of the 1930s, New Deal programs were implemented with the goal of employing teachers while providing an education for adults who had fallen on hard times. In 1933, the Civilian Conservation Corps (CCC) was initiated and developed educational programs for unemployed illiterate and undereducated young men. In 1935, the Works Progress Administration (WPA) was initiated to provide work for unemployed teachers, and in 1938 WPA officials were able to announce that more than 1 million illiterate persons had been taught to read and write. Like Stewart's early materials for the Moonlight Schools, the WPA teachers developed functional materials with adult-oriented content on topics such as health, safety, work, and family life (Cook, 1977, p. 41). In 1941, the urgent demand for workers fueled by the advent of World War II led the government to terminate the WPA.

During World War II, as in World War I, it was discovered that hundreds of thousands of American adults were undereducated and functionally illiterate—that is, having literacy skills at a level lower than those of a fifth-grade student (Cook, 1977, p. 51). General Dwight David Eisenhower, commander of the Allied Forces during the war, was concerned that poorly educated, functionally illiterate adults were a threat to national security, a drain on America's industrial productivity, and a general waste of human talent. After he retired from the army and assumed the presidency of Columbia University, he established there the Conservation of Human Resources project.

Like the CCC, the goal of which was to develop and preserve the nation's natural resources, the Conservation of Human Resources project was intended to develop and preserve the nation's human resources.

Picking up on these concerns about wasting the country's "human resources," Ambrose Caliver of the U.S. Office of Education organized in 1957 the National Commission on Adult Literacy to look for a solution to the adult illiteracy problem in some sort of government program (Rose, 1991, p. 15). Because of its strong focus on employment and illiteracy, however, the commission's work was not wholeheartedly supported by the adult education community as represented by the AEA/USA, with its interest in broad, liberal education for adults.

When the AEA/USA was formed in 1951, the Ford Foundation made an offer of funding support. The Ford Foundation had recently established a program called the Fund for Adult Education with the goal of supporting programmatic and administrative activities that provided liberal adult education (Fund for Adult Education, 1961). To further these goals, Ford's Fund for Adult Education gave grants to create positions for state directors of adult education and to improve the ability of community public schools to provide liberal adult education. This promoted a view of adult education as civic-minded, liberal education with broad purposes as opposed to the economic productivity-oriented focus of the human resources agenda.

These contrasting points of view about the goals of adult education became more important when the AEA/USA adult education community, consisting of public school teachers and administrators, found itself without the strong support it had enjoyed as part of the NEA. In 1952, the National Association of Public School Adult Educators (NAPSAE) was formed as an affiliate of the AEA/USA. In 1953, NAPSAE also affiliated with the NEA, and in 1955 it dropped its affiliation with the AEA/USA and became a department of the NEA, with the full strength of the NEA's strong lobbying experience behind it (Knowles, 1977, p. 231).

While the National Commission on Adult Literacy was lobbying for a federal adult literacy program in the late 1950s, the NAPSAE/NEA was lobbying for an Adult Education Act that would help professionalize the adult education field. As stated by Rose (1991), "As envisioned by this group, adult education would become an equal of the other branches of education, with adequate state and local funding" (p. 15).

By the beginning of the 1960s, the adult education community had become fragmented into several factions: those seeking recognition for adult education as a broad, liberal educational component of the national education system; those who, like Cora Wilson Stewart earlier, sought education for the least educated, least literate adults; and those seeking the conservation of human resources to enhance America's security and increase the industrial productivity of the nation by giving education and job training to adults living in poverty.

As it turns out, none of these groups was having much success getting adult education or adult literacy education implemented in federal legislation. An Adult Literacy Act drafted in 1962 was deemed too narrow, and so it was renamed the Adult Education Act even before it was introduced for legislative hearings. But the U.S. Office of Education considered the term *adult education* too broad. The name finally decided on was the Adult Basic Education Act of 1962, but it went nowhere (Rose, 1991, p. 17).

At the time, President John F. Kennedy, struck by issues of poverty, particularly poverty among African Americans, had placed the adult education issue within the human resources development framework and problems of labor force training. He had been successful in getting the Manpower Training and Development Act and the Area Redevelopment Act for community economic development passed in 1962. But further legislation to combat poverty was stalled. In 1963, Kennedy was assassinated and Lyndon Baines Johnson became president. He would soon find a way to break the logjam and advance his "War on Poverty," which would carry adult education along with it. Once again, leverage for social action in adult education would come from the nation's military.

According to biographer Godfrey Hodgson (2000), in July 1963, Daniel Patrick Moynihan—then an assistant secretary of labor—read an article in the *Washington Post* stating that about half the young men called for examination for military service by the Selective Service System (the "draft") had failed the tests of physical or mental abilities or both. Hodgson reported, "Moynihan had observed how the sacred plea of national security could be used to persuade politicians to support causes they might not otherwise care two pins about" (pp. 81–82). After reading the article, Moynihan got hold of Secretary of Labor Willard Wirtz and convinced him to have the president establish a task force on manpower conservation for which he, Moynihan, would serve as staff leader. Wirtz agreed, and on September 30, 1963, just two months before

Kennedy was assassinated, he established the Task Force on Manpower Conservation, which Johnson continued when he became president.

The task force set out to understand why so many young men were failing the military's standardized entrance screening exam, the Armed Forces Qualification Test (AFQT), and to recommend what might be done to alleviate this problem. Just three months later, on January 1, 1964, Wirtz delivered the task force report to President Johnson. The report was stunning in revealing that half of the young men called for service by the draft were unqualified for military service and a third did not meet the standards of health and education (President's Task Force on Manpower Conservation, 1964). It went on to recommend methods for using the AFQT to identify young adults with remediable problems and to provide them with services by increasing the funding for several ongoing federal government programs (like the Manpower Training and Development Program) and by enacting legislation that would provide additional education and training (pp. 29–33).

In May 1964, President Johnson gave the speech that launched his "Great Society" programs, in which he argued, "The Great Society rests on abundance and liberty for all. It demands an end to poverty and racial injustice, to which we are totally committed in our time" (Davis, 1995, p. 367). With his appeal to "abundance and liberty," Johnson captured the interest of those in Congress concerned with employment, productivity, and poverty ("abundance") as well as those concerned with national security ("liberty"). In August 1964, Public Law 88–452, the Economic Opportunity Act, was passed by the Congress and signed by President Johnson. It contained within it Title IIB: the Adult Basic Education Program (Rose, 1991, p. 14).

Two years later, in 1966, when the Economic Opportunity Act legislation came up for legislative review, the NAPSAE/NEA and the AEA/USA lobbied to move the Adult Basic Education Program from the poverty programs of the Office of Economic Opportunity to the educational programs of the U.S. Office of Education, where it had, in fact, been administered all along. The two organizations also lobbied for a change in title, from the Adult Basic Education Program to the Adult Education Act, seeking to broaden its applicability beyond basic education (Rose, 1991, p. 16). Congress agreed to these changes, and, in November 1966, President Johnson signed an amendment to the Elementary and Secondary Education Act of 1965 that included Title III: the Adult Education Act of 1966. The acorn from which the AELS would grow had finally been planted.

Growth in Funding and Enrollments: 1965–1999

Figure 2.1 shows the funding and enrollment trends for the newly formed AELS from 1965 to 1999. In 1965, the federal adult education program received federal funds of some $18.6 million for some thirty-eight thousand enrollments. By 1999, federal funds had increased to more than $365 million and enrollments to more than 3.6 million (Sticht, 1998, p. 4). While the funding rate grew sporadically, enrollments appear to have grown at a fairly constant rate up to 1997.

Over the years, the federal funding share of adult education has declined and the share of matching funds by states and local education agencies has increased. In 1966, federal funding for adult education was around $20 million for some 377,660 enrollees ($53 per enrollee), while state and local funding was around $10 million ($26 per enrollee). By 1998, federal funds for adult education had risen to more than $345 million for some 4 million enrollees ($89 per enrollee), while around $958 million ($240 per enrollee) was available

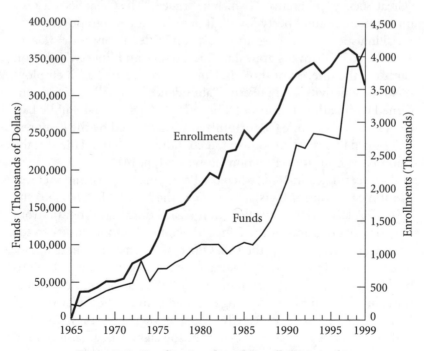

Figure 2.1. Funding Levels and Enrollments in the
Adult Education and Literacy System, 1965–1999.

Source: Sticht, 1998, pp. 3, 4, 33; U.S. Department of Education, 2000.

for adult education from state and local matching funds (U.S. Department of Education, 2000; Sticht, 1998, p. 4).

Four amendments to the Adult Education Act of 1966 contributed to the growth of the AELS over the last third of the twentieth century.

- In 1970, amendments to the Adult Education Act of 1966 lowered the age of those who could participate from eighteen to sixteen years.

- Also in 1970, amendments expanded educational services to go beyond ABE for those students with fewer than nine years of education, those who spoke English as a second language, or those who wanted citizenship classes. New provisions included students needing adult secondary education involving the completion of high school or passing the GED.

- In 1978, amendments expanded services beyond the school-based definitions of basic skills—such as "ninth grade" or "high school"—to include a functional, competency-based definition for adults who might have high school diplomas but whose basic skills were considered too low to permit them to function well in society.

- In 1988, amendments expanded services to permit partnerships with business, labor unions, and educators to provide workplace literacy programs for employees with limited basic skills (U.S. Department of Education, 1991; Rose, 1991).

Another factor contributing to the growth of the AELS during this period was a large influx of immigrants that created heavy demand for English-language education, especially from 1981 to 1990, when some 7.3 million immigrants came to the United States (Sticht, 1998, p. 10).

In addition to the amendments that expanded the number of adults entitled to services under the Adult Education Act of 1966, several amendments expanded the number of education service providers eligible for funding through the act. As described by Rose (1991, pp. 15–31), the major changes included the following:

- Amendments in 1968 permitted state grants to private nonprofit agencies in addition to the public schools and public nonprofit agencies already eligible to receive state grants.

- Amendments in 1978 required state plans to describe how the delivery of educational services could be expanded beyond schools, particularly by public or private nonprofit organizations, and to reach out to those least educated and most in need.

• Amendments in 1984 allowed grants to for-profit agencies.

• Amendments in 1988 permitted special grants to workplace literacy programs, English literacy programs, and programs for commercial drivers, migrant farm workers, and immigrants.

• The National Literacy Act of 1991 (Public Law 102–73) replaced the Adult Education Act of 1966 and further encouraged the expansion of the number of nonprofit education providers eligible for federal funds by including a requirement that every provider in a state have "direct and equitable access" to federal basic grant funds (Moore & Stavrianos, 1995, p. 5).

The changes in the Adult Education Act influencing the eligibility of adult populations and of service providers from 1966 to the end of the century reflect the relative influence of three major groups:

• The professional associations of adult educators who advocated for the broad, liberal education of adults for self-improvement, which eventually became the contemporary call for "lifelong learning." This group followed the lead of the American Association of Adult Education (1926 to 1951) as it transformed first into the American Association of Adult Education in the United States of America (1951–1982) and then into the American Association of Adult and Continuing Education (1985–present).

• The associations for public school teachers and administrators who were in favor of diverse educational programs for adults that would ultimately have equal footing with the K–12 system as part of a public adult education system. This group of mostly public school–based educators formed several professional associations of the National Education Association, Department of Adult Education (1924–1951), then the affiliate of the AEA/USA known as the National Association of Public School Adult Educators (1952), which eventually became a part of the NEA and then became a separate organization known as the National Association for Public and Continuing Adult Education (NAPCAE) (continuing education was added to include the many community college educators that were engaging in noncredit adult education through divisions of continuing education). Other influential organizations include the Council of State Directors of Adult Education and the National Adult Education Professional Development Consortium (NAEPDC) (1990–present), established to provide state adult education staff a presence in Washington, D.C.

• Many community-based adult educators who followed in the footsteps of Cora Wilson Stewart and advocated for basic literacy education for adults. Among the groups exerting particularly strong influence over the last third of the century have been Laubach Literacy (1955–present; Laubach Literacy, 1999) and Literacy Volunteers of America, Inc. (1962–present; Colvin, 1992). The Commission on Adult Basic Education (COABE) (1971–present), which started as a part of the AAACE and is now a separate organization, has also been a strong advocate for adult basic literacy education (Campbell, 2000). In 1981, the National Coalition for Literacy was formed by eleven associations concerned with adult literacy education (Newman & Beverstock, 1990, pp. 168–181). By the end of the century it included more than thirty organizations and was firmly established as the primary advocacy organization for adult literacy education in the United States.

Though it was the second of these groups—the public school teachers and administrators, with some support from the first group of adult educators—that was most influential in naming the Adult Education Act of 1966, it was the third group, the largely community-based groups serving the least educated and relying largely on volunteer tutors, that prevailed over time to get the Adult Education Act recast and renamed the National Literacy Act of 1991. Community-based groups were assisted in this effort by the Business Council for Effective Literacy (BCEL), a nonprofit agency established to help promote the interests of public and private organizations, including businesses and industries, in providing literacy education for adults (McGraw, 1984). The BCEL was instrumental in stimulating an influential report by the Southport Institute for Policy Analysis (Chisman, 1989) that informed the drafting of the National Literacy Act of 1991.

With the passing and signing of the National Literacy Act (NLA) of 1991, the U.S. Department of Education, Division of Adult Education, was renamed the Division of Adult Education and Literacy (DAEL). But just seven years later, in 1998, the NLA of 1991 was gone.

Ironically, the same report that had helped stimulate the drafting of the NLA, with its emphasis on literacy as a broad educational goal, had also emphasized the importance of adult literacy education for workforce development to ensure America's competitive position in the world economy (Chisman, 1989). Armed with this and other influential reports of the 1990s (O'Neil, 1997), advocates of adult education for human resources development, like those who had been so influential in making the Adult Basic Education Program part of the Economic Opportunity Act of 1964, rose to prominence.

This time, however, the argument for adult education as human resources development was not focused on the need to eliminate poverty but to prop up America's economic competitiveness in the new global economy. In this context, the NLA was incorporated into the Workforce Investment Act of 1998 as Title II: The Adult Education and Family Literacy Act (AEFLA) (Tracy-Mumford, 2000, pp. 3–9). Though obviously colored with an orientation toward preparing students for the workforce, by virtue of its inclusion in the Workforce Investment Act of 1998, the AEFLA permits the full array of adult education and literacy services that existed prior to the enactment of the WIA.

At the beginning of the twenty-first century, the WIA/AEFLA is the source of the federal rules and regulations that guide the work of more than four thousand state, local, and community-based organizations that annually receive federal funds for adult education. Among other things, the WIA/AEFLA determines who may attend programs, who may deliver programs, how institutions should develop strategic plans, and how programs should be monitored for the purposes of accountability and quality improvement. The cooperation and coherence that this federal guidance provides for the many disparate programs across the nation has made for a third unique system of education that exists alongside the K–12 and higher education systems, all supported by public funds for the general health and prosperity of the nation.

Yearly, millions of adults who seek education to improve their lives as parents, citizens, workers, and individuals find an opportunity for learning and development in this third branch of public education, the Adult Education and Literacy System of the United States.

Notes

1. Thousands of programs in the United States and its territories provide adult basic education and literacy instruction. In this chapter, the Adult Education and Literacy System is defined as the subset of those programs that must operate in accordance with the provisions of the Adult

Education and Family Literacy Act of 1998 (Title II of the Workforce Investment Act) and that are funded wholly or in part by the federal government and administered by the Division of Adult Education and Literacy in the U.S. Department of Education.

2. Note that a given adult may have had multiple enrollments and may have appeared in more than one of these categories.

3. Given constraints on the length of this chapter and the time provided to prepare it, considerable use has been made of a limited number of mostly secondary sources. In-depth analyses of many important events, institutions, and individuals and their work have been sacrificed to present a concise overview of some four hundred years of the history of adult education and many of the factors that eventually contributed to the rise of the AELS. No history is ever complete, and that is certainly true of the present work. The aim has been to provide those interested in the AELS with a *breadth* of information and references that they may consult for greater *depth* of coverage of various topics, personalities, and issues.

References

Addams, J. (1910). *Twenty years at Hull-House.* New York: Macmillan.

Addams, J. (1930). *The second twenty years at Hull-House.* New York: Macmillan.

Baldwin, J. (Ed.). (1995). *Who took the GED? GED 1995 statistical report.* Washington, DC: GED Testing Service, Center for Adult Learning and Educational Credentials, American Council on Education.

Beder, H. (1991). *Adult literacy: Issues for policy and practice.* Melbourne, FL: Krieger.

Blassingame, J. (1965). The Union Army as an educational institution for Negroes, 1862–1865. *Journal of Negro Education, 34,* 152–159.

Burr, H. L. (1939). *Education in the early navy.* Unpublished doctoral dissertation, Temple University, Philadelphia.

Campbell, A. (2000, January). *A brief history of the National Commission on Adult Basic Education.* Bryan, TX: Querida Enterprises.

Chisman, F. (1989, January). *Jump start: The federal role in adult education.* Southport, CT: Southport Institute for Policy Analysis.

Colvin, R. J. (1992). *A way with words: The story of Literacy Volunteers of America, Inc.* Syracuse, NY: Literacy Volunteers of America.

Cook, W. D. (1977). *Adult literacy education in the United States.* Newark, DE: International Reading Association.

Cornish, D. T. (1952). The Union Army as a school for Negroes. *Journal of Negro History, 37*, 368–382.

Cremin, L. A. (1970). *American education: The colonial experience 1607–1783.* New York: HarperCollins.

Davis, K. C. (1995). *Don't know much about history: Everything you need to know about American history (but never learned).* New York: Crown.

Fund for Adult Education. (1961). *Ten-year report of The Fund for Adult Education, 1951–1961.* New York: Ford Foundation.

Galenson, D. (1979). Literacy and the social origins of some early Americans. *Historical Journal, 22,* 75–91.

Gere, A. R. (1997). *Intimate practices: Literacy and cultural work in U.S. women's clubs.* Chicago: University of Illinois Press.

Gordon, E. E., & Gordon, E. H. (1990). *Centuries of tutoring: A history of alternative education in America and Western Europe.* Lanham, MD: University Press of America.

Gubb, R. (1990). Growth of literacy in colonial America: Longitudinal patterns, economic models, and the direction of future research. *Social Science History, 14,* 451–482.

Herndon, R. W. (1996). Research note: Literacy among New England's transient poor, 1750–1800. *Journal of Social History, 29,* 963–965.

Hodgson, G. (2000). *The gentleman from New York: Daniel Patrick Moynihan.* New York: Houghton Mifflin.

Houle, C. O. (1992). *The literature of adult education: A bibliographic essay.* San Francisco: Jossey-Bass.

Houle, C. O., Burr, E. W., Hamilton, T. H., & Yale, J. R. (1947). *The armed services and adult education.* Washington, DC: American Council on Education.

Hudson, J. (1969). *The history of adult education.* London: Woburn. (Original work published 1851)

Jacobs, H. A. (1987). *Incidents in the life of a slave girl: Written by herself.* Cambridge, MA: Harvard University Press. (Original work published 1861)

Kaestle, C. F. (1991a). Studying the history of literacy. In C. F. Kaestle, H. Damon-Moore, L. C. Stedman, K. Tinsley, & W. V. Trollinger Jr. (Eds.), *Literacy in the United States: Readers and reading since 1880* (pp. 3–32). New Haven, CT: Yale University Press.

Kaestle, C. F. (1991b). The history of reading. In C. F. Kaestle, H. Damon-Moore, L. C. Stedman, K. Tinsley, & W. V. Trollinger Jr. (Eds.), *Literacy in the United States: Readers and reading since 1880* (pp. 33–74). New Haven, CT: Yale University Press.

Keppel, F. P. (1968). *Education for adults.* New York: Columbia University Press. (Original work published 1926)

Kett, J. F. (1994). *The pursuit of knowledge under difficulties: From self-improvement to adult education in America, 1750–1990.* Stanford, CA: Stanford University Press.

Kim, K., & Creighton, S. (2000, March). *Participation in adult education in the United States: 1998–99.* NCES Publication No. 2000–027. Washington, DC: National Center for Education Statistics, U.S. Department of Education.

Knowles, M. S. (1962). *The adult education movement in the United States.* New York: Holt, Rinehart & Winston.

Knowles, M. S. (1977). *A history of the adult education movement in the United States.* Melbourne, FL: Krieger.

Langley, H. D. (1967). *Social reform in the United States Navy, 1798–1862.* Urbana, IL: University of Illinois Press.

Laubach Literacy. (1999). *Only the educated are free—Epictetus.* Syracuse, NY: Author.

Learned, W. S. (1924). *The American public library and the diffusion of knowledge.* New York: Harcourt.

Lockridge, K. A. (1974). *Literacy in colonial New England: An enquiry into the social context of literacy in the early modern West.* New York: Norton.

Long, H. B. (1975). Adult education in colonial America. *Journal of Research and Development in Education, 8,* 1–101.

Main, G. (1991). An inquiry into when and why women learned to write in colonial New England. *Journal of Social History, 24,* 579–589.

McGraw, H., Jr. (1984, January). *Luncheon address.* Paper presented at the National Conference on Adult Literacy. Washington, DC: Division of Adult Education Services, Clearinghouse on Adult Education, U.S. Department of Education.

Moore, M., & Stavrianos, M. (1995, June). Review of adult education programs and their effectiveness: A background paper for reauthorization of the Adult Education Act. Submitted to U.S. Department of Education. Washington, DC: National Institute for Literacy.

Nelms, W. (1997). *Cora Wilson Stewart: Crusader against illiteracy.* Jefferson, NC: McFarland.

Newman, A., & Beverstock, C. (1990). *Adult literacy: Contexts and challenges.* Newark, DE: International Reading Association.

Olson, K. W. (1974). *The G.I. Bill, the veterans, and the colleges.* Lexington, KY: University Press of Kentucky.

O'Neil, H., Jr. (1997). *Workforce readiness: Competencies and assessment.* Mahwah, NJ: Erlbaum.

Perlmann, J., & Shirley, D. (1991). When did New England women acquire literacy? *William and Mary Quarterly, 68,* 50–67.

President's Task Force on Manpower Conservation. (1964, January). *One-third of a nation: A report on young men found unqualified for military service.* Washington, DC: U.S. Government Printing Office.

Quigley, B. A. (1997). *Rethinking literacy education: The critical need for practice-based change.* San Francisco: Jossey-Bass.

Rose, A. D. (1989). Beyond classroom walls: The Carnegie Corporation and the founding of the American Association for Adult Education. *Adult Education Quarterly, 39,* 140–151.

Rose, A. D. (1990). Preparing for veterans: Higher education and the efforts to accredit the learning of World War II servicemen and women. *Adult Education Quarterly, 42,* 30–45.

Rose, A. D. (1991). *Ends or means: An overview of the history of the Adult Education Act.* Columbus, OH: ERIC Clearinghouse on Adult, Career, and Vocational Education. (ERIC Document Reproduction Service No. ED 341 875).

Soltow, L., & Stevens, E. (1981). *The rise of literacy and the common school in the United States: A socioeconomic analysis to 1870.* Chicago: University of Chicago Press.

Sticht, T. (1984, January). Strategies for adult literacy development. Paper presented at the National Conference on Adult Literacy, Washington, DC. San Diego: Applied Behavioral & Cognitive Sciences.

Sticht, T. (1998, September). *Beyond 2000: Future directions for adult education.* Washington, DC: Division of Adult Education and Literacy, U.S. Department of Education.

Sticht, T., & Armstrong, W. (1994, February). *Adult literacy in the United States: A compendium of quantitative data and interpretive comments.* Washington, DC: National Institute for Literacy.

Stubblefield, H. W., & Keane, P. (1994). *Adult education in the American experience: From the colonial period to the present.* San Francisco: Jossey-Bass.

Tracy-Mumford, F. (2000). The year 1998 in review. In J. Comings, B. Garner, & C. Smith (Eds.), *Annual review of adult learning and literacy* (Vol. 1, pp. 1–24). San Francisco: Jossey-Bass.

U.S. Department of Education. (1991). *History of the Adult Education Act: An overview.* Washington, DC: Office of Vocational and Adult Education, Division of Adult Education and Literacy.

U.S. Department of Education. (1998, January). *Adult education: Human investment impact 1992–1996.* Washington, DC: Office of Vocational and Adult Education, Division of Adult Education and Literacy.

U.S. Department of Education. (2000, December). *State-administered adult education program: Program year 1992–1999.* Washington, DC: Office of Vocational and Adult Education, Division of Adult Education and Literacy.

Weinert, R. (1979). *Literacy training in the army.* Fort Monroe, VA: TRADOC Historical Office.

Wesley, E. B. (1957). *NEA: The first hundred years.* New York: HarperCollins.

Woodson, C. G. (1968). *The education of the Negro prior to 1861.* New York: Arno Press. (Original work published 1919)

Yerkes, R. M. (1921). *Psychological examining in the United States Army: Memoirs of the National Academy of Sciences.* Washington, DC: U.S. Government Printing Office.

CHAPTER THREE

Adults with Learning Disabilities

A Review of the Literature

Mary Ann Corley
Juliana M. Taymans

An emerging theme in professional development for adult literacy program staff over the past decade has been the topic of learning disabilities (LD). As adult educators have come to recognize that the effects of LD can play a significant role in the performance and retention of adult learners, many have sought answers to the following questions: What are learning disabilities, and how do they affect adult learners? How can I determine which learners have LD? What strategies are most effective for teaching someone with LD? Interest in what it means to provide effective services for adult learners with LD has not always been this keen.

FRAMING ISSUES AND EVENTS IN THE STUDY OF LEARNING DISABILITIES

The definition of LD, knowledge of its prevalence among adults, and acknowledgment and understanding of the connection between adult literacy and learning disabilities are works in progress. This first section of the chapter brings the reader up to date in each area and defines the parameters used in the authors' search of the literature, the results of which are presented in the balance of the chapter, along with implications for research, policy, and practice.

Definition of Learning Disabilities

In the years following the 1975 enactment of the Education for All Handicapped Children Act, many special educators viewed LD as a developmental delay that would be outgrown as an individual matured. The field was too new at that time to benefit from longitudinal studies that followed students into adulthood. Similarly, the adult literacy field did not readily make connections between clients who seemed to have difficulty learning and existing research on the K–12 special education population. Some early articles (Bowren, 1981; Gold, 1981) questioned the incidence of LD among adult learners and debated appropriate practices for adults with LD. But adult literacy programs were for the most part not yet attending to LD in the design and delivery of services for learners or in staff development.

It is primarily in the past fifteen years that studies on adult populations have caused both the special education and the adult basic education (ABE) fields to acknowledge that LD represents a persistent challenge. An important benchmark in the growing recognition of LD as a lifelong condition was the establishment of the National Adult Literacy and Learning Disabilities Center (National ALLD Center) in 1993 with funds from the National Institute for Literacy. The center's goals were to raise awareness among practitioners, policymakers, and researchers about issues of LD in adults, to add to the knowledge base about LD in adults through a research and development effort, and to build capacity among literacy programs to enhance the quality of services provided for adults with LD. The center represented the first effort to bring together professionals in the fields of adult literacy and learning disabilities on a professional advisory board.

With the recognition of LD as a lifelong condition, new definitions have been crafted, making the important acknowledgments that LD affects individuals of all ages, can occur concomitantly with other disabilities, and can impede social skills. One widely accepted definition is that of the National Joint Committee on Learning Disabilities:

> Learning disabilities is a general term that refers to a heterogeneous group of disorders manifested by significant difficulties in the acquisition and use of listening, speaking, reading, writing, reasoning, or

mathematical abilities. These disorders are intrinsic to the individual, presumed to be due to central nervous system dysfunction, and may occur across the life span. Problems in self-regulatory behaviors, social perception, and social interaction may exist with learning disabilities but do not by themselves constitute a learning disability. Although learning disabilities may occur concomitantly with other handicapping conditions (for example, sensory impairment, mental retardation, social and emotional disturbance) or with environmental influences (such as cultural differences, insufficient/inappropriate instruction, psychogenic factors), it is not the result of those conditions or influences. [1994, pp. 65–66]

Simply stated, LD is an umbrella term for a broad array of disorders in information processing, including disorders in one or more of the basic processes involved in understanding or using spoken or written language. Adults with LD are likely to experience problems that significantly affect their academic achievement and their lives.

Prevalence of Learning Disabilities in Adults

Literacy providers have questions about the prevalence of LD among adults and whether its prevalence in the general adult population is different from that in the population enrolled in adult literacy education. No one study has as yet determined a generally accepted prevalence rate among adults. Varying estimates for specific segments of the population do exist, but the estimates were obtained not through formal evaluation and documentation but through instructor observation, from administrators' educated guesses, and from client self-reports. For example, the U.S. Employment and Training Administration (1991) estimated the incidence of LD among Job Training and Partnership Act Title IIA recipients to be 15–23 percent. When Ryan and Price (1993) surveyed ABE directors nationwide about the prevalence of adults with LD in ABE classes, estimates ranged from 10 percent to more than 50 percent. Other estimates have been proposed for various subpopulations, but all lack validation data. A reasonable estimate of the prevalence rate among the general adult population can be extrapolated from data on the incidence of LD among school-age children.

Data collected by the U.S. Department of Education for the 1998–99 school year indicates that 4.49 percent of the school population ages six to twenty-one have a primary diagnosis of specific learning disability (U.S. Department of Education, 2000). Many believe that this rate is an underrepresentation because operational definitions of LD vary from school system to school system. This may account for the discrepancy in the reported school-age identification rate and estimates derived from other sources. Research based on brain studies supported by the National Institute of Child Health and Human Development (NICHD) indicates that 20 percent of school-age children may be considered reading disabled (Lyon, 1995; Shaywitz, Escobar, Shaywitz, Fletcher, & Makuch, 1992). Although not all children with reading disabilities have LD and not all children with LD have reading disabilities, the percentage of individuals with reading-related disabilities is higher than the standard school-based special education reports would lead us to believe. Given that recent studies point toward LD as a persistent, lifelong impairment, it is reasonable to accept a higher prevalence rate for the general adult population than is reported from special education data. For subsets of the general population, such as persons enrolled in adult literacy programs, we can assume a higher incidence rate (Reder, 1995). Although studies indicate that gender is not a determining factor—equal numbers of males and females have learning disabilities—there is a gender bias in the identification of LD in school-age children, with four times as many boys as girls being so identified (Lyon, 1994; Moats & Lyon, 1993; Shaywitz, Shaywitz, Fletcher, & Escobar, 1990).

Selection Criteria for Publications Included in This Literature Review

The initial computerized database search of Education Resources Information Center, Dissertation Abstracts International, Psychological Abstracts, and Sociological Abstracts yielded 485 references. The search of each database was inclusive of materials dated from January 1990 to October 1999. Descriptors included the terms *LD* plus *adults* plus *research,* and each of the subtopics of this article: *literacy, assistive technology, self-determination and self-advocacy, transition and employment,* and *screening and assessment.* The following criteria were used to determine eligible references: references had to be research-based, and all types of research were acceptable, including quantitative, qualitative, and results from literature reviews. Initially, seventy-three documents were identified as eligible for this literature review. References were added based on resources referenced in the identified documents or resources published after the computerized search was completed. Ultimately, this review was based on ninety-eight references published between 1989 and 2000 as well as selected references published prior to 1989 that supported background information. This literature review organizes the information into two broad categories: what we know about adults with LD and how we serve adults with LD.

WHAT WE KNOW ABOUT ADULTS WITH LEARNING DISABILITIES

To determine what adult life is like for individuals with LD, we can look to seven major studies. Five are follow-up studies, following cohorts of individuals into adulthood; one is a retrospective examination of successful adults with LD; and one is a national survey of adult literacy levels that includes persons with self-reported LD. Findings from these major research endeavors are consistent with those of less extensive investigations, which also are discussed.

Subjects Studied

The seven studies sampled a wide range of individuals with LD. Across these studies, data represent individuals who attended public and private schools, both before and after the federal definition of learning disabilities, and who were from urban, rural, and suburban settings, from different socioeconomic levels and ethnic groups, and in different stages of adulthood.

Two studies of national scope are the National Adult Literacy Survey (NALS) and the National Longitudinal Transition Study (NLTS). The NALS was administered to almost 25,000 randomly selected individuals age sixteen and above across the United States (Kirsch, Jungeblut, Jenkins, & Kolstad, 1993). As part of the NALS interview, participants were asked if they had a learning disability. There were 392 individuals (3 percent) who responded positively to this question (the validity of this self-identification has not been established). The NLTS (for example, Blackorby & Wagner, 1997; Wagner, D'Amico, Marder, Newman, & Blackorby, 1992) investigated a national sample of youth with disabilities zero to two years and three to five years after school exit. Data were compared with that from a sample of individuals without disabilities. Within this study, the postschool outcomes of 337 young adults with LD were examined.

Smaller-scale studies provided a more detailed longitudinal view. Spekman, Goldberg, and Herman (1992) studied factors related to success and life satisfaction for fifty adults with LD, ages eighteen to twenty-five, who had attended the Frostig Center in Los Angeles. Forty-one individuals from this same group were followed up ten years later by Raskind, Goldberg, Higgins, and Herman (1999). Edgar (1995) collected data from two cohorts of students with and without LD who graduated from Washington State public schools in 1985 and 1990 for up to ten years after graduation. The Kauai, Hawaii, Longitudinal Study (Werner, 1993) began studying a multiracial cohort in 1955. Findings from this study compared life indicators for a subset of twenty-two individuals with LD who were assessed at ages one, two, ten, eighteen, and thirty-two against a matched control group.

Finally, Reiff, Gerber, and Ginsberg (1997) studied seventy-one individuals with LD with an average age of 44.9 from twenty-four states across the United States and Canada who had been nominated as successful individuals in their fields. This sample was then divided into highly and moderately successful groups that were matched with each other on gender, race, severity, and types of learning disabilities, and parents' socioeconomic status.

Definition of Success

To identify variables related to success, it is first important to define success. In the referenced studies, researchers attempted to make success as multidimensional as possible by collecting data on educational achievements, career and employment status, independent living, personal and social relationships, and social-emotional adjustment issues. When one cohort was studied over time, success was determined by movement toward acceptable adult behavior, achievements in relation to society's norms, and developmental state. As a result, success for adolescents and young adults looked different from success for older adults. Nondisabled control groups helped determine if persons with LD were different from the norm for their peers. Another success indicator was participants' self-perceptions in relation to their achievements and their satisfaction with their achievements.

Consistent Findings

Given the diversity of individuals studied, it is interesting to note the following consistent findings.

ACADEMIC EXPERIENCE. Academic difficulties faced by schoolchildren with LD persist throughout adulthood. Researchers who traced the academic profiles of persons with LD from elementary school into late adolescence and early adulthood found a consistent pattern of lower-than-expected academic achievement (Spekman et al., 1992; Raskind et al., 1999). Vogel and Reder (1998), in reviewing follow-up studies, found that the high school graduation rate for persons with LD ranged from 32 percent to 66 percent. Ongoing academic difficulties can greatly affect participation and success in postsecondary education. Individuals with LD attend vocational and other noncollege postsecondary programs at a higher rate than their nondisabled counterparts, who attend college and university programs at a higher rate (Murray, Goldstein, Nourse, & Edgar, 2000). It is not surprising that these persons, whose ways of learning often do not match typical school conditions, would gravitate to less academic forms of education. The discouraging news is that they successfully complete these programs at a low rate (Murray et al., 2000; Sitlington & Frank, 1990; Wagner et al., 1991).

EMPLOYMENT. During the past fifteen years, numerous studies have reported the employment status of persons with LD. Peraino (1992), in reviewing eleven follow-up studies of persons with LD, found an average employment rate of 70 percent, with some studies reporting similar employment rates up to five years after high school for persons with LD and their nondisabled peers (Blackorby & Wagner, 1996). Edgar (1995) found that the less-than-full-employment rate for nondisabled individuals zero to five years after high school was partially explained by their enrollment in postsecondary education programs and that individuals with LD engage in postsecondary education at a low rate. Persons with LD who obtain employment upon exiting high school often find themselves in low-wage jobs with little opportunity for advancement and often without health insurance and other benefits (Blackorby & Wagner, 1997; Edgar, 1995).

Reder and Vogel (1997), in a secondary analysis of the NALS data, compared responses of subjects aged sixteen to sixty-four with self-reported learning disabilities (SRLD) with those of subjects who did not report having LD. Persons with SRLD were less likely to be employed full-time (39 percent versus 51 percent) and more likely to be unemployed (16 percent versus 6 percent). They also worked substantially fewer weeks per year, for lower wages, and in lower-status jobs than those in the nondisabled group. Reder (1995) reported that 42.2 percent of families of adults with SRLD were living in or near poverty, compared with only 16.2 percent of the families of their nondisabled peers.

Positive outcomes have also been reported. Employment opportunities seem to improve over time for individuals with LD, with a trend toward higher employment rates the longer youth are out of school (Blackorby & Wagner, 1997; Edgar, 1995; Frank, Sitlington, & Carson, 1995; Scuccimarra & Speece, 1990). Reiff et al. (1997) found that forty-three of forty-six highly successful adults with LD had an annual income of more than $50,000, with twenty-one making $100,000 or more.

STRESS AND SOCIAL-EMOTIONAL ISSUES. Living with a learning disability is a major life stressor that, for many, far outweighs other events or conditions (Raskind et al., 1999). The stress comes from a number of factors. For example, memory difficulties can result in many inconvenient and frustrating experiences, such as not being able to recall a person's name when making introductions or searching thirty minutes to find the car keys before leaving for work. Diagnosed adults have to decide whether to disclose their disability, and undiagnosed individuals have to decide if they are going to communicate to others their strengths and needs. Many adults report hiding their problems with reading, writing, or math as they try to "fake it." Shessel and Reiff (1999) identified the "imposter phenomenon": even some successful individuals feel that they are making false positive impressions and have a fear of failure. These feelings of inadequacy often lead adults with LD to distance themselves from others to avoid being exposed (Spekman et al., 1992). Hoy and Manglitz (1996), in their review of literature on social and affective adjustment of adults with LD, found that adults with LD reported fewer social contacts and a higher incidence of emotional adjustment difficulties than their peers.

PERSONAL SUPPORT. One highly consistent finding from these studies is that support from a significant other is key to successful adult adjustment. Some individuals had family support that allowed them to access specialized services and take extra time to become independent (Spekman et al., 1992). Others were supported by mentors who made them feel special and accepted them as they were. Adults often found support in either intimate or work relationships or both, which helped them gain needed confidence (Gerber & Reiff, 1994). Werner (1993, p. 23) described the impact of support: "The learning disabled youngsters who overcame the odds *all* had at least one person in their lives who accepted them unconditionally, regardless of temperamental idiosyncrasies, physical attractiveness, or level of intelligence."

TOLL OF MULTIPLE RISK FACTORS. For some individuals, LD is accompanied by one or more additional risk factors. Spekman et al. (1992) found that individuals who experienced the least success had required hospitalization or residential placement one or more times. In studying this same group ten years later, Raskind et al. (1999) found a small cluster of individuals who possessed characteristics that should predict success but who had failed to develop an independent adult life. Upon examination, the researchers found that these persons all had developed an additional disability (for example, hearing loss, epilepsy, motor dysfunction). It appeared that this additional challenge affected their ability to become independent.

GENDER. Follow-up studies of individuals with LD during the initial postschool years consistently indicate that males with LD are employed at a higher rate than females with LD (Edgar, 1995; Sitlington & Frank, 1990; Wagner et al., 1992). Edgar's study of two cohorts of graduates from Washington State schools revealed that females with LD were employed at a lower rate than both males with LD and nondisabled females. This in part is explained by the phenomena of early parenthood: females with LD appeared to have children at a younger age and at twice the rate as nondisabled females and to receive public assistance at a higher rate. Edgar (1995, p. 296) concluded that "females with LD are at risk for becoming mothers at an early age without benefit of a supportive partner or financial resources." The risk for females with LD is an amalgam of societal and disability factors. Although great strides have been made, females in general are still striving for career and income equity with males. This study points to the possibility that females may have greater difficulty finding supportive individuals to stand by them in adulthood, especially when they become mothers. The study also calls into question the availability of social contacts to provide childcare and leads into the job market. Because LD is identified at a lower rate in females than in males within the K–12 school system, females with LD who participate in follow-up studies may represent a lower-functioning group of individuals than their male counterparts. Females with LD may come to ABE programs with more family life issues and with fewer supports than males.

SELF-DETERMINATION. The longitudinal research on the status of adults with LD connects well with the growing emphasis on self-determination in disability services. Self-determination, however, has received little attention heretofore in adult literacy.

In 1988, in an effort to improve outcomes for persons with disabilities, the U.S. Department of Education, Office of Special Education and Rehabilitative Services, began an initiative on self-determination that has yielded both conceptual and practical information for working with individuals with LD. Federally funded projects have demonstrated that self-determination skills can be taught (Ward, 1999). Self-determination is a goal for all adults, but it is particularly important for adults with LD because the nature of their disability puts them at risk for leading lives of dependence and for trying to cope with feelings of failure. Guiding persons with LD to become more self-determined is one way to break the cycle of dependence that can be fostered by education, employment, home, and community environments.

Self-determination is both an attitude and a skill. Attitudinally, self-determined persons are positive about themselves; they are goal-directed, with a can-do frame of mind. Behaviorally, self-determined persons with LD have developed a range of competencies that are valued by society and can be used to offset their specific LD. Five factors contribute to self-determination: self-knowledge, the ability to plan, the capacity to act based on self-knowledge and planning, the ability to learn from experience, and the nature of the environment (Hoffman & Field, 1995).

SELF-KNOWLEDGE. Self-knowledge means understanding one's learning disabilities, including specific information processing deficits (such as auditory processing, visual processing, attention, and memory) and how these deficits affect performance in daily life. This knowledge can lead to acceptance of one's disability—that is, the ability to view one's LD as limited or contained rather than all-encompassing. It is this internalization of information into a realistic self-appraisal that helps the individual make both the internal and external changes necessary to accommodate specific learning disabilities, ultimately resulting in a healthy sense of self (Thomas, 1991). Indeed, some highly successful

adults with LD are able to move beyond understanding and acceptance to valuing their disability as something they can use to give
themselves a competitive edge (Shessel & Reiff, 1999; Reiff et al., 1997).

ABILITY TO PLAN. Goal setting is the basis for productive planning.
Learning to differentiate between wants and needs, to make choices that
match one's interests, preferences, and strengths, and to avoid one's areas
of weakness is an important part of this process (Hoffman & Field,
1995). Goal setting and planning require organizational skills and the
ability to follow a process—skills that can pose difficulties for many
adults with LD who struggle with impulsivity, cause-and-effect thinking, and sequencing. Raskind et al. (1999) found that successful individuals with LD were able to use a step-by-step process to achieve goals,
compared with unsuccessful individuals who did not identify goals or
who reported goals that were unrealistic and grandiose for their current
situations. Reiff et al. (1997) determined that a conscious goal orientation was often used to combat fear of failure and instill feelings of control. In a study of tutors and adult beginning readers who used learning
contracts, Ogle (1990) found that adults with learning contracts attended significantly more tutoring sessions and persisted in the program longer than learners without contracts. Tutors and learners alike
agreed that involvement in planning instructional objectives and methods led to increased motivation. The process of focusing, setting goals,
working toward one's goals, and meeting success feeds on itself: successfully achieving goals, no matter how small, sets the stage for more
goal setting and more goal-directed behavior.

CAPACITY TO ACT ON THE BASIS OF SELF-KNOWLEDGE AND PLANNING.
When actions are supported by self-knowledge and planning, it is easier to persist and be successful, despite challenges. Successful adults
with LD are proactive, fitting situations to their strengths while min-
imizing their needs. They learn to persevere despite challenges, and
they learn to seek creative solutions to tasks at hand (Reiff et al., 1997).
In contrast, unsuccessful adults with LD often fail to recognize that
they have power to alter situations and that there are many ways to
achieve a final end (Raskind et al., 1999).

ABILITY TO LEARN FROM EXPERIENCE. When persons understand their
strengths and needs, they are able to evaluate successes and failures in
terms of acknowledged areas of ability and disability. When they meet

with failure at specific tasks, they recognize that it is the LD that got in the way rather than viewing themselves as stupid, inept, or global failures. Moreover, they use the knowledge gained from experience to ensure that, in attempting the same tasks in the future, they will modify their approach and capitalize on their strengths to minimize the chance of repeated failure. Less successful adults with LD do not exhibit the same ability to learn from difficult situations (Gerber, Reiff, & Ginsberg, 1996).

NATURE OF THE ENVIRONMENT. Wehmeyer (1997) described three environmental components that support self-determination. First, individuals must be in situations that help them continue to grow and enhance their abilities. Persons with LD are particularly vulnerable in environments that are not in sync with the way they learn or function. Second, they must learn to use accommodations and supports that can transform challenges into learning and working conditions that set the stage for success. Finally, they must have opportunities to learn, to demonstrate competence, and to become part of the decision-making process that determines the ways in which the environment functions.

The Changing Workplace and Challenges for Persons with Learning Disabilities

Teaching self-determination skills becomes increasingly critical when we consider today's changing workplace. The interpersonal demands of the twenty-first-century workplace can be a challenge: employees are expected to assume greater responsibility, handle diverse tasks, and be team players. Some employees with LD may experience problems when working as part of a team; they may misunderstand oral directions or nonverbal social cues, or they may have difficulty communicating with supervisors or peers (Anderson, 1994; Brown & Gerber, 1994; Dowdy, Smith, & Nowell, 1992). They may have problems requesting and comprehending feedback or constructive criticism of their work performance (Ness & Price, 1990).

Technological advances have resulted in a workplace in constant flux (Dent, 1995). Brown (1997) described both advantages and challenges to persons with LD brought about by the proliferation of technologies in the work environment. Word processing features such as spelling checkers and grammar checkers can help persons with LD with their writing, and automated calendars can help keep track of daily schedules. On the flip side, voice mail requires accurate auditory perception, which can present challenges for some persons with LD. Loss of support staff, as when secretaries and assistants are replaced by personal computers, demands higher literacy skills for all levels of workers (Brown & Gerber, 1994; Mikulecky, 1995). As the NALS indicated, few jobs do not require some reading and writing.

The workplace should be more disability-friendly since the 1992 implementation of the Americans with Disabilities Act (ADA), particularly Title I, which prohibits employment discrimination based on disability. But the workplace is still adjusting to the concept of hidden disabilities such as LD.

Under the ADA, employers are required to provide workplace accommodations, but only for disabilities that have been disclosed. Individuals have the right to determine whether, when, how, and to whom to disclose their disabilities, and many choose to keep their disabilities a secret. Murphy (1992) found that most people are reluctant to disclose that they have LD when they interviewed for jobs. Among the reasons cited were that most employers do not understand LD, that the information might be held against employees, and that most likely nothing could be done about their problems. These responses imply a need for increased knowledge on the part of persons with LD in the areas of self-awareness, civil rights, and the advantages of disclosure. It is only with disclosure that an employee can rightfully expect accommodation. Likewise, employers must understand that the purpose of providing accommodation is not to compensate for lack of knowledge or skills but to help otherwise qualified employees compensate for disabilities as they perform essential job functions.

A model for employment success (Gerber et al., 1996) speaks to the process of reframing, or redefining, the LD experience in a positive light. It involves accepting and understanding one's disabilities and recognizing and valuing one's strengths and talents. It also requires a strong goal orientation on the part of the person with LD and an understanding that there must be a "goodness of fit" between the person's abilities and the work environment and responsibilities (Reiff et al., 1997). The model includes knowing how to request appropriate accommodation. Finally, an element critical to employment success is the formation of personal support networks, or "favorable social ecologies" (Gregg & Phillips, 1996).

HOW WE SERVE ADULTS WITH LEARNING DISABILITIES

There are several components to effective service delivery for persons with LD. Starting with the adult learner's entry into a literacy program, service delivery includes assessment of the learner's needs, interests, academic skill levels, and learning strengths and challenges. From assessment data, there evolves planning appropriate instructional interventions and selecting accommodations or assistive technologies, as needed. Central to effective service delivery is the professional development of instructional and administrative personnel to ensure they understand and employ best practices. Effective service delivery in literacy programs requires that personnel have an understanding of current reading research and a review of the literature on assessment, interventions, and assistive technology for adults with LD.

Reading Research

The ability to read encompasses two distinct abilities: identifying words, or decoding, and comprehending words, sentences, and larger chunks of text. Many adults with LD can be considered to have a reading disability (RD), the general term used to identify individuals who read well below what would be expected for their age and intellect. This definition assumes that reading deficits are not caused by external factors (such as poverty or poor education) or sensory deficits (such as visual or hearing impairments).

Dyslexia is the term commonly used in the literature to denote a specific reading disability (Catts & Kamhi, 1999c). Research into the etiology and symptomatology of dyslexia tells us that specific word identification problems are at its root. Dyslexia is diagnosed by examining an individual's phonological processing abilities, including the processing, storage, retrieval, and use of phonological codes in memory as well as phonological awareness and speech production. Phonological processing is based on an ability to identify, think about, and manipulate the forty-four English phonemes as sounds in individual words (Torgesen & Wagner, 1998). Dyslexia can present as a difficulty in learning to decode and spell printed words. This difficulty often leads to problems with reading comprehension and writing.

CAUSES OF READING DISABILITIES. The literature on causes of RD establishes a strong link between reading disabilities and developmental language disorders (Catts & Kamhi, 1999a). Researchers have been able to trace developmental language delays in young children to subsequent reading deficits (Bishop & Adams, 1990; Catts, 1993). With adults, however, the cause-effect relationship is more tenuous. Poor readers read less (and therefore have different language experiences) than able readers, who develop vocabulary, background knowledge, and familiarity with complex syntax structures through reading rich and challenging textual material. Readers with deficient word identification and comprehension skills often find reading unrewarding, and this lessens their motivation to read. Stanovich and West (1989) developed measures of reading volume for both adults and children and found that the amount of information read has an effect on important language abilities. Adults with reading disabilities can thus be expected to have less well-developed language skills either as a cause or as a result of reading deficiencies (Cunningham & Stanovich, 1998).

Catts and Kamhi (1999b) reviewed research on causes of reading disabilities and identified genetic, neurological, and cognitive-perceptual explanations. There is strong evidence to support dyslexia as a genetically transmitted disorder (DeFries et al., 1997; Catts & Kamhi, 1999b; Light & DeFries, 1995). This means that adults with LD who have children may be trying to cope with their child's disability as well as their own. Some adults become aware of their disability as part of the process during which their child is identified as having LD.

A growing body of research indicates differences in brain structure and function between individuals with RD and normal readers, although with great individual variation (Catts & Kamhi, 1999b). Recent technologies, such as magnetic resonance imaging (MRI) and examination of blood flow in different regions of the brain, allow for noninvasive brain studies. This emerging area of research is too new to have direct application to the development of relevant educational diagnoses or interventions. Thus we are faced with a chicken-or-egg dilemma: are the neurological differences between able and disabled adult readers the result of organic anomalies or of years of poor reading skills that have affected the brain?

ADULTS WITH READING DISABILITIES. Some adults with LD have reading disabilities and can be characterized as slow readers compared with their nondisabled peers. Slow reading rates can be caused by lack of skills needed for automatic word identification as well as by ineffective reading comprehension strategies or ineffective reading instruction (Bruck, 1992; Stanovich, 1986). There is convincing evidence that dyslexics' phonological processing deficits are not the result of developmental delays and that they continue into adult life. These deficits may represent an important barrier to the acquisition of fluent word recognition and consequently may affect reading comprehension.

In a recent synthesis of research on metacognition (the ability to monitor and reflect on one's thinking), Collins, Dickson, Simmons, and Kameenui (1998) identified a body of research indicating that individuals with RD can learn to become effective and active readers through instruction aimed at increasing such metacognitive skills as self-regulation. Self-regulation is the ability to use self-talk to engage in the cognitive activities needed to complete a challenging task. For example, self-regulated learners regularly stop during reading to covertly ask themselves questions to check on comprehension. Additionally, a self-regulated learner will actively try to figure out new vocabulary in a reading through a variety of means, such as using context clues; analyzing the word for meaning using prefixes, suffixes, and roots; or stopping to look up the word in the dictionary. It may be crucial for adult literacy programs to incorporate the direct teaching of reading strategies in a way that helps adults with LD apply strategies to meet their specific reading needs.

Assessment

An important question for literacy providers concerns the assessment process for learners suspected of having LD: How do I know if a learner has LD? Literacy practitioners report that it is not uncommon to find among their adult learners some individuals who seem to have great difficulty learning and retaining information. Most of these adult learners have never been diagnosed for the presence of LD (Riviere, 1998).

Vogel (1998) presents arguments both for and against formal diagnostic testing. Those who question the value of diagnostic testing suggest that the label *LD* may increase the adult's sense of inadequacy and further discourage risk taking (Alderson-Gill & Associates, 1989; Ross-Gordon, 1989). In addition, the cost of diagnostic evaluations can be prohibitive. Literacy programs typically do not have access to free diagnostic testing and often refer learners to publicly supported diagnostic services, such as vocational rehabilitation. Eligibility criteria can be a barrier to services, particularly if the client is not looking for a job or for job advancement.

In addition, Ross-Gordon (1996) points out that the sociocultural dimensions of LD assessment for participants in adult literacy programs have largely been ignored. For example, the gender bias discussed earlier (Lyon, 1994) means that women are more likely to enroll in adult literacy programs undiagnosed. Culturally biased testing also can lead to over- or underidentification of cultural or linguistic minority students (Ross-Gordon, 1998).

Despite these arguments, Vogel (1998) points out that diagnosis is necessary for appropriate service delivery. A formal diagnosis allows persons with LD to access those rights provided for by law, such as accommodations for General Educational Development (GED) testing as well as accommodations for instruction and the workplace. Some adults with LD have confirmed that a diagnosis helps lift some of their insecurity and sense of inadequacy (Hatt, 1991). As suggested in the self-determination literature, to act as their own best advocates, individuals with LD need an accurate understanding of their learning strengths and challenges; LD assessment can provide this understanding. Ross-Gordon (1998) suggests a middle ground: rather than referring all learners for diagnostic testing, literacy providers should refer only those learners for whom test results would yield a benefit that would not otherwise be obtained. The literacy provider should discuss advantages of diagnosis with the learner and then allow the learner to decide whether to seek diagnostic testing (Fowler & Scarborough, 1993; Ross-Gordon, 1989).

Before referring learners for formal assessment, literacy programs have the option of conducting LD screening. Staff members should understand how LD screening fits into the overall assessment process. Its purposes are to determine if a learner is likely to have LD and to refer likely candidates for more formal diagnostic testing, as appropriate (Payne, 1998; National ALLD Center, 1999). The advantages of LD screening are that it is inexpensive, quick, and appropriate for large numbers of persons, sometimes in a group setting, and that it does not require extensive staff training (Mellard, 1998). Screening provides a superficial assessment of several ability areas and can help determine the need for further assessments. Staff should know how to identify, select, and use screening tools and understand how LD screening results can affect programs and learners (Mellard, 1998).

As part of the research and development on *Bridges to Practice: A Research-Based Guide for Literacy Practitioners Serving Adults with Learning Disabilities,*[1] the National ALLD Center (1999) conducted focus groups throughout the nation. The groups consisted of literacy teachers and tutors, administrators, and researchers in ABE, ESL, GED, and correctional education, as well as library literacy personnel. Participants were asked to share best practices in LD screening and instruction. Transcripts of focus group sessions were organized into a set of statements about screening and intervention, and this set of statements, in questionnaire form, was mailed to literacy practitioners nationwide (Sturomski, Lenz, Scanlon, & Catts, 1998). From the responses, ten standards were developed for selecting screening materials. The standards serve as guidelines for making decisions and are essential for a complete evaluation of screening instruments. There are both administration standards, such as "Guidelines regarding whether to refer the individual for further testing are clear and reasonable," and technical development standards, such as "The screening material accurately predicts who may have a learning disability." The nationally validated standards were then applied to fourteen screening instruments with high frequency of use in literacy programs, and report cards were developed on each of the instruments. These report cards have been published in *Bridges to Practice, Guidebook 2: The Assessment Process* (National ALLD Center, 1999). The report cards can guide literacy program staff in selecting appropriate LD screening instruments. A literacy program that strives to be responsive to the needs of all learners will have a process in place for screening learners for LD and for making referrals, as appropriate, for diagnostic testing.

Instructional Interventions

There is a wealth of research on effective instructional interventions for school-aged students with LD. This abundance is in stark contrast with the paucity of research on instructional interventions for adults with LD. The bulk of the adult research has focused on instructional support interventions with college students (Scanlon & Mellard, 1997), whereas investigations of LD instructional interventions in ABE programs are mostly descriptive and lack experimental control. One reason for this is the lack of specialized services and personnel typically found in the college setting. This section of the literature review draws on research across K–12, college, and ABE programs, with an emphasis on interventions that could be offered by ABE teachers and tutors.

INSTRUCTIONAL MODELS AND PRINCIPLES. Research on instructional variables positively associated with successful learning for students with LD strongly supports combining direct instruction with strategy instruction, two models that have much in common. Both are designed to teach a graduated series of steps or procedures and to provide ample opportunity for practice to promote overlearning, and they allow a teacher to closely monitor students' progress. Strategy instruction explicitly teaches covert mental processes through cognitive modeling and often incorporates a mnemonic as a way of remembering the steps of the cognitive task. For example, a simple three-step strategy for paraphrasing uses the mnemonic RAP (Schumaker, Denton, & Deshler, 1984). *R* stands for "read the paragraph." *A* stands for "ask yourself, what are the main ideas and details of this paragraph?" *P* stands for "put the main ideas and details in your own words." This three-step procedure is a strategy because it provides three prompts to help learners engage in self-talk to determine what is important in a paragraph and to use their own words to remember what the paragraph is about. In teaching this strategy, an instructor would model the three steps of paraphrasing by thinking aloud and engaging learners in explicitly discussing the thinking processes used in each step.

Swanson (1999) reviewed 180 intervention studies and determined that a combination of both direct instruction and strategy instruction for students with LD produced a larger effect than either instructional method by itself. Swanson defined direct instruction as a bottom-up approach that teaches subskills as a way of mastering important basic skills, and strategy instruction as a top-down approach that emphasizes rules and procedures to be applied across settings. Swanson identified many commonalities between the two instructional models, given that each is focused on explicit teaching: instruction in which the teacher describes and models a skill or higher-order thinking task and then provides the learner with multiple opportunities for practice.

Hughes (1998) reviewed research on college students and adolescents with LD and identified principles of effective instruction that support Swanson's findings. These principles, easily incorporated into direct and strategy instruction, and are listed in Exhibit 3.1.

- *Teach important skills.* Include adults in deciding what is important to learn and identify functional skills.
- *Teach less better.* When you teach fewer skills, students can have enough practice to master them.
- *Teach explicitly.* Clearly identify what is being taught rather than using discovery techniques.
- *Teach contextually.* Teach skills that can be practiced and applied to real-life situations.
- *Explain what is to be learned and why it is important.* Explaining purpose and relevance can increase motivation.
- *Check the old before teaching the new.* Many individuals have difficulty retaining what they have previously learned. Include practice exercises of previously learned material to check on retention and allow for reinforcement.
- *Model what is to be learned.* A clear demonstration helps students see the important components of the skill or strategy to be learned.
- *Use supportive practice.* Learners with LD need guided practice before they are asked to apply a skill independently.
- *Use controlled materials.* New learning should be applied in easy materials and the task difficulty gradually increased.
- *Provide practice, practice, practice (and more practice).* Individuals with LD often have difficulty retaining new information or skills. Practice to the point of automaticity helps new learning stick.
- *Require frequent responses.* Students benefit from active and frequent questioning to maintain attention and involvement.
- *Provide corrective feedback.* Specific and immediate positive and corrective feedback is a powerful force in guiding the learning process.
- *Promote generalization.* One common attribute of individuals with LD is difficulty in applying new learning to situations beyond the instructional setting. Having learners identify real-life tasks in which new learning can be applied is important in making new learning functional.
- *Be prepared.* Learners with LD benefit from well-organized and explicit instruction. This takes planning.

Exhibit 3.1. Instructional Principles.

Source: Adapted from Hughes, 1998.

Instruction is a means to two ends. One is the development of learner competence. The student learns the skill, strategy, or content that is the focus of instruction (for example, learning to read, learning information needed to pass the GED tests). The other is helping the learner become a more confident, knowledgeable, and self-sufficient learner. How intervention programs are structured is a crucial variable affecting whether self-determination is promoted or hindered (Ryan & Deci, 2000).

METACOGNITION AND SELF-REGULATED LEARNING. In comparison with their peers, students with LD are less likely to identify and use effective strategies for learning (Swanson, 1999). While ABE researchers identify adults as self-directed learners (Merriam & Brockett, 1997), adults with LD often lack feelings of self-efficacy because they have a history of educational failure (Adelman & Vogel, 1991). They may be less willing to initiate, to become active partners in learning, and they may not possess the self-knowledge crucial for self-directed learning. Students with LD need instruction that helps them develop metacognition, or awareness of their own thinking processes (Borkowski & Muthukrishna, 1992). Metacognition can be divided into three parts: being planful before engaging in a learning task; being active and efficient during learning by using strategies and monitoring comprehension and performance; and being self-aware—evaluating one's learning and making adaptations to increase success when faced with a similar task. Engaging in metacognition allows learners to become self-directed, self-regulated learners.

Instructors can help students become metacognitive by teaching them how to analyze tasks and to select from various strategies for accomplishing those tasks. Strategies for comprehending textbook chapters can be different from strategies for comprehending literature. Learners need a repertoire of strategies and then must be able to apply the most useful and relevant strategy to the task at hand. For example, in reading literature the reader may want to use visual imagery to picture characters and action. In textbook reading, headings, charts, pictures, and end-of-chapter questions may be used as guides for identifying important content. Both strategies are important, but they must be applied to the type of reading task they are designed to meet. Self-regulation depends on prior beliefs and knowledge. Learners need to develop a repertoire of learning strategies from which to choose for various learning tasks, and they need to build an experience base of successful learning in order to believe that they can be successful. Successful learning is dependent on instruction that is offered at the learner's current level of performance. Models of instruction to develop metacognition are rooted in Vygotsky's (1978) concept of scaffolding and interactive dialogue between teacher and learner. Scaffolded instruction is based on what the learner already knows as a guide to determine the next step for instruction. Teachers model important cognitive processes and guide students as they practice and gradually learn these processes to the point of independent performance. Ross-Gordon (1998, p. 81) contrasts adult basic education and special education teaching models as "placing the teacher at the side of the learner as a guide or facilitator rather than in front of the learner as director of the learning experience."

The principles of strategy instruction can be in direct alignment with adult learning principles. For example, Palincsar and Brown (1984) developed a reading comprehension instructional model called reciprocal teaching. In this model, the teacher is a facilitator who engages in collaborative problem solving with students to discuss, evaluate, and adapt strategies to achieve reading goals. Using principles from reciprocal teaching and other strategy instructional models, Butler (1993) developed a Strategic Content Learning model to tutor college students. Each student chose a task important to current or future academic work and then was tutored to help approach the task strategically. Results from the six case studies provided evidence that students' performance on their chosen task improved and that they became more self-regulated in their learning. Pre- and post-data also indicated gains in metacognitive knowledge and increased perceptions of self-efficacy.

Highly structured reading instruction approaches are being used for adult students deficient in basic sound-symbol relationships. The Orton-Gillingham (Orton, 1966) approach to teaching reading has been used successfully with dyslexic students of all ages for more than thirty years. The Wilson Reading System (WRS) has incorporated Orton-Gillingham principles of multisensory, cumulative, and sequential instruction to teach analytic and synthetic reading skills. The program uses a highly structured form of direct instruction, which allows for individualized teaching based on continuous assessment of student progress. Although no controlled studies of the WRS are available, program evaluation and descriptive measures such as retention rate offer an initial base of support for this program's effectiveness (Wilson, 1998).

In summary, effective instruction for adults with LD is a combination of keeping in mind the big-picture goal of developing self-determined metacognitive learners and of employing instructional models that guide interactions between teachers or tutors and learners to accomplish specific learning tasks. Effective instruction also includes understanding various assistive technologies that can help learners meet with success.

Assistive Technology

Assistive technology (AT) refers to devices that can be used to compensate for disabilities. It is defined by the Technology-Related Assistance Act of 1988 as "any item, piece of equipment, or product system acquired commercially off-the-shelf, modified, or customized, that is used to increase, maintain or improve the functional capabilities of individuals with disabilities." Persons with LD have deficits in the ways they process information; AT can provide a means of modifying the way they receive or express information in a manner that accentuates their strengths. Raskind (1994) points out that the purpose of AT is not to "cure" a learning disability but to help people work around their difficulties. Studies indicate that persons with LD can function effectively and enjoy greater freedom and independence using appropriate AT. Gerber, Ginsberg, and Reiff (1992) reported that highly successful adults with LD tend to use technology, and Raskind, Higgins, and Herman (1997) found that adults who used AT in the workplace attributed their achieving job independence, satisfaction, and success to their use of technology.

AT for persons with LD can include, but is not limited to, recorded books, computers, tape recorders, readers, spellers, calculators, organizers, and word-processing programs. Both high-tech devices such as optical character recognition (OCR) systems or speech recognition and low-tech tools such as organizers are referred to as AT. Several studies have found AT to be effective in addressing the language-based difficulties experienced by persons with LD. Elkind, Black, and Murray (1996) found that adults with dyslexia read faster and comprehended better using an OCR and speech synthesis system than when reading without this support. In addition, the use of systems such as OCR and recorded books open up a world of subject matter for the learner. This may be especially useful for GED test preparation as well as for acquiring strategies for future learning related to life and to work. Higgins and Raskind (1997) found OCR and speech synthesis systems to be of greatest support to persons with severe reading disabilities. College students with LD have demonstrated improved writing performance with word processors (Collins, 1990; Primus, 1990). The use of organizer systems can help persons with LD to overcome some of the limitations associated with difficulties in memory and planning functions.

Raskind (1998, p. 261) stresses that "not all assistive technologies are appropriate for all individuals in all situations." Further, he suggests that in selecting appropriate technology for an individual with LD, four elements must be considered: the individual, the task and functions to be performed, the specific technology itself, and the specific contexts of interaction. The selection of an appropriate technology will depend on the individual's strengths and weaknesses in areas such as reading, writing, math, spelling, listening, memory, and organization as well as on the individual's prior experience with and interest in using AT. The goal of using AT is to allow individuals with LD to function effectively in their various roles as family members, employees, lifelong learners, and citizens. The use of AT can make the difference between an individual's self-reliance and dependence on others.

IMPLICATIONS FOR RESEARCH, POLICY, AND PRACTICE

It becomes apparent, in reviewing the literature on LD and adult literacy, that this is a field still in its infancy, with seemingly limitless opportunities for development and growth. This is at once discouraging and exciting: We want answers *now* about proven strategies for serving all adult learners, but we recognize and appreciate that we and our adult learners can have a hand in shaping future research, policy, and practice.

Few literacy programs now have comprehensive services for adults with LD, and not all current practices are grounded in research. There is a need for reliable, field-tested practices on assessment of adults with LD as well as on curriculum development, instructional strategies, and professional development of program staff. Although there exists an extensive research base on best practices for children and adolescents with LD, we cannot apply this information with confidence to adults until we have appropriate studies.

To serve adult learners effectively, first and foremost we need the increased knowledge that research can provide. Next, we need policy changes, both nationally and locally, to support improved practice. Finally, we need systemic program changes to ensure that services are responsive to persons with LD. Systemic reform is needed at every level of service delivery and, most particularly, in the professional development of literacy program staff.

Research

Research on adults with LD is perhaps the greatest and most immediate need; it should guide the profession of adult literacy education. From research flows the development of policy initiatives and improved practice.

DIVERSITY ISSUES, INCLUDING GENDER, RACE, AND CULTURE. We've learned from the literature review that issues of diversity (gender, race, culture) regarding adults with LD have received minimal attention from the LD field (Ross-Gordon, 1996). We've also learned that 43 percent of adults participating in the NALS with self-reported LD were at or below poverty level (Reder, 1995). And we've learned that females with LD are underidentified in school and consequently enter adult literacy programs undiagnosed (Lyon, 1994). Possible research questions include the following:

- How do different minority groups construct the term *learning disability?*
- What types of instructional strategies, curriculum materials, counseling, and other support services are most appropriate, given specific cultural mores?
- What is the extent of gender, race, and primary language bias in the LD identification process?
- How do we appropriately identify LD in persons for whom English is not the primary language?
- What tests are valid and reliable for LD screening for native speakers of other languages?
- In the case of students in classes in English for speakers of other languages (ESOL), how can we know whether a student's difficulty in learning tasks is a result of LD or of language and cultural acquisition problems?
- Is there a difference in the instructional methods effective for persons with LD and those effective for persons with a history of low educational achievement as a result of poverty?

ASSESSMENT. The issue of when and for whom diagnostic testing is appropriate must be clarified for literacy providers. The question of how to fund the cost of diagnostic testing must also be addressed.

- What are appropriate uses of diagnostic testing and LD labeling of adults?
- Are there times when diagnostic testing is not appropriate?
- When are learners' interests best served by identification?
- Do models exist for obtaining diagnostic evaluations at reasonable cost for GED candidates and other learners?

READING. The NICHD has been investigating child reading acquisition and instructional interventions for the past several years. Current research on the K–12 population, if replicated with adult subjects, would provide new directions for the field of adult literacy education.

- What do we know about how adults with LD learn to read?
- What role does phonological awareness play in reading acquisition in adults?
- How effective is strategy instruction compared with other methods?
- How can assistive technology enhance reading instruction?

INSTRUCTIONAL INTERVENTIONS. There is a need to determine if the interventions that are effective for children and adolescents with LD are effective and appropriate for adults.

- What instructional interventions are most effective for adults with LD?
- Do instructional interventions differ for different types of LD?
- What assistive technologies are most effective for adults with LD?
- What curricular materials are particularly effective for adults with LD?
- What research-based practices supported by the K–12 literature have the most promise for teaching adults with LD?

EMPLOYMENT. Few follow-up studies have followed persons with LD past early adulthood. Additional follow-up studies are needed to provide better information about the employment success of adults with LD.

- What is the long-term occupational, economic, and employ-ment status of adults with LD?

- How do men and women with LD differ in these categories from the general population?

- How can we design programs to enhance employment success for persons with LD and, in particular, for women with LD?

- In what ways are persons with LD who disclose different from those who do not?

- What accommodations are most frequently requested and which are most effective in enhancing job success?

- What are the differences in job success of employees with LD when employers are given awareness training?

- What are the most commonly reported problems and strategies used on the job by persons with LD?

- Are there model programs for incorporating preemployment skills and literacy skills for persons with LD?

SELF-DETERMINATION. We have seen that, more than any skill, the de-velopment of self-determination is critical to the success of the indi-vidual with LD, but we recognize that literacy programs are only now becoming aware of this fact.

- How does the typical functioning of an adult basic educa-tion program encourage and hinder the development of self-determination for persons with LD?

- How can professional development encourage teachers to infuse activities into the curricula that foster self-advocacy and self-determination on the part of learners?

- What effect do support groups have on the academic and employment success of adults with LD?

- What is the effect of literacy instruction that incorporates the development of self-determination on the academic and employment success of adults with LD?

PROFESSIONAL DEVELOPMENT. Unless effective professional develop-ment is an integral part of a literacy program's plan, it is unlikely that the program will be able to meet the needs of all learners. Everyone who has an effect on the learning environment—from administrators to counselors and assessment specialists to teachers, volunteers, and support staff—must continually improve their knowledge, skills, and attitudes about LD issues.

Borkowski and Muthukrishna (1992) emphasize that instructors must be given time to develop their own mental models of effective instruction. Teacher beliefs about and experiences with instruction are powerful determiners in their readiness to incorporate research-based practices into their teaching. Until a research base on instructional models for adults with LD is developed, appropriate instruction for students with LD can be based on the extensive literature from special education, reading research, and college support services. The challenge is not a lack of information on effective instructional models appropriate to the ABE setting but the lack of system support that allows for focused, sustained professional development opportunities for ABE practitioners. Providing professional development for this teaching force, largely composed of part-time professionals and volunteers, will be a challenge, but it can be the first step in building research-validated practices for teaching adults with LD in adult basic education programs.

- What models of professional development have the greatest effect on changed instructional practices for serving persons with LD?

- What difference have the *Bridges to Practice* materials (National ALLD Center, 1999) and training made in the design and delivery of program services for adults with LD?

- What difference have the program changes listed above made on learner performance and success?

ROLE OF THE COMMUNITY. It has long been acknowledged that adults with learning disabilities need a support system to help them realize their potential. It would be helpful to understand the extent and the nature of support that truly makes the difference between self-determination and dependence for persons with LD.

- What role does a community play in serving adult learners with LD?

- In what ways can a community help adults with LD on their journey toward self-determination?

• In what ways does community involvement make a difference in the adult education program's ability to serve adults with LD?

Policy

State and federal governments need to become proactive in developing policy for adults with LD. A first priority is to promote high-quality professional development for literacy staff members. Another priority is to encourage publishers of textbooks and instructional materials to develop products that are sensitive to the needs of persons with LD. Also, in recognition of the need for professional development of instructional, administrative, and support services staff, a third priority is for the establishment of a national professional development and resource center to provide continuing support to literacy programs serving adults with LD.

Research on participation and success rates of individuals with LD in all types of postsecondary education is discouraging. These findings bring into question how well our secondary schools are preparing individuals with LD for the range of postsecondary opportunities. Better communication between secondary education and ABE systems might influence secondary education programs' effectiveness in preparing students with LD to participate and succeed in postsecondary education. The poor success rate of persons with LD in postsecondary education and the lack of research on this group in ABE point to the need for additional support services personnel, such as counselors, screening and intake specialists, diagnosticians, job coaches, and LD instructional specialists as an integral part of the adult literacy program. Although this may be an additional expense, such an investment may yield significant results in successful program completion.

In light of the requirements of the Workforce Investment Act of 1998, adult literacy programs have a mandate to prepare learners for the world of work. For learners with LD to be successful in obtaining and retaining employment, community agencies must integrate and coordinate services, including educational diagnostic services to identify the presence of LD and suggest interventions, counseling services, advocacy groups, job-training services, and educational services. This opens up the whole assessment issue: whether, when, and to whom to refer learners for diagnostic evaluations for LD. Instruction, job coaching, and other postplacement services may need to follow the learner into the workplace and continue until the learner has mastered the essential functions of the job. Accountability measures may need to include postplacement follow-up to determine worker success after exiting an ABE program. Again, this calls for coordination among adult service agencies.

Education is needed to increase employer awareness of LD. It is likely that poor employee evaluations and job loss have often resulted because of employers' lack of knowledge about LD and appropriate job accommodations. The attributes of persons with LD, including those of creativity, persistence, and willingness to work hard, if recognized and encouraged in the right environment, can make these individuals valued and contributing employees. With the ADA, a mandate is in place. The appropriate implementation of this policy calls for a continued, concerted effort from governmental agencies, the business community, advocacy groups, educators, LD professional associations, and the media to help change negative perceptions and to recognize, support, and encourage the career development of employees with LD.

Practice

Literacy programs have only recently begun to consider changes to enhance services to persons with LD. The *Bridges to Practice* materials (National ALLD Center, 1999) and training represent a first effort to encourage systemic reform of literacy programs and services, but resultant changes have not yet been measured across programs. Ways to build on the *Bridges to Practice* resources should be explored: every component of service delivery, from intake and assessment through planning and instruction, must be considered for its responsiveness to persons with LD. Programs also must look beyond their walls to collaboration with other community agencies.

Coordinated local program efforts can enhance employment opportunities and job success for adults with LD among diverse service providers (such as ABE, vocational rehabilitation, public assistance). The literacy field would benefit from the dissemination of model demonstration projects on interagency coordination that avoids replication of intake, screening, referral, documentation of disability, and determination of eligibility across agencies.

Within ABE programs, allocation of staff responsibility should be examined to determine how screening for LD might best be accomplished. Because screening may lead to referral for further diagnostic services, it is important for ABE staff to identify and establish relationships with organizations providing those services. Once an individual has a diagnostic profile, program staff need to understand how that information should inform instruction. Finally, when a person has documentation of LD, program staff should be skilled in helping the individual learn how to appropriately disclose the disability to employers, coworkers, and other educational program staff. Learning when and how to disclose one's disability is a complex issue that deserves attention and support from ABE programs.

The research reviewed herein has direct implications for how the adult literacy field defines its services. The development of self-determination, which can be fostered both directly and indirectly, is critical for many persons with LD. Demonstration projects (Ward & Kohler, 1996) recommend the following strategies: direct teaching of self-determination, including problem solving, self-development, and self-advocacy; mentoring and modeling; and involvement in goal setting and planning. These projects reported that it was necessary to provide learners with multiple opportunities for practice and to allow learners to have a voice in choosing and evaluating learning goals. The K–12 literature indicates that there is a direct link between the development of self-determination and metacognition or, more specifically, between metacognitive deficits and reading problems. It is time for adult literacy programs to explore how to incorporate instruction in these areas and to evaluate their impact for both diagnosed learners and those with suspected but undiagnosed LD.

The issues identified here imply a need for ongoing professional development of program administrative, instructional, and support staff. Ideally, professional development would include information not only about LD but also about the change process and strategies for initiating and sustaining change. However, this may not be feasible for a number of reasons. First and foremost, adult literacy teaching and tutoring is for the most part a part-time venture. This often means that programs experience frequent staff turnover and may find it difficult to provide ongoing professional development beyond the basics. Typical professional development for new literacy providers generally covers such essential topics as adult learning, effective instructional practices, and use of selected instructional materials. It is only in recent years that some literacy programs have begun to include general information about LD in staff development workshops. In addition, many ABE instructors, teaching in churches, homes, libraries, community centers, and social service agencies, work without the support of other teachers or staff nearby. Therefore, it may not be practical for many programs to include more in-depth professional development such as peer coaching and team teaching. And the addition of resource specialists to a program's budget means that resources and budget line items must be reallocated.

Each program must make decisions about how to deploy resources for the benefit of all learners, based on its history of financial and community support, level of involvement of community stakeholders in the program's design and delivery of services, and the program's vision and mission statement. A literacy program whose vision includes the concept of "success for all learners" cannot ignore the need to provide improved services to persons with LD and to help all learners reach their full potential.

Note

1. A major accomplishment of the National ALLD Center was the research, development, and publication of *Bridges to Practice: A Research-Based Guide for Literacy Practitioners Serving Adults with Learning Disabilities* (1999), a series of guidebooks with accompanying video and professional development manual. The purpose of the program is to encourage systemic reform of literacy programs to enhance services for adults with LD.

References

Adelman, P. B., & Vogel, S. A. (1991). The learning disabled adult. In B.Y.I. Wong (Ed.), *Learning about learning disabilities* (pp. 563–594). San Diego: Academic Press.

Alderson-Gill & Associates. (1989). *Study of literature and learning disabilities.* Ottawa, Ontario: Learning Disabilities Association of Canada.

Americans with Disabilities Act of 1990, PL 101–336. 42 U.S.C.

Anderson, C. (1994). Adult literacy and learning disabilities. In P. J. Gerber & H. B. Reiff (Eds.), *Learning disabilities in adulthood: Persisting problems and evolving issues* (pp. 121–129). Austin, TX: PRO-ED.

Bishop, D.V.M., & Adams, C. (1990). A prospective study of the relationship between specific language impairment, phonological disorders and reading retardation. *Journal of Child Psychology and Psychiatry, 31,* 1027–1050.

Blackorby, J., & Wagner, M. (1996). Longitudinal postschool outcomes of youth with disabilities: Findings from the National Longitudinal Transition Study. *Exceptional Children, 62*(5), 399–413.

Blackorby, J., & Wagner, M. (1997). The employment outcomes of youth with learning disabilities: A review of findings from the National Longitudinal Transition Study of Special Education Students. In P. J. Gerber & D. S. Brown (Eds.), *Learning disabilities and employment* (pp. 57–74). Austin, TX: PRO-ED.

Borkowski, J. G., & Muthukrishna, N. (1992). Moving metacognition into the classroom: "Working models" and effective strategy teaching. In M. Pressley, K. R. Harris, & J. T. Gutherie (Eds.), *Promoting academic competence and literacy in school* (pp. 477–501). Burlington, MA: Academic Press.

Bowren, W. F. (1981). Teaching the learning disabled to read. *Adult Literacy and Basic Education, 5*(3), 179–194.

Brown, D. S. (1997). The new economy in the twenty-first century: Implications for individuals with learning disabilities. In D. S. Brown & P. J. Gerber (Eds.), *Learning disabilities and employment* (pp. 19–37). Austin, TX: PRO-ED.

Brown, D. S., & Gerber, P. J. (1994). Employing people with learning disabilities. In P. J. Gerber & H. B. Reiff (Eds.), *Learning disabilities in adulthood: Persisting problems and evolving issues* (pp. 194–203). Austin, TX: PRO-ED.

Bruck, M. (1992). Persistence of dyslexics' phonological awareness deficits. *Developmental Psychology, 28,* 874–886.

Butler, D. L. (1993). Promoting strategic learning by adults with learning disabilities: An alternative approach. *Dissertation Abstracts International, 56–11A,* 4349.

Catts, H. W. (1993). The relationship between speech-language impairments and reading disabilities. *Journal of Speech and Hearing Research, 36,* 948–958.

Catts, H. W., & Kamhi, A. G. (1999a). Language and reading: Convergences and divergences. In H. W. Catts & A. G. Kami (Eds.), *Language and reading disabilities* (pp. 1–24). Boston: Allyn & Bacon.

Catts, H. W., & Kamhi, A. G. (1999b). Causes of reading disabilities. In H. W. Catts & A. G. Kami (Eds.), *Language and reading disabilities* (pp. 95–127). Boston: Allyn & Bacon.

Catts, H. W., & Kamhi, A. G. (1999c). Defining reading disabilities. In H. W. Catts & A. G. Kami (Eds.), *Language and reading disabilities* (pp. 50–72). Boston: Allyn & Bacon.

Collins, T. (1990). The impact of microcomputer word processing on the performance of learning disabled students in a required first year writing course. *Computers and Composition, 8,* 46–68.

Collins, V. L., Dickson, S. V., Simmons, D. C., & Kameenui, E. J. (1998, June). *Metacognition and its relation to reading comprehension: A synthesis of the research.* Eugene, OR: National Center to Improve the Tools of Educators, University of Oregon.

Cunningham, A. E., & Stanovich, K. E. (1998). What reading does for the mind. *American Educator, 22*(1&2), 8–15.

DeFries, J. C., Filipek, P. A., Fulker, D. W., Olson, R. K., Pennington, B. F., Smith, S. D., & Wise, B. W. (1997). Colorado learning disability research center. *Learning Disability Quarterly, 8,* 7–19.

Dent, H. S. (1995). *Job shock.* New York: St. Martin's Press.

Dowdy, C., Smith, T., & Nowell, C. (1992). Learning disabilities and vocational rehabilitation. *Journal of Learning Disabilities, 25,* 442–447.

Edgar, E. (1995). *First decade after graduation. Final report.* Seattle, WA: University of Washington. (ERIC Document Reproduction Service No. ED 397 573).

Education for All Handicapped Children Act of 1975, PL 94–142, 20 U.S.C. § 1400 *et seq.*

Elkind, J., Black, M. S., & Murray, C. (1996). Computer-based compensation of adult reading disabilities. *Annals of Dyslexia, 46,* 159–186.

Fowler, A. E., & Scarborough, H. S. (1993). *Should reading-disabled adults be distinguished from other adults seeking literacy instruction? A review of theory and research.* (NCAL Technical Report TR93–07). Philadelphia: University of Pennsylvania. (ERIC Document Reproduction Service No. ED 363 732).

Frank, A. R., Sitlington, P. L., & Carson, R. R. (1995). Young adults with behavioral disorders: A comparison with peers with mild disabilities. *Journal of Emotional and Behavioral Disorders, 3,* 156–164.

Gerber, P. J., Ginsberg, R., & Reiff, H. B. (1992). Identifying alterable patterns in employment success for highly successful adults with learning disabilities. *Journal of Learning Disabilities, 25,* 475–487.

Gerber, P. J., & Reiff, H. B. (1994). *Learning disabilities in adulthood: Persisting problems and evolving issues.* Stoneham, MA: Butterworth-Heinemann.

Gerber, P. J., Reiff, H. B., & Ginsberg, R. (1996). Reframing the learning disabled experience. *Journal of Learning Disabilities, 29*(1), 98–101.

Gold, P. C. (1981). The DL-LEA: A remedial approach for non-readers with a language deficiency handicap. *Adult Literacy and Basic Education, 5*(3), 185–192.

Gregg, N., & Phillips, C. (1996). Adults with learning disabilities: Empowering networks of inclusion, collaboration, and self-acceptance. In N. Gregg, S. Hoy, & A. F. Gay (Eds.), *Adults with learning disabilities: Theoretical and practical perspectives* (pp. 1–20). New York: Guilford Press.

Hatt, P. (1991). Learning disabilities: To label or not to label. *Literacy/ Alphabetisation, 15*(3), 4–5. (ERIC Document Reproduction Service No. ED 350 394).

Higgins, E. L., & Raskind, M. H. (1997). The compensatory effectiveness of optical character recognition/speech synthesis on reading comprehension of postsecondary students with learning disabilities. *Learning Disabilities: A Multidisciplinary Journal, 8*, 75–87.

Hoffman, A., & Field, S. (1995). Promoting self-determination through effective curriculum development. *Intervention in School and Clinic, 30*, 134–141.

Hoy, C., & Manglitz, E. (1996). Social and affective adjustment of adults with learning disabilities: A life-span perspective. In N. Gregg, C. Hoy, & A. F. Gay. *Adults with learning disabilities: Theoretical and practical perspectives.* New York: Guilford Press.

Hughes, C. (1998). Effective instruction for adults with learning disabilities. In B. K. Lenz, N. A. Sturomski, & M. A. Corley (Eds.), *Serving adults with learning disabilities: Implications for effective practice* (pp. 34–50). Washington, DC: National Adult Literacy and Learning Disabilities Center, Academy for Educational Development. (ERIC Document Reproduction Service No. 430 078).

Kirsch, I. S., Jungeblut, A., Jenkins, L., & Kolstad, A. (1993). *Adult literacy in America: A first look at the results of the National Adult Literacy Survey.* Washington, DC: National Center for Education Statistics, U.S. Department of Education.

Light, J. G., & DeFries, J. C. (1995). Comorbidity of reading and mathematics disabilities: Genetic and environmental disabilities: Genetic and environmental etiologies. *Journal of Learning Disabilities, 28*, 96–106.

Lyon, G. R. (1994). *Frames of reference for the assessment of learning disabilities: New views on measurement issues.* Baltimore: Brookes.

Lyon, G. R. (1995). Research initiatives in learning disabilities: Contributions from scientists supported by the National Institute of Child Health and Human Development. *Journal of Child Neurology, 10* (Suppl. 1), S120-S126.

Mellard, D. F. (1998). Screening for learning disabilities in adult literacy programs. In B. K. Lenz, N. A. Sturomski, & M. A. Corley (Eds.), *Serving adults with learning disabilities: Implications for effective practice* (pp. 13–28). Washington, DC: National Adult Literacy and Learning Disabilities Center, Academy for Educational Development. (ERIC Document Reproduction Service No. 430 078).

Merriam, S. B., & Brockett, R. G. (1997). *The professional practice of adult education: An introduction.* San Francisco: Jossey-Bass.

Mikulecky, L. (1995). Literacy practices in today's workplace. *Linkages, 2*(1), 1–2. (Newsletter of the National Adult Literacy and Learning Disabilities Center, Academy for Educational Development, Washington, DC).

Moats, L. C., & Lyon, G. R. (1993). Learning disabilities in the United States: Advocacy, science, and the future of the field. *Journal of Learning Disabilities, 26,* 282–294.

Murphy, S. T. (1992). *On being LD: Perspectives and strategies of young adults.* New York: Teachers College, Columbia University.

Murray, C., Goldstein, D. E., Nourse, S., & Edgar, E. (2000). The postsecondary school attendance and completion rates of high school graduates with learning disabilities. *Learning Disabilities Research and Practice, 15,* 119–127.

National Adult Literacy and Learning Disabilities Center (NALLD). (1999). *Bridges to practice: A research-based guide for literacy practitioners serving adults with learning disabilities.* (A project of the National Institute for Literacy). Washington, DC: Academy for Educational Development.

National Joint Committee on Learning Disabilities. (1994). Learning disabilities issue on definition. In *Collective perspectives on issues affecting learning disabilities: Position papers and statements* (pp. 61–66). Austin, TX: PRO-ED.

Ness, J., & Price, L. A. (1990). Meeting the psychosocial needs of adolescents and adults with learning disabilities. *Intervention in School and Clinic, 26*(1), 16–21.

Ogle, M.T.P. (1990). The outcomes of using 'learning contracts' with adult beginning readers in a one-to-one literacy program. *Dissertation Abstracts International, 51,* 1875.

Orton, J. L. (1966). The Orton-Gillingham approach. In J. Mondy (Ed.), *The disabled reader: Education of the dyslexic child* (pp. 245–253). Baltimore: Johns Hopkins University Press.

Palincsar, A. S., & Brown, A. L. (1984). Reciprocal teaching of comprehension fostering and comprehension monitoring activities. *Cognition and Instruction, 1,* 117–175.

Payne, N. (1998). The rationale, components, and usefulness of informal assessment of adults with learning disabilities. In S. A. Vogel & S. Reder (Eds.), *Learning disabilities, literacy, and adult education* (pp. 107–131). Baltimore: Brookes.

Peraino, J. M. (1992). Post-21 follow-up studies: How do special education students fare? In P. Wehman (Ed.), *Life beyond the classroom.* Baltimore: Brookes.

Primus, C. (1990). *Computer assistance model for learning disabled* (Grant No. G008630152–88). Washington, DC: Office of Special Education and Rehabilitation Services, U.S. Department of Education.

Raskind, M. H. (1994). Assistive technology for adults with learning disabilities: A rationale for use. In P. J. Gerber & H. B. Reiff (Eds.), *Adults with learning disabilities* (pp. 152–162). Austin, TX: PRO-ED.

Raskind, M. H. (1998). Literacy for adults with learning disabilities through assistive technology. In S. A. Vogel and S. Reder (Eds.), *Learning disabilities, literacy and adult education.* Baltimore: Brookes.

Raskind, M. H., Goldberg, R. J., Higgins, E. L., & Herman, K. L. (1999). Patterns of change and predictors of success in individuals with learning disabilities: Results from a twenty-year longitudinal study. *Learning Disabilities Research & Practice, 14*(1), 35–49.

Raskind, M. H., Higgins, E. I., & Herman, K. L. (1997). Technology in the workplace for persons with learning disabilities: Views from the inside. In P. J. Gerber & D. S. Brown (Eds.), *Learning disabilities and employment* (pp. 307–330). Austin, TX: PRO-ED.

Reder, S. (1995). *Literacy, education, and learning disabilities.* Portland, OR: Northwest Regional Educational Laboratory.

Reder, S., & Vogel, S. A. (1997). Life-span employment and economic outcomes for adults with self-reported learning disabilities. In P. J. Gerber & D. S. Brown (Eds.), *Learning disabilities and employment* (pp. 371–394). Austin, TX: PRO-ED.

Reiff, H. B., Gerber, P. J., & Ginsberg, R. (1997). *Exceeding expectations: Successful adults with learning disabilities.* Austin, TX: PRO-ED.

Riviere, A. (1998). *Screening for adults with learning disabilities: The role of the practitioner in the process.* Washington, DC: National Adult Literacy and Learning Disabilities Center, Academy for Educational Development.

Ross-Gordon, J. M. (1989). *Adults with learning disabilities: An overview for the adult educator* (Information Series No. 337). Columbus, OH: ERIC Clearinghouse on Adult, Career, and Vocational Education. (ERIC Document Reproduction Service No. ED 315 664).

Ross-Gordon, J. M. (1996). Sociocultural issues affecting identification and service delivery models for adults with learning disabilities. In N. Gregg, C. Hoy, & A. F. Gay (Eds.), *Adults with learning disabilities: Theoretical and practical perspectives* (pp. 85–126). New York: Guilford Press.

Ross-Gordon, J. M. (1998). Literacy education for adults with learning disabilities. In S. A. Vogel & S. Reder (Eds.), *Learning disabilities, literacy, and adult education* (pp. 69–87). Baltimore: Brookes.

Ryan, A. G., & Price, L. (1993). Learning disabilities in adult basic education: A survey of current practices. *Journal of Postsecondary Education and Disability, 10*(3), 31–40.

Ryan, M. R., & Deci, E. L. (2000). Self-determination theory and the facilitation of intrinsic motivation, social development, and well-being. *American Psychologist, 55*(1), 68–79.

Scanlon, D., & Mellard, D. F., with Garrison, S., Lancaster, S., Mellard, J., & Rausch, T. (1997, August). *What we know about literacy practices for adults with learning disabilities: A review of published research.* Washington, DC: The National Adult Literacy and Learning Disabilities Center, Academy for Educational Development.

Schumaker, J. B., Denton, P. H., & Deshler, D. D. (1984). *The paraphrasing strategy.* Lawrence, KS: University of Kansas.

Scuccimarra, D. J., & Speece, D. L. (1990). Employment outcomes and social integration of students with mild handicaps: The quality of life two years after high school. *Journal of Learning Disabilities, 23*(4), 213–219.

Shaywitz, S. E., Escobar, M. D., Shaywitz, B. A., Fletcher, J. M., & Makuch, R. (1992). Evidence that dyslexia may represent the lower tail of a normal distribution of reading ability. *New England Journal of Medicine, 326*, 145–150.

Shaywitz, S. E., Shaywitz, B. A., Fletcher, J. M., & Escobar, M. D. (1990). Prevalence of reading disability in boys and girls: Results of the Connecticut Longitudinal Study. *Journal of the American Medical Association, 264*, 998–1002.

Shessel, I., & Reiff, H. B. (1999). Experiences of adults with learning disabilities: Positive and negative impacts and outcomes. *Learning Disability Quarterly, 22*, 305–316.

Sitlington, P. L., & Frank, A. R. (1990). Are adolescents with learning disabilities successfully crossing the bridge into adult life? *Learning Disability Quarterly, 13*, 97–111.

Spekman, N. J., Goldberg, R. J., & Herman, K. L. (1992). Learning disabled children grow up: A search for factors related to success in the young adult years. *Learning Disabilities Research and Practice, 28,* 602–614.

Stanovich, K. E. (1986). Matthew effects in reading. Some consequences of individual differences in the acquisition of literacy. *Reading Research Quarterly, 21,* 360–407.

Stanovich, K. E., & West, R. F. (1989). Exposure to print and orthographic processing. *Reading Research Quarterly, 24,* 402–433.

Sturomski, N., Lenz, K., Scanlon, D., & Catts, H. (1998). The National Adult Literacy and Learning Disabilities Center: Standards, criteria, procedures, and strategies for screening and teaching adults with learning disabilities. In S. A. Vogel & S. Reder (Eds.), *Learning disabilities, literacy, and adult education* (pp. 93–105). Baltimore: Brookes.

Swanson, H. L. (1999). Instructional components that predict treatment outcomes for students with learning disabilities: Support for a combined strategy and direct instruction model. *Learning Disabilities Research, 14,* 129–140.

Technology-Related Assistance for Individuals with Disabilities Act of 1988, PL 100–407, 29 U.S.C. § 2201 *et seq.*

Thomas, J. L. (1991). Examining self-acceptance of learning disability in young adults through counseling and vocational outcomes. *Dissertation Abstracts International, 52,* 3269–3280.

Torgesen, J. K., & Wagner, R. K. (1998). Alternative diagnostic approaches for specific developmental reading disabilities. *Learning Disabilities Research and Practice, 13*(4), 220–232.

U.S. Department of Education. (2000). *To assure the free appropriate public education of all children with disabilities: Twenty-second annual report to Congress on the implementation of the Individuals with Disabilities Education Act.* Jessup, MD: Author.

U.S. Employment and Training Administration. (1991). *The learning disabled in employment and training programs* (Research and Evaluation Series 91-E). Washington, DC: U.S. Department of Labor.

Vogel, S. A. (1998). Adults with learning disabilities: What learning disabilities specialists, adult literacy educators, and other service providers want and need to know. In S. A. Vogel & S. Reder (Eds.), *Learning disabilities, literacy, and adult education* (pp. 5–28). Baltimore: Brookes.

Vogel, S. A., & Reder, S. (1998). Educational attainment of adults with learning disabilities. In S. A. Vogel & S. Reder (Eds.), *Learning disabilities, literacy and adult education* (pp. 43–68). Baltimore: Brookes.

Vygotsky, L. S. (1978). *Mind in society: The development of higher psychological processes.* Cambridge, MA: Harvard University Press.

Wagner, M., D'Amico, R., Marder, C., Newman, L., & Blackorby, J. (1992). *What happens next? Trends in post school outcomes of youth with disabilities: The second comprehensive report from the National Longitudinal Transition Study of Special Education Students.* Menlo Park, CA: SRI International.

Wagner, M., Newman, L., D'Amico, R., Jay, E. D., Butler-Nalin, P., Marder, C., & Cox, R. (1991). *Youth with disabilities: How are they really doing? The first comprehensive report from the National Longitudinal Transition Study of Special Education Students* (pp. 1–15). Menlo Park, CA: SRI International.

Ward, M. J. (1999, October). The special education self-determination initiative. In *National leadership summit on self-determination and consumer-direction and control: Invited Papers.* Bethesda, MD.

Ward, M. J., & Kohler, P. D. (1996). Teaching self-determination: Content and process. In L. E. Powers, B.H.S. Singer, & J. Sowers (Eds.), *Promoting self-competence in children and youth with disabilities: On the road to autonomy* (pp. 275–322). Baltimore: Brookes.

Wehmeyer, M. L. (1997). Self-directed learning and self-determination. In M. Agran (Ed.), *Student-directed learning: A handbook of self-management.* Pacific Grove, CA: Brooks/Cole.

Werner, E. E. (1993, February). A longitudinal perspective on risk for learning disabilities. Paper presented at the Annual Conference of the Learning Disabilities Association of America, San Francisco. (ERIC Document Reproduction Service No. ED 357 559).

Wilson, B. (1998). Matching student needs to instruction: Teaching reading and spelling using the Wilson Reading System. In S. A. Vogel & S. Reder (Eds.), *Learning disabilities, literacy, and adult education* (pp. 213–235). Baltimore: Brookes.

Workforce Investment Act of 1998, PL 105–220.

CHAPTER FOUR

Literacy Assessment in Adult Basic Education

John Kruidenier

Adult basic education programs, sometimes called adult basic and secondary education programs, typically serve adults over the age of sixteen who do not have a high school diploma and are no longer eligible for traditional secondary education programs. Although adult basic education (ABE) is situated apart from the elementary, secondary, and college education systems, it does not exist in a vacuum. This is especially true of literacy education assessment in adult basic education now, at the turn of the century. Adult literacy assessment is affected by changing definitions of literacy, changes in the needs of federal and state funders, and changes in assessment tools and practices. These changes will be discussed in detail in this chapter in order to present a broad picture of the current state of literacy assessment in adult basic education. Because none of these changes are completely new, a brief history will be presented to put them in context. Literacy must be defined before it is possible to know how to assess it, and assessment must be defined before it is possible to know how best to implement it. This chapter thus begins with definitions of literacy and then describes assessment in adult basic education within this definitional framework. Implications for practice, research, and policy follow.

DEFINING ADULT LITERACY ASSESSMENT

This section presents various views of literacy and identifies three dimensions that appear to be especially important for adult literacy: context, practice, and ability. A working definition of literacy assessment is then presented, and important characteristics of both traditional and newer forms of assessment are introduced.

Views of Literacy

A straightforward, though narrow, definition of literacy is *the ability to read and understand written text.* This definition is roughly doubled in complexity when written expression is added to the way in which literacy is viewed: *the ability to write understandable text.* Even more complex and expansive views of literacy are possible. There is no single, fixed view of literacy. The existence of multiple viewpoints makes sense given the following statements about literacy, all of which are true: reading ability itself is a continuum (adults are described as high- and low-literate); reading is both a psychological or cognitive phenomenon and a sociocultural phenomenon (occurring *within* and *outside* the individual); writing is a form of literacy that is virtually inseparable from reading; numeracy, or the ability to read, write, and manipulate numbers is considered a form of literacy by many; literacy may develop differently in different types of individuals (native-language learners and those attempting to become literate in a second language, those with and without a specific learning or reading disability, females and males); and oral communication differs from written communication along a continuum from the less formal to the more formal (Harris & Hodges, 1995, p. 140).

THE ROLE OF CONTEXT. Expansive definitions of literacy abound. Most dictionaries define a literate person not only as one who can read and write but also as one who is well-informed, educated, or cultured. Although this is a relatively old definition, it has led recently to a phenomenon that might be called "literacy with an adjective." More than thirty-five types of literacy are listed in the International Reading Association's literacy dictionary (Harris & Hodges, 1995, p. 141). Some of these are more directly related to reading and writing, such as family literacy and adult literacy, while many others are more expansive, such as computer literacy, cultural literacy, and media literacy, to name just a few.

Implicit in the *literacy with an adjective* phenomenon is the view that literacy is more than reading, writing, and computing with efficiency and understanding. It is also the ability to practice reading and writing in specific situations to obtain or communicate specific information (Guthrie & Greaney, 1991; Smith, 1995, 2000; Reder, 1994). Although the number of situations or contexts linked with literacy may be new, the central role of context in defining literacy is not.

One dimension of the history of the development of reading and writing over the past six thousand years is the expansion in the number of situations in which literacy may be used and the number of people using it (Kaestle, Damon-Moore, Stedman, Tinsley, & Trollinger, 1991; Venezky, 1991). Literacy was originally a craft confined to a select group of clerics and government and business bureaucrats (ecclesiastical, governmental, and business literacy). It was then extended to many societies' elite classes (cultural literacy, perhaps, is added to the mix of literacies). Finally, after the invention of the printing press in the fifteenth century and through the second half of the nineteenth century, literacy was put within reach of most people (Kaestle et al., 1991).

Perhaps the most expansive view of literacy is critical literacy, wherein reaction to a text is considered to be grounded in one's social, political, or economic situation (Brookfield, 1997; Fehring & Green, 2001; Hiebert, 1991). Literacy in this context is "reading the world" (Freire & Macedo, 1987), and its goal is to continue the spread of literacy to adults as a form of empowerment. All that we express about a text we read is bound to our past experience, which is shaped by society (Alvermann, Young, Green, & Wisenbaker, 1999).

LITERACY PRACTICES. Literacy practices are closely related to context. Practices describe how individuals use reading and writing in various situations and include, for example, reading books, newspapers, or magazines, reading job-related texts, writing letters, and so on (Guthrie & Greaney, 1991; Smith, 1995, 2000; Diehl & Mikulecky, 1980; Mikulecky & Drew, 1991; Sticht, 1995; Kirsch, Jungeblut, Jenkins, & Kolstad, 1993).

Practices are sometimes associated with specific contexts. Guthrie and Greaney (1991) found that adults do most of their reading at work while scanning brief documents such as tables, schedules, memos, and bulletins. The next largest amount of time is spent reading books during leisure time, and then newspapers and magazines, also during leisure time. Some practices, however, may occur in several contexts. Reading a newspaper, for example, could take place when looking for a job, buying a house, or learning about a political candidate. Literacy practices, because they are not always linked to one specific context, could be considered a separate dimension in definitions of literacy.

PSYCHOLOGICAL PROCESSES. Context is an important dimension in definitions of literacy. It incorporates all that might be going on around or outside an individual. An equally important dimension is what goes on within individuals as they read and write, what enables an individual's literacy practices in various situations. Like the issue of context, the study of psychological or cognitive processes involved in reading also has a history, although it stretches over roughly the last one hundred years instead of thousands of years.

As Stahl (1999) notes, the history of reading instruction in the United States over the last century reflects the changing views of the internal mechanisms or cognitive processes involved in reading and writing. Instruction in reading at the turn of the century focused on the ability to decode text. By mid-century, the focus had shifted to an emphasis on meaning, typically the ability to read a passage and answer factual questions about it.

In the 1980s, according to Stahl, the definition of reading shifted again to include an emphasis on meaning construction, the ability to combine ideas that exist in memory with ideas derived from a text being read (Anderson, 1984; van Dijk & Kintsch, 1983; Lesgold, Roth, & Curtis, 1979). In this view, constructing the meaning or mental representation of a text while reading involves the actions of many processes:

> Many different processes are involved in constructing these representations. To mention just a few, there is word identification, where, say, a written word like *bank* must somehow provide access to what we know about banks, money, or overdrafts. There is a parser that turns phrases like *the old men and women* into propositions [ideas in memory] ... There is an inference mechanism that concludes from the phrase *The hikers saw the bear* that they were scared. There are macrooperators that extract the gist of a passage. There are processes that generate spatial imagery from a verbal description of a place. [Kintsch, 1988/1994, p. 951]

Next, continues Stahl, the whole language movement brought with it a new emphasis on reading as a response to a text, along with issues such as motivation to read and an appreciation of literature (for example, Cramer & Castle, 1994). More recently, "balanced" reading instruction has emerged, in which decoding, meaning construction, and motivation or engagement are all considered important aspects of the reading process (Stahl, 1999; Baker, Dreher, & Guthrie, 2000; Pressley, 1998; Snow, Burns, & Griffin, 1998; National Reading Panel, 2000).

Results from studies of basic reading and writing abilities indicate that within individuals both reading and writing are cognitive processes made up of several components (Perfetti, 1985; Curtis, 1980; Perfetti & Curtis, 1987; Chall & Curtis, 1987; Carr & Levy, 1990; Snow & Strucker, 2000; Gregg & Steinberg, 1980; Torrance & Jeffery, 1999; Levy & Ransdell, 1997; Kruidenier, 1991). This is an attractive notion for some educators because it suggests that teachers can focus on specific aspects of the reading and writing process during assessment and instruction.

Components or aspects of the reading process that are typically addressed by instruction include word analysis (phonemic awareness and phonics), word recognition, fluency (accuracy, rate, and prosody in the reading of connected text), word meaning, and reading comprehension and metacomprehension (knowledge of comprehension strategies) (Chall, 1994; Chall & Curtis, 1992; Curtis, 1999; Curtis & Chmelka, 1994; Roswell & Natchez, 1979; Strucker, 1997a, 1997b; Kruidenier, 1990). Although components of the writing process are not as well defined through research, they include both general or global processes as well as lower-level processes (Flower & Hayes, 1981; Hayes, 1996; Torrance & Jeffery, 1999; Levy & Ransdell, 1997; Kruidenier, 1991, 1993). The more general or global processes include planning (generating and organizing ideas), forward production (translating ideas into text), and editing and revising. Lower-level processes include word production (spelling) and sentence production (syntax and morphology). An additional component of both the reading and writing process is motivation or engagement (Beder, 1990; Guthrie & Wigfield, 1997; Baker, Dreher, & Guthrie, 2000).

These aspects or components of reading and writing processes develop over time. Individuals may be described as being at various levels or stages in the development of their literacy abilities (Chall, 1996; Adams, 1990; Collins & Gentner, 1980; Bereiter, 1980). This is the basis for some assessments that place readers at a developmental level based on ability. It is also the basis for some forms of diagnosis that describe students' strengths and weaknesses. One component or aspect of the reading process may develop at a rate different from that of another. Looking at these different rates across components yields profiles of literacy abilities (Chall, 1994; Strucker, 1992, 1997b; Snow & Strucker, 2000). The notion that component processes are active whenever reading and writing take place and that they develop over time is another important dimension in views of literacy.

The definition of literacy that will be used in this chapter to discuss adult literacy assessment includes the three dimensions described thus far: context, practices, and ability. It might be summarized as follows: *Literacy is the ability to read (construct meaning from text) and write (create text that is meaningful). Reading and writing are processes, consisting of specific subprocesses or components operating in memory within individuals. These processes are expressed through literacy practices in specific contexts among individuals.*

As important as describing what will be included in a discussion of adult literacy assessment is a description of what will not be covered. First, although the assessment of numeracy, mathematics, or quantitative literacy could easily be incorporated into this definition, it is left out because it is beyond the scope of this chapter. Also left out of the discussion are literacy contexts that are not fairly directly related to adult literacy or that have not received as much attention in the adult literacy literature. Contexts that will be considered are those especially important to adults, including the workplace (Diehl & Mikulecky, 1980; Mikulecky & Lloyd, 1997; Sticht, 1995), the home or family (National Center for Family Literacy, 1996), and health and community settings (Davis, Crouch, & Long, 1992; Nurss, Parker, Williams, & Baker, 1995).

The assessment of specific types of adult learners is also beyond the scope of this chapter. Second-language adult learners, adults with learning disabilities, and other subgroups of adult learners will not be considered separately. The purpose of literacy assessment is not to identify a learning disability, although good assessments of literacy should provide adequate information on instructional planning for all adults, including those with a reading disability. One possible exception would be testing that attempts to measure native-language literacy to help determine the global literacy ability of students in English for speakers of other languages (ESOL) classes. Readers interested in adults with learning disabilities may want to focus on the discussion of assessments that provide the most information about beginning readers (Snow & Strucker, 2000; Corley & Taymans, Chapter Three of this volume).

Views of Educational Assessment

Assessment in education is defined by Harris and Hodges (1995) as "gathering data to understand the strengths and weaknesses of student learning" (p. 12). Using the description of literacy provided in this chapter, literacy assessment might be defined as gathering data to understand the strengths and weaknesses of student reading and writing abilities and practices in various contexts. Adult literacy assessment has been heavily influenced by several developments in the field of educational assessment: standardized testing and more recent innovations in assessment, including criterion-referenced testing and performance or alternative assessment.

STANDARDIZATION: TESTING, VALIDITY, AND RELIABILITY. Educational testing, including tests of literacy ability, has a long history. School examinations in China were administered as early as the twelfth century B.C. (Nitko, 1983). The first recorded reading assessments in England and France occurred in the fourteenth century A.D. or earlier and consisted of oral reading (reading aloud) (Resnick & Resnick, 1977; Venezky, 1991). The history of educational assessment in the United States in the past hundred years, however, is dominated by the development of standardized testing. During the first half of the twentieth century, testing was heavily influenced by theories of mental abilities developed in the field of psychology and by the use of individually administered IQ tests, first in France by Binet and Simon and then in the United States in the early 1900s (Nitko, 1983, p. 445). The first group-administered intelligence test, which included a silent reading comprehension section, was developed by the U.S. Army during World War I (the Army Alpha) (Sticht, 1995).

Advances in the field of statistics beginning in the mid-1800s also contributed to the development of standardized tests. Statistical analysis of *raw scores* (usually the total number of correct answers) enabled one person's score to be compared with the scores of all others taking a test in numerically objective, accurate, and precise ways.

With compulsory education in the 1920s and 1930s came the rapid development and increased use of standardized achievement and intelligence tests, as well as their misuse by Social Darwinists and the eugenics movement (Nitko, 1983). These tests were considered to be standardized because administration and scoring procedures were the same for all examinees. Exam questions were presented in the same way to everyone, and tests were all scored in the same way, using detailed examination guides and trained examiners. (See Exhibit 4.1 for a description of some common assessment terms, such as *standardized*.)

Standardized Assessment: Administration and scoring procedures are standardized, or the same, for all examinees. Exam questions are presented in the same way to everyone taking the test, and tests are all scored in the same way, using detailed examination guides and trained examiners.

Norm-Referenced Assessment: One person's score may be compared to the scores of a representative group of those taking a test (a norm group). Several types of norm-referenced scores have been developed that can be used to compare one person's raw score to another's. Among others, these include *percentile ranks* and *stanines* (what percentage of students score below a given raw score), *scale scores* (comparing one person's score to a norm group using a scale that, unlike percentile ranks, is an equal-interval scale), and *grade-equivalent scores* (which relate a raw score to the typical or average performance of students at specified grade levels).

Criterion-Referenced Assessment: A test taker's performance is compared to the domain of performances being assessed. Assuming that ability can be represented along a continuum from no or little ability in a domain to higher levels of competency, for example, a criterion-referenced test is used to determine where along the continuum a learner should be placed. *Performance standards* specify the domain of instructionally relevant tasks that a learner should know at a given level or point along the continuum. *Minimum competencies* specify the lowest level of performance that is acceptable. Criterion-referenced measures focus on determining what an individual already knows and therefore what needs to be taught as opposed to an individual's standing relative to a group of peers.

Performance-Based Assessment: Performance-based assessments are used to evaluate a student's ability to complete tasks that require the application of knowledge or skills they have learned in a realistic, or authentic, situation. Generally, performance tasks involve lengthy written (or spoken) responses or participation in group or individual activities.

Validity: A test is considered valid if it is judged to adequately measure the domain of knowledge that it was designed to measure.

Reliability: A test is judged to be reliable primarily by means of statistical measures that indicate how reliable its scores are, including reliability coefficients that measure how consistent its scores are and a standard error of measurement that suggests how accurate they are. Statistical measures of reliability are tools that are used to address the broader, more qualitative aspect of a test's validity. Reliability is a necessary, but not sufficient, condition for validity.

Exhibit 4.1. Assessment Terms.
Source: Adapted from Nitko, 1983, 1996.

By referencing one person's score to the scores of a representative group of those for whom the test was developed (a norm group), examiners could compare learners' abilities and use this information in the process of making decisions on, for example, which candidates to admit to an educational program and where to place them. Over the years, several types of norm-referenced scores have been developed that can be used to compare one person's raw score to another's: *percentile ranks* and *stanines* (what percentage of students score below a given raw score), *scale scores* (comparing one person's score to a norm group using a scale that, unlike percentile ranks, is an equal-interval scale), and *grade-equivalent scores* (which relate a raw score to the typical or average performance of students at specified grade levels) (Nitko, 1996).

Standardization of testing has also led to relatively specific, agreed-upon methods for evaluating a test using the concepts of validity and reliability. A test is considered valid if it is judged to adequately measure the domain of knowledge that it was designed to measure. A test is judged to be reliable primarily by means of statistical measures that indicate how reliable its scores are, including reliability coefficients that measure how consistent the scores are and a standard error of measurement that suggests how accurate they are. The statistical measures of reliability are tools that are used to address the broader, more qualitative aspect of a test's validity (Nitko, 1996). A test must be reliable to be valid; reliability is a necessary but not sufficient condition for validity. For adult literacy assessment, these developments in standardized testing culminated in the development of norm-referenced tests for use specifically with ABE students in the 1950s and 1960s, including, for example, the Adult Basic Learning Exam (ABLE) (Karlsen & Gardner, 1986).

Standardized tests have played a significant role in what Linn (2000) has identified as the five prominent "waves of reform" that have swept through education since World War II:

1. The movement toward grouping or tracking in the 1950s to handle the diverse population of elementary and secondary students entering public schools. (Standardized tests were important in placing students.)

2. Large, federal expenditures for compensatory education in the 1960s through the Elementary and Secondary Education Act.

(Tests were used to satisfy congressional demands for evaluation and accountability.)

3. Minimum-competency testing in the 1970s and 1980s.

4. High-stakes standardized testing in the 1980s and 1990s. (Teachers and administrators were held accountable for test results.)

5. Current reform efforts. (These include the high-stakes accountability element of earlier reforms along with "ambitious content standards," assessment and accountability based on these performance standards, performance-based assessment, and inclusion.)

INNOVATIONS: CRITERION-REFERENCED AND PERFORMANCE-BASED ASSESSMENT. Several innovations in assessment also occurred during the post–World War II period. Minimum-competency testing, the third reform wave, is a type of criterion-referenced testing originally developed for the military (Sticht, 1995) in the 1960s by Glaser and others as an alternative to norm-referenced testing (Glaser, 1963, cited in Nitko, 1983, p. 445). Instead of comparing a test taker's score to others' scores (a norm group), criterion-referenced tests compare the test taker's performance to the domain of performances being assessed (Nitko, 1996). Assuming that reading ability can be represented along a continuum from no or very few literacy abilities (competencies) to advanced forms of literacy, for example, a criterion-referenced reading test is used to determine how literate a learner is, or where along the continuum that learner could be placed. Similarly, performance standards specify the domain of instructionally relevant tasks that a learner should have mastered at a given level or point along the continuum (Nitko, 1983). Criterion-referenced measures focus on determining what an individual already knows and therefore what needs to be taught as opposed to an individual's standing relative to a group of peers.

The last current wave of reform described by Linn (2000) includes the development of performance-based assessment. Performance assessments are used to evaluate how well students complete tasks that require the application of knowledge or skills in a realistic, or authentic, situation. A performance assessment designed to assess adult literacy students' reading, for example, might have them use a manual to troubleshoot a specific problem in a workplace setting (Sticht, 1972; Mikulecky & Lloyd, 1997). Or, to assess writing, students might be asked to help construct a portfolio of their best written work generated in a classroom setting (Fingeret, 1993). Generally, performance tasks involve lengthy written (or spoken) responses or participation in group or individual activities (Nitko, 1996). Assessing specific literacy practices, such as how frequently newspapers are read at home, is also a form of performance assessment, although it is often based on retrospective self-reports rather than direct observation by an examiner.

Performance assessments, like standardized tests, can be evaluated for validity—that is, judged on the basis of how well they measure the literacy task they purport to evaluate and how consistently they are administered and scored. Performance assessment also includes the use of one or more scoring rubrics to increase reliability. *Rubrics* are sets of rules that can be used as a guide for scoring and administration (Nitko, 1996) and usually include some sort of scale or checklist. Scoring guides for the holistic or analytic scoring of student writing samples are an early example of this type of rubric. Numbered quality scales are established (a scale from 1 to 4, for example, with 4 being the highest), and descriptions of what is expected of an essay at each level are provided. Evaluators read each essay and assign it a score based on which level of quality it most closely matches.

Performance assessment is conceived of by some as an alternative to standardized, norm-referenced, and criterion-referenced testing (for example, Garcia & Pearson, 1991). As will be shown later in this chapter, performance assessment is an important part of the reforms under way in adult literacy, including the new National Reporting System for adult literacy (DAEL, 2000).

WHY ASSESS?

Recent reports suggest that many adult educators remain unconvinced that assessment is an important part of the teaching process (General Accounting Office, 1995; Kutner, Webb, & Matheson, 1996; Condelli, Padilla, & Angeles, 1999). These are educators who have, in the past, not used any formal assessment tools or procedures when teaching reading and writing, who have used them only for posttesting, not diagnosis (Beder, 1999), or who have been reluctant to use them because of possible negative side-effects (Ehringhaus, 1991). A review of eleven states' assessment systems (Kutner et al., 1996), for example, found that

Administering standardized assessment instruments is not a priority for most programs; pretests are often administered only to participants whose literacy is considered to be at a sufficient level and very few programs have post-test data, even for learners remaining in a program for a substantial number of hours. Furthermore, standardized assessment instruments are often selected for ease of administration rather than because they reflect the content of what is being taught. [p. 2]

Tests are not directly related to the instruction offered by local adult education programs. [p. 12]

Instructors . . . may need assistance in becoming familiar with the relationship between learner competencies, curriculum, and assessment measures. [p. 17]

Many within and outside the field of adult literacy have described the possible negative effects of assessment, particularly when standardized tests are used. Students, for example, may be anxious about testing, and negative results from tests may lead to a loss of self-esteem and motivation (Ehringhaus, 1991). A standardized test may be culturally biased, particularly when normed on groups that are different either culturally or in some other significant way from those taking the test, and this may lead to misdiagnosis (Garcia & Pearson, 1991; Joint Task Force on Assessment, 1994; Askov, Van Horn, & Carman, 1997).

When used professionally and carefully to minimize possible negative side-effects, however, assessment can be beneficial. The most common uses of assessment in adult literacy include

- Screening to place students in appropriate programs
- Diagnosis of individual strengths and weaknesses in literacy to help plan for instruction
- Measurement of individual growth
- Self-evaluation and personal growth
- Program evaluation and accountability (Askov et al., 1997; Askov, 2000)

These uses are generally accepted in areas of education other than adult literacy as well (Joint Task Force on Assessment, 1994; Joint Committee on Standards for Educational and Psychological Testing, 1999).

Given the apparent usefulness of assessment, is there evidence that it really works, that it leads to improved student learning? Linn (2000) examined test score trends over the last several decades following the use of high-stakes accountability testing. He found a pattern of early gains in average achievement test scores followed by a leveling off. The examination of large-scale assessment programs, however, is difficult and controversial because of the large number of uncontrolled variables that may affect results. Few carefully controlled studies of the direct effects of assessment in education exist, and there may be none in the field of adult literacy. In a comprehensive review, Dochy and colleagues (Dochy, Segers, & Buehl, 1999) found eleven experimental studies of progress assessment in education. In these studies, teachers assessed students at least twice to measure progress. Most of these studies indicate that the assessment of progress for instructional purposes, when compared with no progress assessment, leads to greater student gains. The researchers suggested that progress assessment may give teachers a better understanding of student ability and thus lead to better, more focused instruction, or that frequent testing may provide students with explicit information about what they need to know.

Very few assessment models in adult literacy go beyond the model described by Askov (Askov et al., 1997): diagnostic pretests to determine strengths and weaknesses, instruction based on these assessment results, informal assessment during instruction, and posttests to determine gains. One model for assessment and instruction that adds the research-based notions of literacy components and developmental levels (discussed earlier) to this general model is described by Chall (1994; see also Curtis, 1999; Curtis & Longo, 1997; Strucker, 1997a; Kruidenier, 1990). This model, originally developed for use in literacy instruction with children (Chall & Curtis, 1987, 1990, 1992), suggests that each aspect or component of the reading process be assessed to determine a learner's developmental level for each one (for example, word analysis, word recognition, fluency or oral reading of connected text, oral vocabulary, silent reading comprehension, and motivation).

This form of assessment results in a comprehensive profile of relative student strengths and weaknesses in reading (Roswell & Chall, 1994; Strucker, 1992, 1997b; Snow & Strucker, 2000; Chall & Curtis, 1992; Curtis, 1999). The profile is used to design a program of instruction that addresses all aspects of the reading process while taking into account the unique needs of each learner. Instruction is built around each component, ensuring that developmentally appropriate materials and instructional methods are provided for both strengths and weaknesses. Ongoing, informal assessment is used to continually adjust instruction as needed. Addressing all components during instruction ensures that no one aspect of the reading process is overemphasized (Strucker, 1997b).

In the description of this model, Chall (1994) notes that assessment also takes into account adult needs and interests and elicits the adult learner's collaboration. The unique needs and abilities that adults bring to literacy instruction are an important theme in adult education (Kasworm & Marienau, 1997; Sticht & McDonald, 1992; Curtis, 1990). Kasworm and Marienau (1997) propose five key principles for assessment derived from "commonly held premises about adult learning" (p. 7):

- Assessment recognizes that adults come to literacy instruction with a wide variety of experiences and an extensive knowledge base and that what they learn will be applied to specific situations.

- In addition to the need to improve their literacy abilities, adults also have affective needs and should be involved in the assessment process through, for example, self-assessment and the sharing of assessment results.

- Giving adults feedback promotes learning.

- Assessment should take into account, and use, adults' involvement in work, family, and community.

- Adults' prior experienced-based learning gives them the knowledge to participate in the design of assessment programs and to be actively involved in their own assessment (through the use of procedures such as portfolio assessment).

The use of assessment for instruction has not been the focus of very much research in the field of adult literacy. The modern history of adult literacy assessment in the United States has instead been dominated by large-scale assessments of adults' functional literacy abilities and federal adult literacy legislation.

Large-Scale Assessments

Aside from intelligence testing during World War I, direct assessment of the literacy abilities of large groups of adults first occurred in the 1930s in the United States and then not again until the 1970s (Kaestle et al., 1991). Before this, from about 1840 to 1930, national assessments of literacy consisted of asking adults if they were able to read and write a simple message. These self-reports of a literacy practice were obtained during each national census. From 1940 onward, literacy was measured by asking how many grade levels in school adults had completed (Kaestle et al., 1991; Ehringhaus, 1990). This last criterion for literacy demonstrates a central problem with criterion-based approaches generally—their arbitrariness. The grade-level criterion for being considered literate gradually increased from grade 3 to grade 12 over the years as the literacy demands of society apparently increased (Ehringhaus, 1990).

The first direct assessment of adult functional literacy abilities was conducted by Buswell in the 1930s (1937; cited in Kaestle et al., 1991, p. 94). As a test of functional literacy, it measured the ability of adults to locate information in texts encountered in everyday life, such as catalogs and telephone directories.

Although occurring much later, during the minimum-competency wave of reform (Linn, 2000), a series of large-scale assessments of adult literacy conducted in the 1970s also included measures of functional or everyday literacy. The Survival Literacy Study, the National Reading Difficulty Index, the Functional Literacy: Basic Reading Performance Test, the Adult Functional Reading Study, the Adult Performance Level Study, and the English Language Proficiency Study all asked adults to read and respond to functional reading material. This material included, for example, classified ads, product advertisements, legal documents, schedules, and other texts people may encounter in their daily lives. The Survival Literacy Study and Adult Performance Level Study also included writing tasks or items that assessed writing ability (Kaestle et al., 1991).

All these assessments were standardized and all except one were criterion-referenced tests. The determination of functional literacy for the criterion-referenced tests was based on the percentage of questions answered correctly. The literate/illiterate cut-off varied from a low of 75 percent correct to a high of 90 percent. Several of these tests included additional percent-correct cut-offs to establish three levels of literacy instead of just one: literate, marginally literate, and illiterate.

Kaestle and colleagues note the two problems related to the validity of these national assessments, which are issues commonly associated with criterion-referenced tests. Functional literacy competency was defined by means of specific test content, which may not apply to certain subgroups of adults. In addition, the percent-correct criteria were arbitrary and not always clearly defined.

Similar problems have been seen in the two most recent national adult literacy assessments: the Young Adult Literacy Survey, or YALS

(Kirsch & Jungeblut, 1986), and the NALS (Kirsch et al., 1993). Both defined five levels of functional competencies. Although the YALS and NALS used item-response theory, a statistical technique that is more sophisticated than a simple determination of an individual's percentage of correct answers, arbitrary cut-off scores were still used. To be placed at level 3 out of a possible five levels of literacy ability, for example, an adult's answers must indicate that the adult has an 80 percent chance of getting items of average difficulty correct at level 3. Level 3 is the functional literacy standard for the National Governors Association. When the arbitrary 80 percent cut-off is reduced to 65 percent, the criterion used for the National Assessment of Educational Progress, the number of adults in the United States classified as literate increases by 15 percent (Sticht, 1998; Kirsch et al., 1993).

The choice of content for the NALS test items defined what was meant by functional literacy. The content was similar to content used in earlier functional literacy tests, although it was grouped into three categories—prose, document, and quantitative passages from everyday life—suggesting three forms of functional literacy. Item format, which included questions about prose, document, or quantitative texts, also suggested a view of literacy that focused on reading comprehension as opposed to other aspects of the reading process, such as word recognition or word analysis. NALS responses were not limited to multiple-choice selections but included extended written responses as well.

Large-scale assessments of adults' literacy practices began in the early 1900s in the United States. These included self-reports, responses to questions such as "Have you read a book in the last month?" (Kaestle et al., 1991, p. 180). Studies of reading habits or practices have been undertaken regularly since, and surveys of reading practices have recently been used in large-scale studies of adult literacy (the YALS and NALS). The type and frequency of reading practices are now associated with reading ability and used to measure literacy development (Smith, 1995; Mikulecky & Lloyd, 1997; Sticht, Hofstetter, & Hofstetter, 1996) as well as the literacy demands of various jobs (Sticht, 1995).

National Legislation and Effects on Assessment Practices

As mentioned, the federal government's role in adult education began in the military with the assessment of recruits during World War I and still continues (Sticht, 1995). The federal role in civilian adult literacy programs began in the 1960s, during the compensatory education reform movement (Linn, 2000) and the passage of the Elementary and Secondary Education Amendments (PL 89–750), of which the Adult Education Act of 1966 was a part. This federal role has continued through the Elementary and Secondary School Improvement Amendments of 1988 (PL 100–297), the National Literacy Act of 1991 (PL 102–73), and the Adult Education and Family Literacy Act of 1998 (Title II of the Workforce Investment Act, PL 105–220).

This legislation has funded states' adult literacy programs based on the number of adults in a state who are over the age of sixteen, are out of school, and do not have a high school diploma. It has also affected assessment activities in adult education. Legislative guidelines and language have generally reflected the waves of education reform described by Linn (2000), bringing the accompanying innovations and changes in assessment practices to adult literacy programs.

THE ADULT EDUCATION ACT (AEA) OF 1966. The AEA did not require the use of assessment for program evaluation, only that programs would enable adults to "acquire skills necessary for literate functioning" (Merrifield, 1998). The overall program lacked realistic goals, specific criteria, and ways to measure progress toward goals, according to an independent government review (General Accounting Office, 1975). The 1988 amendments to the AEA listed specific topic areas to be addressed for program evaluation and mandated the use of standardized tests (Condelli, 1996), part of a larger reform wave in education in which standardized tests were used for accountability. The amended AEA specified that at least one-third of the adults in each state's AEA-funded programs be assessed using valid and reliable norm-referenced, criterion-referenced, or competency-based tests (Sticht, 1990).

Despite these efforts, a review by Padak and Padak (1994) found assessment practices in adult education to be haphazard. This review was based on three statewide surveys of evaluation and assessment practices in adult literacy programs, and more detailed descriptions of nineteen programs. The authors found that evaluations were either not being done or were reported in ways that made interpretation difficult and suggested several reasons for this pattern of poor assessment practices. First, many programs had flexible open-entry, open-exit policies for their adult students. Reporting data on progress that takes into account different amounts of time in a program requires a level of sophistication in the analysis of data that local programs did not have. Second, programs relied on volunteers, who may not have the knowledge needed to conduct assessments or to understand the need for assessment. Third, evaluations were often tied to funding and may have tended to overstate successes and obscure weaknesses (Padak & Padak, 1994).

THE NATIONAL LITERACY ACT (NLA) OF 1991. The NLA incorporated elements of the last wave of reform described by Linn (2000). Accountability requirements were increased by asking states to develop "indicators for program quality" in three areas: recruitment, retention, and improvement of students' literacy skills. These indicators were envisioned as a step toward the development of measurable performance standards. Quality indicators were to be developed first (for example, students remain in the program long enough to meet their educational needs), measures were to be established next (for example, hours of instruction student receives), and then performance standards established (for example, 80 percent of students stay at least fifty hours) (Condelli, 1996, p. 1).

Most states, in fact, voluntarily developed performance standards for these and additional areas following the development of model standards by the U.S. Department of Education (DOE). The additional standards were related to program planning, curriculum and instruction, staff development, and support services (Condelli, 1996). The NLA also incorporated new literacy assessment techniques, allowing states to report learner gains using standardized tests, teacher reports, learner self-reports, measures of improvement in job or life skills, and portfolio assessment and other alternative performance assessments (General Accounting Office, 1995).

The NLA required that states use their new quality indicators (and, presumably, the associated performance standards) to evaluate the effectiveness of local programs, although it did not provide evaluation guidelines. A review of usage of indicators and standards found that by 1996 they were being used in virtually all states to evaluate local program effectiveness, to determine which programs needed assistance, and to improve the quality of state programs. A little more than one-half of all states were using them to make funding decisions, reducing or eliminating funding to those programs not meeting specified standards (Condelli, 1996).

Despite the DOE's attempt to provide states with technical assistance related to performance standards, assessment and evaluation, and data collection and reporting systems, several reports were extremely critical of the federal and state adult literacy delivery systems and of assessment practices in particular (General Accounting Office, 1995; Kutner et al., 1996; see also Stein, 1997). Many of the criticisms questioned the validity of the assessment procedures used. As mentioned earlier, validity in assessment refers to how well an assessment measures the domain of knowledge or behaviors it is designed to measure (Nitko, 1996). If the domain is not well defined, measurement may not be adequate. As evidence of this problem, critics pointed to the inconsistent definitions of learner progress across states, poorly defined objectives, and the use of different standardized tests in different states (General Accounting Office, 1995; Kutner et al., 1996).

Given the very broad definitions of literacy currently used in adult literacy (see "Views of Literacy," earlier in this chapter), it is not surprising that different definitions of literacy exist or that some objectives associated with broader definitions (for example, functional literacy) may be difficult to measure. To a certain degree, questioning the external or domain-related validity of a particular standardized test (or of standardized, norm-referenced, and criterion-referenced tests generally) is simply one way to express disagreement with the aspects of literacy (the skills, contexts, or practices) on which the assessment focuses (see Stein, 1997, and Merrifield, 1998, for examples of this type of criticism).

In addition, multiple and perhaps conflicting definitions of the literacy domain might be expected in a system that has multiple funders with different interests and views (Merrifield, 1998). Fifty-nine percent of adult literacy programs are funded through local education agencies (primarily local school districts), 15 percent by community colleges, 14 percent by community-based programs, and 12 percent by other agencies (General Accounting Office, 1995; Beder, 1999).

The other major criticism of the validity of assessment practices had to do with serious questions related to the reliability of the data collected for assessment, or how consistent the collection of data was. The General Accounting Office report (1995) found that data collected from local programs often had gaps or was inaccurate (see also Kutner et al., 1996).

This problem may be related to several factors. First, learner attendance in adult literacy programs has traditionally been poor. Many barriers to attendance exist, such as the need for childcare and transportation, and the demands of work (Merrifield, 1998; Comings,

Parrella, & Soricone, 1999), and poor attendance makes it difficult in some cases to give assessments and collect data. Second, adult literacy program staff have traditionally had limited expertise. In 1995, 80 percent of staff were part-time, 60 percent of programs had no full-time staff, and many staff were volunteers (General Accounting Office, 1995; Stein, 1997). Finally, program resources have traditionally been inadequate and may not be capable of supporting the training and monitoring activities necessary for reliable data collection practices (Beder, 1999; Stein, 1997; Merrifield, 1998; Sticht, 1998).

Whatever the causes or reasons, large-scale, independent evaluations of adult literacy assessment over the past ten years have consistently found that assessment practices are frequently haphazard and ineffective. As noted, assessment—particularly the use of standardized approaches to assessment, such as standardized tests—has simply not been a priority. Standardized tests were often chosen not for instructional purposes but for ease of administration (Kutner et al., 1996). When pilot-testing a management information system for adult literacy providers, Condelli and colleagues learned from a user survey that providers liked the system's ability to generate government reports automatically but resisted collecting assessment data and entering it into the system (Condelli et al., 1999).

THE ADULT EDUCATION AND FAMILY LITERACY ACT (AEFLA) OF 1998. In the wake of the evaluations discussed in preceding sections, the most recent federal adult literacy legislation, implemented in 1998, again attempts to strengthen accountability through the use of more uniform performance standards. In addition, the Adult Education and Family Literacy Act (Title II of the Workforce Investment Act, 1998, PL 105–220) provides for funding incentives for states based on the performance of their adult literacy programs, a form of high-stakes assessment. The AEFLA expects all states, in turn, to base funding decisions for local programs at least in part on their performance.

Performance measures to be used for accountability include "(i) demonstrated improvements in reading, writing, and speaking the English language, numeracy, problem solving, English language acquisition, and other literacy skills, (ii) placement in, retention in, or completion of, postsecondary education, training, unsubsidized employment or career advancement, and (iii) receipt of a secondary school diploma or its recognized equivalent." States may add their own measures but are required to use these. Levels of performance must be "expressed in objective, quantifiable, and measurable form" in order to show progress. This information must be reported to the Department of Education and made public; a state-by-state comparison of assessment results must be compiled and disseminated by the DOE (Title II, Chapter 1, Sec. 212 of the Workforce Investment Act). All local programs are required to use these measures.

Specific guidelines for measures to be used in assessing adult learners, recording assessment results, and reporting the results through a computer-based system are provided by the National Reporting System (NRS), implemented in the summer of 2000 (DAEL, 2000; Garner, 1999). Criticism of the generally poor state of assessment procedures in adult literacy and the need for "uniform valid and reliable data" to evaluate program effectiveness were major factors in developing the NRS (DAEL, 2000, p. 2). The NRS provides states with specific guidance on the types of standards, measures, and collection procedures that must be used by adult literacy providers accepting state and federal funds. It also provides states with technical and training assistance to support data collection and reporting procedures.

Gain in reading or writing ability is a key measure, "probably the most important single measure in the NRS" (DAEL, 2000, p. 38). Every adult entering a program must be pretested to determine a beginning literacy level and posttested before leaving to determine gain. Programs may use either standardized tests (norm- or criterion-referenced) or performance assessments with standardized scoring rubrics. Although any state-approved assessment may be used for determining beginning and ending levels, each ABE student must be placed in one of six basic education levels defined by the NRS. The first four levels cover, roughly, literacy development through the beginning of secondary education: beginning ABE literacy, beginning basic education, low intermediate basic education, and high intermediate basic education. The last two levels cover adult secondary education: low adult secondary education and high adult secondary education.

Performance standards, or entry-level descriptors, are given for each level. These descriptions of what an adult at each level is expected to be able to do are keyed to scores from common standardized literacy tests. Performance standards for six ESOL levels are also provided. States report to the federal government the number and percent of learners who advance one or more levels.

In summary, a wide variety of basic reading and writing assessment instruments may be used by states and local programs as long as they are either standardized norm- or criterion-referenced tests or performance assessments with standardized scoring rubrics. Results from these assessments are not reported directly but are translated into the NRS literacy levels, which are then used for reporting purposes.

In addition to basic reading and writing abilities, specific literacy contexts are highlighted in the AEFLA. As in earlier federal legislation, the overall goal of the AEFLA is to increase adults' self-sufficiency and functional literacy. As part of the WIA, however, a greater emphasis is placed on workplace literacy. Along with performance standards for basic reading and writing, the NRS also describes performance standards for numeracy and for functional and workplace skills in terms of reading and writing. Follow-up measures related to employment, collected after students have left a program, are also required (whether a former learner has entered employment, retained employment, entered postsecondary education, or obtained a General Educational Development [GED] credential or diploma).

Secondary measures, recommended but not required, are also specified for family literacy programs. These measure progress toward the goal of assisting parents in obtaining the skills necessary to be full partners in their children's educational development. These are measures of literacy practices, such as the frequency of helping children with schoolwork and the number of contacts with teachers (measures of involvement in children's education), and the frequency of reading to children, visits to the library, and book purchases (measures of involvement in children's literacy activities).

The use of uniform measures across states and a uniform, computer-based system for collecting data is designed to increase the validity and usefulness of data collected to evaluate the effectiveness of adult literacy legislation and funding. Additional procedures are recommended by the NRS to improve the validity (and reliability) of the data collected. These include staff development activities for local teachers, volunteers, and other staff; Web-based resources; organized and concrete data-handling procedures; increased resources for data collection; ongoing monitoring of data collection and recording; and formal audits of local program data.

Assessment for Instruction

As discussed, much of the literature related to assessment in adult literacy has been dominated by large-scale, national assessments of functional literacy. Although federal and state legislation have attempted to shape the use of assessment, it has focused primarily on accountability.

The use of assessment in adult literacy instruction, presumably the primary function of assessment, has not been studied in detail.

No national survey or observational studies of local programs' use of assessment for instruction exist. Therefore, it is not possible to determine how closely local practices approximate assessment models described by experts such as Askov (Askov et al., 1997), Chall (1994), and others. State accountability assessment plans, required by national legislation over the past decade, are currently in a state of flux because of new regulations (the AEFLA of 1998 and the NRS). However, past analyses of state plans do provide some very general information about how reading and writing abilities are assessed in local ABE programs. Some information about the role of the other two major dimensions of literacy, context and practices, is also available. These three dimensions of literacy will frame the discussion of assessment for instruction that follows. Ability and literacy practices will be discussed separately, while literacy context will be discussed in relation to each.

ABILITIES: ASSESSING ASPECTS OF THE READING AND WRITING PROCESS

Until recently, many local adult literacy programs did not pretest incoming learners' reading and writing abilities. According to one survey conducted in the early 1990s (Beder, 1999; Young, Fitzgerald, & Fleischman, 1994), more than one-third did not pretest. Lack of pretesting abrogates the use of the assessment models described earlier (Askov et al., 1997; Chall, 1994): pretesting to determine strengths and weaknesses in terms of components, use of pretest results to formulate a plan for instruction, ongoing assessment to adjust instruction as needed, and posttesting to measure the effects of instruction.

Most programs, however, have regularly pretested learners, using standardized tests, locally developed measures, or a combination of the two. With implementation of the NRS, all programs are now required to pretest, although not necessarily for instructional purposes. Of the standardized tests that state and local programs report using, the Test of Adult Basic Education (TABE) has consistently been used by more adult literacy programs than any other standardized test (Ehringhaus, 1991; Kutner et al., 1996; Beder, 1999). Reports of its use vary from about 70 percent to 80 percent among programs that use assessment regularly (Kutner et al., 1996; Beder, 1999). The Adult Basic

Learning Examination (ABLE) and Wide Range Achievement Test (WRAT) are the next most frequently used tests (reports of 20 percent), followed by the Comprehensive Adult Student Assessment System (CASAS) (14 percent) and the Slosson Oral Reading Test (SORT) (12 percent) (Beder, 1999).

Assuming these assessments are used for instruction, how well do they measure learner reading and writing processes, and how useful are they in an assessment model that incorporates the concepts of instructional components and developmental levels? To help answer these questions, each component (such as comprehension, vocabulary, fluency, and so on) is discussed in terms of the way it is, and could be, used in adult literacy programs. This part of the chapter is organized as follows:

- For each component, norm-referenced, criterion-referenced, and performance or informal assessments are discussed.
- The most commonly used ABE assessment instruments are presented first.
- Other ABE assessments and non-ABE assessments are presented when a component is not addressed by one of the common tests, or when another test suggests a significant alternative approach to assessment. Table 4.1 provides a summary of the components measured across tests. All the tests discussed (common ABE assessments, other ABE assessments, and non-ABE assessments) are listed in Table 4.2, categorized by type.

Specific issues related to the literacy context addressed by a test and test reliability and validity are discussed when a test is first mentioned, and then as needed. This includes the types of scores offered by an assessment instrument and the norming group on which the scores are based. The list of tests in Tables 4.1 and 4.2 is not meant to be exhaustive, and many tests that may be just as appropriate to use with adults as those listed are not included. To name just a few, the Test of Applied Literacy Skills (TALS) (Educational Testing Service, 1991), the Peabody Picture Vocabulary Test (PPVT) (Dunn & Dunn, 1997), the Test of Word Reading Efficiency (TOWRE) (Torgesen, Wagner, & Rashotte, 1999), and the Comprehensive Test of Phonological Processing (CTOPP) (Wagner, Torgesen, & Rashotte, 1999) are not discussed.

Assessment	Reading						Writing					
	C	OV	SV	F	WR	WA	P	V	S	W	P	R
Common ABE												
TABE	x		**						x	x		
ABLE	x	*	x						x	x		
WRAT					x					x		
CASAS Reading	x											
CASAS Writing							x				x	
SORT					x							
Other ABE												
READ	x				x							
DAR	x	x		x	x	x				x		
TOFHLA	x											
Woodcock	x	x	x			x			x	x		
REALM					x							
AMES												
GED Practice	x						x					
Non-ABE												
GORT	x		x									
TAAS						x						
WPT							x		x	x	x	
TOWL							x	x	x	x		x

Table 4.1. **Reading and Writing Component Scores Provided by Common ABE Assessments, Other ABE Assessments, and Non-ABE Assessments.**

Key: C = comprehension; OV = oral vocabulary; SV = silent vocabulary; F = fluency; WR = word recognition; WA = word analysis; P = written product; V = writing vocabulary; S = sentence production; W = word production; P = planning; R = revising.

* Assesses oral vocabulary for adults completing one through four years of formal schooling.

** For the 1987 edition only. The 1994 edition of TABE does not provide a separate vocabulary subtest score.

Reading

Assessment of the following components of the reading process will be discussed: reading comprehension, vocabulary, fluency (reading accuracy and rate), word recognition, and word analysis.

READING COMPREHENSION. Reading comprehension assessment measures students' ability to understand or generate meaning from a text that is read. This aspect of the reading process is what most people associate with literacy or reading ability.

Assessment	Standardized	Norm-Referenced	Criterion-Referenced	Performance	Informal
Common ABE					
TABE	x	x			
ABLE	x	x			
WRAT	x	x			
CASAS Reading	x	x	x		
CASAS Writing	x		x	x	
SORT	x	x			
Other ABE					
READ			x		x
DAR	x		x		
TOFHLA	x		x		
Woodcock	x	x	x		
REALM			x		
AMES	x	x			
GED Practice					x
Non-ABE					
GORT	x	x			
TAAS			x		
Adams			x		x
WPT	x	x		x	
TOWL	x	x		x	

Table 4.2. Common ABE Assessments, Other ABE Assessments, and Non-ABE Assessments, Categorized by Type.

Norm-Referenced Assessment. The TABE (CTB/McGraw-Hill, 1987, 1994a, 1994b),[1] ABLE (Karlsen & Gardner, 1986), and CASAS (CASAS, 1989) all measure reading comprehension by asking students to answer multiple-choice questions about what they have read. The ABLE and CASAS also include a number of *cloze,* or fill-in-the blank, items. Although the CASAS reading test includes some word analysis test items, most are comprehension items. All three tests are normed on representative samples of adults from various settings. The TABE and ABLE provide separate norm-referenced scores (percentile ranks and so on) for some of these groups (vocational-technical programs, prisons, ABE programs, and others).

The tests' content reflects the literacy contexts represented. All of these tests contain adult-oriented reading material, a mix of material from educational, daily life, and employment-related contexts. The reading passages in the ABLE seem to contain more academic passages, or what might be expected in a K–12 school context, such as literature (for example, fiction and poetry) and content-oriented material (for example, science, social studies, or history). The TABE has somewhat more reading related to daily life and employment than the ABLE. In addition to passages from works of fiction and factual passages about topics such as boats, it also has students read and respond to advertisements, letters, and passages of dialogue. Alternate versions of the TABE are also available that focus on any one of four work contexts: health, business, trade, and general occupational (CTB/McGraw-Hill, 1994a, 1994b). These versions, however, are available only for more advanced ABE learners.

At the other end of the continuum, perhaps, is the CASAS system, which includes two CASAS tests, the Beginning Literacy Reading Assessment portion of the Life Skills Assessment and the Reading portion of the Basic Skills for Assessment in Employability. As their names suggest, they almost exclusively address daily life and employment-related contexts, respectively. The CASAS Life Skills assessment, for example, has students read ads, price tags, restaurant menus, food labels, medical forms, and passages about legal issues and community services. The CASAS assessments also contain what, in the NALS framework, are quantitative items, displays such as graphs and other items that require numerical computations or numeracy skills.

The skills measured on the TABE and ABLE were obtained by examining ABE curriculum guides, texts, instructional programs, and objectives from other achievement tests. The CASAS system is based on more than three hundred competencies related to the Secretary's Commission on Achieving Necessary Skills (SCANS) competencies (1991) identified by the U.S. Department of Labor to help apply teaching and learning in a real-world context. One competency, for example, is described as the ability to "interpret advertisements, labels, or charts to select goods and services."

These tests actually consist of three or four separate tests, called *levels,* each at a different level of difficulty. A short "locator" test is given to determine which level a learner takes. All three tests are able to measure gain through the use of scale scores, which provide a single numerical scale that covers all levels of a test. The TABE and ABLE, but not the CASAS, provide reliability data in their manuals.

Criterion-Referenced Assessment. In addition to being norm-referenced, the CASAS could also be considered a criterion-referenced test. Test questions are keyed to its list of SCANS-based competencies, and the competencies are keyed to suggested instructional material. Instructors may examine a learner's individual responses on a test, note which items are missed, and provide instruction in the corresponding competency. In addition, each scale score is keyed to one of four presecondary ABE literacy levels: Beginning/PreLiteracy, Beginning Basic Skills, Intermediate Basic Skills, and Advanced Basic Skills. Two secondary literacy levels are also described: Adult Secondary and Advanced Adult Secondary. These are all similar to the NRS entry-level performance standards for ABE.

The TABE and ABLE provide criterion referencing in the form of mastery levels for reading comprehension subskills such as Event Interpretation, Main Ideas, and Details. Mastery levels and criteria for establishing mastery levels, however, are poorly defined. The ABLE reports the average number of items correct for the norm group in each subskill within a level. Each level may span several grade or ability levels. The examiner must decide whether or not this constitutes mastery of a subskill. The TABE provides a three-level index of mastery for each subskill (Not Mastered, Partial Mastery, and Mastery) based on number correct, but it does not provide a rationale for each cutoff score. In addition, the ABLE and TABE mastery levels are based on a relatively small number of test items, too few to be truly useful for placement and instruction. Both should be considered informal, as opposed to criterion, measures.

Any norm-referenced test, such as the TABE, ABLE, and CASAS, may be used as an informal, criterion-referenced test as an examiner becomes familiar with its content and comes to understand how various norm-referenced scores reflect actual reading behavior (Joint Committee on Standards, 1999). The NRS and the CASAS system, for example, key scale scores to entry-level performance standards for specific ABE reading levels. Although the NRS does not endorse the TABE or vouch for the validity of its scale scores, it does suggest that a TABE reading scale score between 542 and 679 is associated with the Beginning Basic Education level, which is described as follows: "Individual can read and print numbers and letters, but has a limited understanding of connected prose and may need frequent rereading" (see DAEL, 2000, p. 14, for the full description).

Particularly for the inexperienced examiner, the scores 542 and 679 may seem arbitrary and difficult to interpret. Relating scale scores to performance standards simulates what a TABE examiner may come to know only after extensive experience in using the test and providing a wide range of students with instruction.

The perceived benefit of Grade Level Equivalent scores, which associate raw scores with the abilities of average students at various grade levels, is that unlike scale scores, they intuitively make sense. Unfortunately, they often make too much sense—the concept of grade-in-school is so familiar that inexperienced examiners may easily misinterpret Grade Equivalents (GEs). GEs, like scale scores, are not derived consistently across tests, so GEs from different tests may have different implications. The TABE derived its GEs by equating TABE scores with California Achievement Test scores, for example. The ABLE GEs were formulated by giving the ABLE to a sample of elementary and secondary school students. The CASAS determined GEs simply by asking students who took the CASAS how many grade levels in school they had completed.

Although norm-referenced GEs are usually reported in terms of years and months (for example, 7.6), average scores for students are actually obtained at only one or two points during the year. Additional points along the GE continuum, as with scale scores, are determined through extrapolation and interpolation. GEs, then, illustrate that the interpretation of norm-referenced tests for criterion-referenced purposes requires a fairly high degree of expertise in both testing and teaching.

In addition to using norm-referenced tests for criterion-based decisions, there are several tests that were constructed as criterion-referenced tests that may be used in adult literacy programs. Two of these are the Reading Evaluation Adult Diagnosis (READ) (Colvin & Root, 1982) and the Diagnostic Assessments of Reading (DAR) (Roswell & Chall, 1992). Both are similar to informal reading inventories, tests that measure oral reading and reading comprehension by having students read and answer questions about passages written at different levels of difficulty. The levels of difficulty usually correspond to school grade levels or Grade Equivalents.

Both use a simple form of adaptive testing. In adaptive testing, items are first ordered according to difficulty. Both the READ and the DAR, for example, contain reading comprehension test passages beginning at, roughly, GE 3 and continuing through successive grade levels to GE 12. The examiner finds the highest level passage at which a student exhibits mastery (answers a specified number of questions correctly, for example). The level of this passage (somewhere between GE 3 and GE 12) is the student's score. A unique feature of adaptive testing is that the learner need not respond to all of the test items, saving time and perhaps avoiding frustration.

The READ, developed for Literacy Volunteers of America (LVA), contains passages that represent a more adult-oriented context than the DAR. The DAR, however, is a more reliable test. The level of the DAR content, corresponding to school grade levels, was validated on a large, national sample of students at various grade levels. No validity checks for the READ are reported.

The Test of Functional Health Literacy in Adults (TOFHLA) (Nurss et al., 1995) is an example of a criterion-referenced assessment that focuses on a specific, fairly narrow context. Adults' ability to read and understand health-related texts (X-ray preparation, Medicaid rights, and a consent form) is measured using a multiple-choice cloze passage. The cloze score is combined with the score on a separate numeracy test, and this combined score is used to place the learner at one of three literacy levels (low, marginal, and adequate functional health literacy). Reliability coefficients are presented in the TOFHLA manual.

Performance Assessment. Performance assessment includes the evaluation of student portfolios, demonstrations, projects, oral retellings, and other alternatives to norm-referenced and criterion-referenced test content. Because performance assessments may include tasks normally used for instructional purposes, they have the potential to link instruction directly to assessment (Fingeret, 1993; Leipzig & Afflerbach, 2000; Padak, Davidson, & Padak, 1994).

Although it is conceivable that a performance assessment could focus narrowly on only one aspect of the reading process, most view performance assessments as situated, holistic evaluations, in contrast with tests that focus on specific parts, aspects, or components of reading and writing processes (Garcia & Pearson, 1991; Paris, Calfee, Filby, Hiebert, Pearson, Valencia, & Wolf, 1999). Most performance assessments, then, measure more global skills, such as reading comprehension.

Performance assessments are considered by many to be a more valid measure of the domain of reading comprehension behaviors (for example, Padak et al., 1994). They are able to measure metacomprehension abilities such as strategy use and comprehension monitoring, and they use an extended, constructed response mode as opposed to multiple-choice or short-answer formats (Martinez, 1999). The fact that they use an extended response mode, however, also makes it more difficult for performance assessments to establish consistent scoring procedures. Perhaps because performance assessment is just beginning to be used extensively, procedures for establishing and measuring reliability are not well developed (Merrifield, 1998; Leipzig & Afflerbach, 2000).

Performance assessments may be used to assess reading and writing ability to satisfy assessment requirements in the NRS. It is not clear yet, however, how many states and local programs will actually use performance assessments or what form they will take as they incorporate the concepts of ability levels and standardized scoring rubrics that are a part of the NRS. As the NRS has evolved over the past decade, however, at least some states have developed performance assessments. A review of eleven states' ABE literacy assessment systems, based on interviews with state officials and published state plans, showed that at least five were adopting published performance assessments (Kutner et al., 1996). Although very little detail was provided, these included learner portfolios, writing samples, classroom demonstrations, and reading aloud, as well as documentation of specific practices.

Performance tasks such as project-based learning have been used by local programs for some time, although scoring rubrics and other ways of evaluating student learning gains have lagged behind (for example, see Wrigley, 1998). As performance tasks and related scoring rubrics evolve, more detailed descriptions of existing performance assessment systems, including direct observations, will be needed, as will research related to reliability and validity.

Informal Assessment. The Tests of General Educational Development (GED) are administered by the American Council on Education (American Council on Education, 1993) and adults who pass the GED receive a high-school-level educational diploma. Many programs for advanced ABE learners base their curriculum on the GED. Although local programs cannot administer the actual GED, GED practice tests are available as informal measures (GED Testing Service, 1997). Test content consists of passages, as well as charts, tables, and other graphics, that cover high school subject matter at the twelfth grade level, including social studies and science, and literature and the arts. Test takers read the passages and answer multiple-choice questions. Although norm tables with percentile ranks and scale scores are provided (based on a national sample of high school seniors) the results are informal because the norms are based on standard administration procedures in official testing centers. As an informal assessment of reading comprehension, the GED practice tests would be suitable for learners who are reading at the high school level or above.

VOCABULARY (ORAL). Vocabulary, or knowledge of word meanings, may be measured either orally or silently. In oral measures, students hear a word and tell what it means, choose the correct illustration of the word, or choose the correct orally presented definition. In silent measures, students must read silently and answer questions about a word. "Silent vocabulary" will be discussed in more detail in the next section.

Norm-Referenced Assessment. Of the commonly used adult literacy assessment instruments (the TABE, ABLE, CASAS, WRAT, and SORT), only the ABLE assesses oral vocabulary, and it does so only for adults who take the lowest level of the test (level 1, for adults with one to four years of formal schooling). Sentences are dictated to students, who must decide which of three alternatives best completes each sentence. A multiple-choice vocabulary item assessing knowledge of a word such as *foot* might ask, *A foot is made up of . . . 12 inches, 3 inches, 8 inches,* with the student marking the correct answer on an answer form. The context represented by test items is roughly the same as in the ABLE reading comprehension assessment; words are drawn from work situations, daily life, and academic texts, with most being from the social, physical, and natural sciences.

Tests not commonly used by adult literacy programs that measure oral vocabulary at all levels are available. The Woodcock-Johnson Diagnostic Reading Battery (Woodcock, 1997) measures both oral and silent vocabulary. Students' oral vocabulary is measured by having them listen to a tape on which they hear a word, then respond with a one-word antonym or synonym.

The Woodcock is normed on children and adults ranging from two to ninety-five years old and provides scale scores, percentile ranks, age equivalents, grade equivalents, and a mastery score. Extensive data on the test's reliability is provided. GEs are determined by obtaining the average scores for the norm group in a given grade level during each month of the school year, without extrapolating or interpolating. Like the DAR, the Woodcock uses adaptive testing and does not have separate tests for students at different levels of ability (as the TABE, ABLE, and CASAS do). The Woodcock is also different from the TABE and ABLE in that it does not provide an overtly adult context, using more school-like content.

Criterion-Referenced Assessment. As with reading comprehension, the ABLE provides criterion-referenced scores (mastery levels) for vocabulary knowledge and support for item analysis. The same problems related to validity exist for these measures that were discussed above for the ABLE criterion-referenced reading comprehension measures.

Of the criterion-referenced tests not commonly used in adult literacy, the DAR measures vocabulary by asking learners to define words rather than using a multiple-choice or short answer format. While this makes the test more difficult to score, it may be a more valid measure of vocabulary knowledge. As with reading comprehension, the DAR vocabulary subtest yields a "validated" GE score.

The Woodcock mastery score (Relative Proficiency Index) is based on one of its norm-referenced scale scores. It indicates what percentage of material a test taker would be expected to know when compared with individuals at the same age (or grade) level. Unlike the ABLE, it uses a sufficient number of items overall for reliable indexes of mastery.

VOCABULARY (SILENT). Silent vocabulary assessment, in which students silently read and answer questions about a word and its meaning, is not as pure a measure of vocabulary as oral assessment. When the learner must read the questions silently, vocabulary knowledge is confounded with other aspects of reading ability, such as decoding. This measure may not be as valid as an oral measure, but it is easier to administer and score.

Norm-Referenced Assessment. The ABLE uses the same item format for silent vocabulary assessment on levels 2 and 3 (for students with five to eight and nine to twelve years of school) as it does for oral vocabulary on level 1, except that the items are read silently by the student, not dictated by a teacher. The CASAS and most recent TABE (CTB/McGraw-Hill, 1994a, 1994b) do not have a separate subtest for vocabulary knowledge. The 1987 TABE does have a separate vocabulary assessment test. It contains multiple-choice items that are a little more varied than those on the ABLE. In addition to asking students to complete a sentence with the correct word, as on the ABLE, the TABE asks students to find synonyms and antonyms for an underlined word or word part (such as a prefix) in a phrase or sentence. The student reads a phrase (such as <u>Over</u> *the mountain*) and must select from a list of four options the word with the same meaning as the underlined word (such as *above, below, near, through*). As with the TABE reading comprehension subtest, the 1987 TABE vocabulary assessment emphasizes functional contexts (life and work-related contexts) somewhat more than the ABLE.

Some tests provide both oral and silent vocabulary measures. The Woodcock, for example, has separate oral and silent vocabulary subtests, and the norm-referenced scores are directly comparable.

Criterion-Referenced and Informal Assessment. The ABLE and the 1987 TABE provide support for item analysis and mastery cutoffs for total vocabulary scores and vocabulary subskill scores. Again, problems with these criterion levels are the same as those discussed earlier. The Woodcock mastery score is more robust because it is based on more items and is referenced to the performance of the norm group.

FLUENCY. Assessments of reading fluency measure learners' ability to read connected text accurately, at a reasonable rate, and with appropriate prosody (intonation and phrasing).

Norm-Referenced Assessment. The TABE, ABLE, and CASAS do not measure oral reading fluency directly, nor do they provide a score for reading fluency. The TABE, because it is timed, penalizes those test takers who read slowly.

An example of a norm-referenced test that does measure reading fluency is the Gray Oral Reading Test (GORT), now in its third edition (Weiderholt & Bryant, 1992). The GORT is normed on students in grades 2 through 12, not on adults. On this individually administered, adaptive test, students are asked to read aloud from short passages that become progressively more difficult (sentences increase in length and complexity, and vocabulary increases in difficulty). As learners read, their oral reading errors and the time that it takes to read a passage are recorded. Three separate scores—one for rate, one for accuracy, and a total score—may be converted into percentiles, scale scores, and grade equivalents. Student miscues (reading errors such as mispronunciations, omissions, repetitions, and self-corrections) may be analyzed qualitatively to look for patterns in the errors. A low rate score accompanied by many self-corrections, for example, might be interpreted differently from a low rate score accompanied by many omissions and mispronunciations. The GORT manual suggests using the procedures described by Goodman and Burke (1972) to conduct the error analysis.

Criterion-Referenced Assessment. The DAR is an example of a criterion-referenced assessment that measures fluency in oral reading. Like the GORT, the DAR oral reading subtest is an adaptive test. A student's score indicates the highest level passage that is mastered, with passages spanning GE 1 through GE 11–12. Mastery is defined as pronouncing roughly 95 percent of the words in a passage correctly, as in traditional Informal Reading Inventories (IRIs). As mentioned earlier in the comprehension section, the DAR is similar to IRIs, but differs in the care taken to establish content validity. The difficulty and grade placement levels of oral reading passages are based on readability measures, experts' judgments, and two research studies in which the passages were given to a wide range of students of different ability levels to verify that student scores on the passages accurately differentiated students at different grade levels and were adequately correlated with a norm-referenced test.

Performance Assessment. Oral reading is a natural performance task that usually involves the analysis of oral reading errors. Miscue analysis is one example of methods used to analyze these errors (Goodman, 1999; Goodman, Watson, & Burke, 1987; Leipzig & Afflerbach, 2000). With this method, miscues are not treated as errors but are evaluated in terms of whether or not they maintain a text's syntactic and semantic integrity. Other informal assessments, such as IRIs, look at the number and type of errors (mispronunciations, self-corrections, and so on).

WORD RECOGNITION. Word recognition assessments measure students' ability to pronounce individual words presented in isolation. Students may read a word list rather than a passage of text, for example.

Norm-Referenced Assessment. The ABLE, TABE, and CASAS do not have separate word recognition subtests. The WRAT (Wilkinson, 1993) and SORT (Slosson & Nicholson, 1990), although not used as frequently in adult literacy programs, do measure isolated word recognition.

On the WRAT, students are asked to read aloud a list of words that increase in difficulty (*cat* and *red* are at the beginning, for example, and *disingenuous* and *inefficacious* are at the end). The test ends when the student either is unable to pronounce ten consecutive words or gets to the end of the list. On the SORT, an adaptive test, students are also asked to read isolated words, but they are asked to pronounce words from lists ranging in difficulty from the primary level through high school. Both are normed on children and adults, and both provide norm-referenced scores derived from raw scores. The WRAT and SORT GE scores are not interpolated or extrapolated scores (there is no need for this because all learners take the same test, there are no separate levels, and an adequate sample is drawn from each grade level). Manuals for both provide reliability data.

Criterion-Referenced Assessment. Although the CASAS does not give a separate score for word recognition, it does include "discrimination among sight words" as one of its reading comprehension objectives, and several items on the reading comprehension subtest address sight words directly. Item analysis support is given on the CASAS for sight words, although this measure has the same problems as the TABE and ABLE mastery measures discussed earlier.

The DAR and READ also use word lists as a part of their criterion-referenced assessments. The student's score for word recognition is the grade level of the most difficult list on which mastery is exhibited. On these adaptive tests, mastery is determined by the percentage of words pronounced correctly—70 percent of the words on a DAR list, for example. Although the DAR provides information on validity, the READ manual contains none.

The Rapid Estimate of Adult Literacy in Medicine (REALM) (Murphy, Davis, Long, Jackson, & Decker, 1994) is an example of a context-specific word recognition assessment. Modeled after the WRAT and SORT, the REALM consists of three word lists containing medical terms (for example, *flu, infection, osteoporosis*). Raw scores are converted into GEs that are anchored to descriptions of patients' abilities to read medical-related texts. The GEs were obtained by correlating the REALM with the SORT.

WORD ANALYSIS. Word analysis assessment measures students' ability to recognize, produce, and manipulate individual phonemes or speech sounds (phonemic awareness) in words or syllables that they hear. It also measures their ability to match sounds with letters and letter combinations (their knowledge of letter-sounds correspondences) and to blend letter-sounds into words while reading or spelling (phonics ability). Higher-level word analysis assessment measures students' knowledge of meaningful word-parts, such as compounds, prefixes, and suffixes.

Norm-Referenced Assessment. None of the norm-referenced tests commonly used in adult literacy give a separate score for word analysis. Several other norm-referenced tests, however, do measure aspects of phonemic awareness and phonics. The Woodcock looks at students' ability to sound out words (in the Word Attack subtest), to supply missing phonemes in words (Incomplete Words), and to blend isolated sounds into words (Sound Blending). The ability to sound out words is measured by having students read phonologically regular nonsense words. The nonsense word *stad,* for example, can be pronounced (it rhymes with *had*) even though it is not a real word. Using nonsense words ensures that students are actually sounding out a word as opposed to saying a word that they have memorized (as they might have memorized irregular words such as *enough* and *though*). Scores on the Incomplete Words and Sound Blending tests can be combined to obtain an overall Phonological Awareness score. On these subtests, students listen to a word with one or two missing phonemes (*si__ter*) and must say the complete word (*sister*), or they are asked to listen to the individual parts of a word (*c-a-t* or *b-at*) and then must say the word (*cat* and *bat*).

Criterion-Referenced Assessment. The TABE, ABLE, CASAS, and WRAT do have items that test for knowledge of certain word analysis or phonemic awareness skills when measuring some more inclusive component of the reading process. The WRAT, for example, which measures sight word knowledge, asks beginning readers to read isolated upper- and lowercase letters. The easiest level of the TABE has items for matching and recognizing letters and for identifying beginning, middle, and end sounds in words. The CASAS reading comprehension subtest includes items that measure the ability to recognize and discriminate upper- and lowercase letters. The 1987 TABE vocabulary subtest tests knowledge of affixes, and both the TABE and ABLE spelling subtests test knowledge of various word parts, such as affixes, vowels, consonants, and vowel digraphs. The TABE, ABLE, and CASAS support item analysis and provide mastery level scores, but, as said before, these scores are not easily interpreted.

The Adult Measure of Essential Skills (AMES) (Steck-Vaughn, 1997) is a newer test of adult literacy that, like the TABE and ABLE, is normed on groups of adults, places questions in an adult context (home, community, workplace, and school), and has forms at different levels for adults who are at different levels of literacy development. Unlike the TABE and ABLE, however, it has a separate auditory discrimination subtest for nonreaders (for those "who have had from one to two years of schooling"). Students are asked to find words that have the same sound as a stimulus word in beginning, medial, and ending positions. A student might be shown three pictures (of a *house, cat,* and *dog,* for example) and then asked by the examiner to locate the one that begins with the same sound as a word pronounced by the examiner (such as *hat*). Unfortunately, this subtest has not been separately normed, and results are combined with other subtest results to obtain a norm-referenced total reading score.

The Test of Auditory Analysis Skills (TAAS) (Rosner, 1979) is an example of a criterion-referenced word analysis test of phonological awareness. It is a short, thirteen-item test that measures the ability to manipulate phonemes and syllables by asking students to say a word after removing a phoneme or syllable. The student might be asked to say *boat* without the /b/ sound, for example (*oat*). It gives a GE score from kindergarten through grade 3, based on the number of correct items.

The Word Analysis assessment of the DAR measures a student's knowledge of letter-sound correspondences using a series of twelve subtests that correspond roughly to the order in which word analysis skills are introduced to, or learned by, beginning readers: matching words, matching letters, naming lowercase and uppercase letters (prereading subtests), consonant sounds, consonant blends, short vowel sounds, rule of silent *e*, vowel digraphs, diphthongs, vowels with *r*, and polysyllabic words. These tests of basic word analysis ability are given only to those students who score below the fourth-grade level on the DAR Word Recognition subtest. It is assumed that those scoring above level 3 on Word Recognition will have mastered basic word analysis skills.

Mastery levels on the twelve DAR Word Analysis subtests are determined individually for each subtest, based on the number of correct responses. GE scores are not provided for these subtests. In addition to simple matching and naming tasks for the pre-reading subtests, students are asked to say the sounds of individual consonants when presented with the letter that represents the sound or to read words containing specific letter-sound correspondences. To assess knowledge of vowel digraphs (two-letter vowel combinations that represent one sound), for example, a student might be asked to read a word list including the word *seat* to assess knowledge of the sound that the digraph *ea* makes. Correct answers, indicating that the student knows the *ea* sound, would include any one-syllable word with a medial /e/ sound, such as *beat* or *seam,* as well as *seat.*

Several informal tests of basic word analysis are also available, such as Adams's Test of Phonemic Awareness (Adams, 1998).

Writing

Assessment of the following components of the writing process will be discussed: the production of written products, writing vocabulary, sentence production, word production, planning and monitoring, and revising and editing.

WRITTEN PRODUCTS. Essays, reports, stories, and other written products produced in response to a task have increasingly been scored holistically. Readers rate a written product on a scale (usually an ascending four- or five-point scale) using guidelines that describe the characteristics of products at each point along the scale. Analytic scoring is also used, where several specific traits, such as style or mechanics, are scored separately. This form of performance assessment, consisting of a writing task and scoring rubric, is one of the few that have led to norm-referenced performance assessments, what Nitko (1996) calls structured, on-demand performance assessments.

Norm-Referenced Assessment. None of the most commonly used assessments in adult literacy provide norm-referenced scores for whole written products. There are, however, other norm-referenced writing assessments that do evaluate student essays, stories, and descriptions. The Writing Process Test (WPT) (Warden & Hutchinson, 1992), for example, is a group-administered, structured performance assessment that uses an analytic scoring procedure to evaluate a student's composition. Students are given an academic or school-like writing task, such as writing a personal essay for a school newspaper. Their response, a written product, is evaluated analytically by giving a score for ten features: purpose and focus, audience, vocabulary, style and tone, support and development, organization and coherence, sentence structure and variety, grammar and usage, capitalization and punctuation, and spelling. These scores are summed to produce a total score, which can then be converted into one of several standardized scores, including percentile ranks and two scale scores.

Although the norming group for this test includes students in grades K–12 and not adults, the manual suggests that the test can be used in ABE settings and can also be used to evaluate any writing assignment. When used with adults, then, it becomes an informal criterion-referenced test because there are no adult norms.

A more varied norm-referenced writing assessment is the Test of Written Language (TOWL) (Hammill & Larsen, 1996). Its measure of story writing uses an analytic scoring rubric that considers aspects of both sentence-level and story-level production. Like the Writing Process Test, it was normed on a K–12 population and its content reflects an academic context. In addition to measuring whole, written products, it also measures five components of the writing process with a more traditional, short-answer format.

Scoring a test that uses an analytic scoring rubric requires more training than is required for scoring a multiple-choice test. Analytic scoring is more subjective than multiple-choice scoring, and the reliability coefficients reported in the Writing Process Test manuals are generally somewhat lower than those reported for the TABE or ABLE. When judging an entire essay, the evaluator may find many different responses to be "correct." As the use of a five-point scoring scale suggests, several types of responses may fall between "correct" and "not correct." When judging whether a student has "used techniques to engage a reader," for example, a scorer selects one of five responses (sophisticated, competent, partly competent, not yet competent, and problematic). These are keyed to more detailed criteria. For a piece to be judged sophisticated, for example, it must be one that "uses techniques (e.g., questions, humor, direct address, references to audience) effectively to engage [the] audience throughout the writing." A competent piece, on the other hand, shows "some evidence of techniques to engage the audience, but not all are effective; a clear effort is made once but not carried throughout."

Performance Assessment. Of common adult literacy tests, only the CASAS Functional Writing Test gives scores for complete written products. The CASAS writing test is a structured, on-demand performance assessment (Nitko, 1996) that measures a learner's ability to produce one or more of three types of adult-oriented texts. The first text type is descriptive and is derived from a picture task. The test taker looks at a drawing of a street scene and writes about what is happening in the picture. The second text type is a form, such as an employment application, and the task for the learner is to complete it. The third type is a description of a common process depicted in a picture, such as obtaining money from an ATM.

The CASAS writing test provides both analytic and holistic writing scores. Analytic scoring is used for two of the tasks, the picture task and the form task. When scoring the description, for example, evaluators give it a score (from 0 to 6) in each of the following five categories: content; organization; word choice; grammar and sentence structure; and punctuation, spelling, and capitalization. These scores are first weighted and then summed to yield a total that is used to place students at one of six writing ability levels, from a Beginning Literacy level through an Advanced level. A text produced for the Process Task is scored holistically, with evaluators assigning a single score on a scale from 0 to 5, using a scoring rubric that focuses on content, organization, word choice, and mechanics (grammar, spelling, and so on). CASAS will ensure the reliability of scores for the different tasks only if test administrators receive training from CASAS or the essays are sent to CASAS for scoring.

Informal Assessment. The GED practice tests (GED Testing Service, 1997) may be used informally to measure advanced ABE learners' written products (those ready to take the GED high school equivalency exam). Learners are given a statement (about the effects of watching television, for example) and directions about what to write (a two-hundred-word essay on whether they agree with the statement, for example). The essays are scored holistically. Although scoring guides and sample essays are provided, the results are reliable only for trained examiners.

WRITING VOCABULARY. Although there is considerable overlap, writing vocabulary and reading vocabulary assessment may measure somewhat different abilities. While reading vocabulary assessment typically measures the ability to recognize or state the meaning of a word, writing vocabulary assessment measures how effectively a learner uses or produces a concept while composing.

Norm-Referenced Assessment. None of the tests commonly used in adult literacy provide norm-referenced measures of a student's ability to use specific vocabulary words while writing. As described earlier, the TABE and ABLE do assess students' knowledge of word meanings, but the assessment requires reading, not writing. The nonadult TOWL is an example of a norm-referenced test for writing vocabulary. Students are asked to write sentences that contain specific vocabulary words. As with the WRAT word recognition reading test, students are given progressively more difficult words until they reach their ceiling, missing a specified number of words in a row (or completing the test). The test begins with words like *see, eat,* and *help* and ends with words like *evade* and *inept.* Percentiles, scale scores, and grade equivalents can be derived from students' raw scores.

Criterion-Referenced Assessment. The Writing Process Test provides a criterion-referenced score for the use of words to communicate purpose and style. This vocabulary score is one of the ten analytic scores the test provides to evaluate a whole written product. The criteria range from sophisticated ("uses precise, fresh, vivid words to communicate purpose and style") to problematic (vocabulary is "inadequate, incorrect, or confusing") on a five-point scale.

The CASAS Functional Writing Test also contains an analytic score for vocabulary in which a student's choice of words is evaluated according to specified criteria. Although this is not a direct, controlled measure of writing vocabulary, the scoring rubric might be used as a guide for the assessment of vocabulary used in naturally occurring student writing, such as texts collected for a portfolio.

SENTENCE PRODUCTION: CAPITALIZATION, PUNCTUATION, AND SENTENCE STRUCTURE (SYNTAX AND USAGE). None of the commonly used adult literacy assessments ask learners to actually write sentences. Sentence production ability is instead evaluated indirectly with measures of capitalization and punctuation knowledge (these are usually measured together) and knowledge of the structure of sentences (both grammar or syntax and conventional usage).

Norm-Referenced Assessment. Capitalization, punctuation, and sentence structure knowledge are all measured by the ABLE and TABE using a multiple-choice format. On the TABE, a Language score is obtained, in part, by asking students to read a sentence or passage and then select the best way to punctuate or capitalize a part of the selection from among four or five choices. For example, if a sentence such as *It is I think very hot outside* is given, the correct answer among the choices would be *It is, I think, very hot outside* as opposed to *It is I, think, very hot outside*. The Language score on the TABE is also derived from responses to multiple-choice questions related to knowledge of English language *usage,* or phrase- and sentence-level syntactic structures, and *paragraph development,* or specific paragraph-level skills. For sentence-level structures, students are tested on their ability to recognize the correct use or form of basic syntactic structures: nouns, verbs, modifiers, and simple sentences. For paragraph-level structures, students are asked to recognize the best topic sentence, the best sequence for sentences in a paragraph, and the best way to combine two simple sentences into one, more complex, sentence.

Unlike the TABE, the ABLE measures only capitalization, punctuation, and sentence-level structures. Neither test measures these skills on the levels of the test designed for beginning readers (for students with one to four years of schooling on the ABLE and for students at about GE 0–2 on the TABE).

Norm-Referenced Performance Assessment. The Writing Process Test and the TOWL (normed on children) provide examples of ways in which extended learner-generated writing may be used to assess sentence production ability. The Writing Process Test contains a norm-referenced score for fluency that is derived from a combination of analytic scores for the following features: sentence structure and variety, grammar and usage, capitalization and punctuation, and spelling. The TOWL scores student stories analytically for both contextual conventions (spelling, capitalization, and punctuation) and contextual language (sentence construction, grammar, and quality of vocabulary). These measures of students' extended writing can be compared with students' scores on style and sentence-combining subtests that require one-sentence responses to stimuli (dictated sentences or short sentences that are to be combined into one longer sentence).

The Woodcock-Johnson Tests of Achievement (Woodcock & Johnson, 1989) measure a learner's ability to write sentences, evaluating both the quality of the written product and fluency (speed) and then combining these measures into one written expression score. In one task used to generate sentences, the student is shown a picture and three words and then asked to write a sentence containing each of these elements as quickly as possible. The student might be shown, for example, a picture of a house and the words *door, man,* and *knock* and be expected to produce *the man will knock on the door of the house* (students are not penalized for capitalization and punctuation errors). The Woodcock-Johnson Achievement test gives the same types of scores (percentiles, scale scores, age and grade equivalents, and mastery scores) as the Woodcock-Johnson Diagnostic Reading test discussed above. These tests, part of the Woodcock-Johnson Psycho-Educational Battery, are constructed so that standard scores from one may be compared with standard scores from the other. Reading results, for example, can be compared directly with writing results.

Criterion-Referenced Assessment. The CASAS Functional Writing Test contains a separate analytic score for grammar and sentence structure. The scoring rubric for grammar and sentence structure, like the rubric for writing vocabulary discussed earlier, might be used as a guide for evaluating sentence structure in naturally occurring written work.

WORD PRODUCTION: SPELLING (SOUND-LETTER CORRESPONDENCE) AND MORPHOLOGY (DERIVATION, INFLECTION, AND COMPOUNDS). Word production ability is most often measured with spelling tests. Spelling tests may be used to test for specific subskill knowledge, such as knowledge of sound-letter correspondences, derivations, inflections, and compounds. Reading teachers sometimes use spelling tests to measure word analysis ability.

Norm-Referenced Assessment. The TABE and ABLE measure spelling by asking students to read a sentence with a missing word and to then choose the correct spelling of the missing word from among a short list of words. Although only one of the words on the list is spelled correctly, all might be confused with the correct spelling. The following is an example of this type of spelling item: *The _____ is dry. strem, streme, stream, streem.*

This example tests students' knowledge of vowel digraphs (the two-letter vowel combination *ea*). The TABE and ABLE also use the spelling subtest to measure knowledge of consonant variants (consonant digraphs like the *ph* in *phone,* for example) and structural forms, such as contractions and affixes. The TABE level L, for adults reading at about GE 0–2, does not contain a spelling subtest. The sentences and possible responses for the level 1 on the ABLE (the level for adults with one to four years of schooling) are dictated.

The WRAT spelling subtest is also oral, although it is more like a traditional spelling test, in which the teacher dictates a word, uses the word in a sentence, and then directs students to write the correct spelling without the benefit of being able to select from among a list of possible answers. The TOWL spelling subtest, like most of the other TOWL subtests, requires extended writing. In this case, students write dictated sentences.

Criterion-Referenced Assessment. Both the Writing Process Test and the TOWL have analytic scores that evaluate spelling in context (in a learner's story, for example). The Woodcock provides a mastery score for spelling.

PLANNING AND MONITORING. Planning includes what a student does before or during writing to generate ideas and organize them coherently, based on the writing task and intended audience. Creating a working outline for a written product is an example of a planning behavior. While writing, writers may monitor their composing to ensure that it conforms with their plans, to change plans, and to check spelling and other lower-level processes.

Norm-Referenced Assessment. None of the common adult literacy assessments measure planning ability in writing. The Writing Process Test does provide norm-referenced scores for *development,* derived from the sum of analytic scores for purpose, audience, vocabulary, style and tone, support and development, and organization and coherence. *Development* is described as the ability to handle the broader concerns of topic, audience, and ideas, as opposed to *fluency* or the ability to handle the more mechanical aspects of writing (sentence structure, grammar, and so on).

Criterion-Referenced Assessment. The CASAS Functional Writing Assessment provides two measures that are very roughly related to generating and organizing ideas: a measure of an essay's content, which is an overall assessment of the quality of the ideas in an essay and the degree to which the ideas expressed address the writing task, and a measure of the degree to which a final written product is well organized. These measures address neither the writer's ability to handle demands related to an audience nor the writer's ability to plan before beginning to write or during the writing process.

The Writing Process Test is unique in that it does attempt to measure writers' views of their own writing ability and use of specific planning and revising strategies. Writers rate their writing using the same analytic scoring features that the examiner uses to evaluate the writing. Teacher and writer ratings can then be compared. Writers' evaluations of their own writing are not very reliable, especially among less experienced writers, according to the test publisher's research. However, self-evaluation provides a natural way for adults to be more directly involved in the assessment process.

REVISING AND EDITING. Revising and editing both involve making changes to what has been written. Although the two overlap to some degree, editing is a more local activity, involving changes in sentence-level structures as students write or as they read over what they have written. Revising is more global and involves adding, deleting, moving, or otherwise changing sentences or paragraphs within a text to better express an idea.

Norm-Referenced, Criterion-Referenced Assessment. Only one assessment was located that provided norm-referenced or criterion-referenced scores for general revising and editing processes. The TOWL has one subtest that measures an aspect of editing. On the *logical sentences* subtest, students rewrite illogical sentences so that they make better sense. If given the sentence *John washed the sky,* for example, the student would be expected to rewrite the sentence so that it made sense (*John washed his car,* for example).

As discussed, the Writing Process Test is unique in that it does attempt to measure writers' view of their own writing ability and use of specific revising strategies. Both writers and examiners use analytic scoring rubrics to evaluate the revising process. The writers, for example, rate the degree to which they agree with statements such as the following (using a four-point scale): *As I rewrote, I thought about the assignment.*

Informal Assessment. Although none of the commonly used adult literacy tests evaluate the way in which students edit or revise their own work, both the TABE and ABLE language subtests do ask students to make decisions about secondary texts that are similar to decisions that writers make when editing or revising their own text. A careful item analysis by an examiner can serve as an indirect, informal evaluation of some aspects of these processes. To measure capitalization and punctuation skills, for example, the ABLE asks students to read a sentence that may or may not contain an error and then to select a better version of the sentence or a part of the sentence if there is an error. A student may be given a sentence like the following: *Should I wash the* cloths. The student selects the best alternative to the underlined part of the sentence from a list like the following: *a. Correct b. Clothes. c. cloth? d. clothes?*

The TABE indirectly measures more sophisticated editing and revising abilities as part of its language expression measure: recognizing correct sentence structures, combining sentences, working with topic sentences, and sequencing sentences in a logical manner.

Motivation

Motivation is an important aspect of reading and writing, especially for adult learners, most of whom are not required to attend literacy classes and who must find the time and energy to do so. Motivation, attitude, and engagement in literacy are frequently associated with time spent reading and reading achievement (Smith, 1990; Guthrie & Wigfield, 1997; Mikulecky & Lloyd, 1997). Motivation has traditionally been assessed in adult literacy during intake interviews, when new learners are asked about their goals and interests (Askov et al., 1997).

Normally, change in motivation to read is not measured, and none of the assessments considered so far contain a measure for motivation. Examples of measures that do exist, in addition to the informal measures mentioned earlier (Askov et al., 1997), are measures developed primarily for research purposes (Beder, 1990; Guthrie & Wigfield, 1997), for statewide performance assessment programs at the K–12 level (Leipzig & Afflerbach, 2000), and in assessments of K–12 literacy curricula (Au, 1997). Among the items in the questionnaire used by Wigfield are, for example, *I have favorite subjects that I like to read about* and *I like to read about new things.* Students indicate their degree of agreement on a four-point scale (Guthrie & Wigfield, 1997, p. 432).

Au's evaluation of a literacy curriculum involved the use of a performance assessment with children. The assessment included grade-level benchmarks to measure ownership of literacy (ownership is considered an aspect of motivation). Teachers used checklists, anecdotal records, collections of student products, and questionnaires to evaluate progress in meeting the benchmarks. Some examples of the benchmarks used are "enjoys writing" (kindergarten) and "makes connections between reading and writing" (grade 3) (Au, 1997, p. 178).

Assessments developed for research and large-scale assessment may provide items that have more validity than those developed by teachers for local programs (those used during intake interviews, for example). The reliability of motivation questionnaires may be problematic because they are fairly transparent, especially for adults, and the natural tendency is to respond in the way that you think the examiner would want you to respond.

PRACTICES: ASSESSING THE USE OF READING AND WRITING PRACTICES

The frequency of reading practices, such as document, book, newspaper, or magazine reading, is positively associated with literacy ability (Smith, 1995; Sheehan-Holt & Smith, 2000). A goal for many adult literacy programs is to increase both the amount of time adults spend reading and the volume of material they read. Although there are no standardized assessments of literacy practice, it can be assessed informally when a teacher is interested in whether or not a literacy program has positively affected the frequency of specific reading practices.

Assessment of literacy practices involves self-reports and the use of diaries to record what is read (Alvermann et al., 1999; Kirsch & Jungeblut, 1986; Mikulecky & Lloyd, 1997; Smith, 2000; Sticht, 1995). In a study of after-school "read and talk" clubs, adolescents were expected to keep a daily log in which they answered questions about what they read, where they read, why they read, how much time they spent reading, and how much they used the library as a source for reading (Alvermann et al., 1999). Assessment may be associated with a specific setting or context, such as family literacy practices (National Center for Family Literacy, 1996) or workplace practices (Mikulecky & Lloyd, 1997; Sticht, 1995). Mikulecky and Lloyd, for example, in a study of workplace literacy, asked participants, "Tell me the sorts of things you read and write on the job during a normal week" (1997, p. 563).

Direct observation and recording of literacy practices can also be used (Sticht, 1995). Direct observation is more reliable than self-reports, although it is more difficult to implement. Interview questions that elicit self-reports must be constructed carefully. Small changes in the phrasing of questions can have a large impact on the information obtained. For example, the question, "Have you completed a book in the past month?" would probably result in fewer positive responses than, "Have you read in a book in the past month?" (Kaestle et al., 1991, p. 189).

Change in literacy practices over time can be assessed by collecting practices data more than once (Mikulecky & Lloyd, 1997), as is required by the NRS. Self-reports can be used to obtain the data specified in the NRS, such as family literacy practices, and to evaluate a program of instruction. The NRS, for example, suggests that family literacy programs ask adults about practices such as how frequently they read to their children. Unlike more typical forms of performance assessment, results from the assessment of literacy practices are not tied to developmental levels. It is not known, for example, precisely how growth in the frequency or number of reading practices is related to growth in literacy ability.

THE STATE OF ABE
LITERACY ASSESSMENT

The most frequently used literacy assessments in adult basic education (the TABE, ABLE, WRAT, CASAS reading tests, and SORT) each provide norm-referenced scores for one or two components of the reading process. The TABE, ABLE, and CASAS measure comprehension, the ABLE has a separate vocabulary measure, and the WRAT and SORT have scores for word recognition. These assessments do not have norm-referenced scores for fluency, word analysis, or aspects of the writing process other than sentence production and spelling. Some have criterion-referenced measures for word analysis and a few additional components of the writing process, but they generally rely on too few items or are otherwise difficult to interpret.

Norm-referenced, criterion-referenced, and standardized performance assessments for adults that measure other components do exist, including measures of fluency (the GORT and DAR), word analysis (the Woodcock and DAR), and written products (the CASAS Functional Writing Assessment and Woodcock). Two criterion-referenced or performance-based assessments that were developed primarily for the K–12 level might also be used with adults to measure written products and writing vocabulary (the TOWL and the Writing Process Test) and planning and revising or editing (the Writing Process Test).

Of all the tests mentioned here, only the DAR and the Woodcock (Reading) attempt to measure all aspects of the reading process, and only the Woodcock (Achievement) attempts to measure multiple components of both the reading and writing process. Unfortunately, the DAR has only one form, which makes it difficult to use for both pre- and posttesting, and the Woodcock is available only to those with specified credentials (requiring a fairly high level of expertise).

There are no formal, adult-oriented assessments of the motivational aspect of reading and writing. Assessments of motivation designed for research with adults (Beder, 1990) or at the K–12 level (for example, Guthrie & Wigfield, 1997) might serve as examples. There are also no formal assessments for literacy practices, although research may again serve as a guide for the creation of questions that help to generate reliable self-reports of adult practices (Purcell-Gates, Degener, Jacobson, & Soler, 2000; Mikulecky & Lloyd, 1997; Kaestle et al., 1991).

Most of the common adult literacy assessments (the TABE, ABLE, and CASAS) use adult-oriented contexts, including functional, life-skills, and workplace content for test items. The ABLE has the most academic content, while the CASAS has the most functional content. Although the WRAT and SORT do not use adult contexts, there are other word recognition tests that focus on specific contexts, such as health and medicine (the TOFHLA and REALM).

Performance assessments have the potential to measure many aspects of reading and writing ability. Although there is no detailed, comprehensive survey of their use in adult literacy, K–12 and adult education literature indicate that they have traditionally focused primarily on reading comprehension, written products, and oral reading. They are, for example, used to measure aspects of reading comprehension that common assessments do not, such as comprehension monitoring and strategy use. They are also used to gauge the ability to use reading and writing in naturally occurring situations. Methods to use in evaluating the reliability and validity of performance assessments are still evolving (Leipzig & Afflerbach, 2000).

Most of the common adult literacy assessment instruments are group-administered tests (the TABE, ABLE, and CASAS). They provide brief scripts for test administrators to use and so can be administered fairly easily and reliably. The WRAT and SORT are somewhat more difficult to administer. They are given individually and the tester must be able to interpret and score oral responses as either correct or incorrect, and must know when to end the testing. Less frequently used tests, such as the DAR, Woodcock, and CASAS writing test are more complex to administer. Performance assessments, because they are a newer form of assessment and do not have established procedures for constructing tasks and developing scoring rubrics, are perhaps the most complex assessments to administer. Setting up performance assessment systems is an extended, iterative process even for those who are experts (for example, see Paris, 1999).

The amount of training that adult literacy staff need in order to reliably administer literacy assessments varies along with the complexity of the assessments. Training is necessary, however, when scoring and interpreting even the simplest tests. A task as simple as using a norms table to convert a raw score into a percentile rank or GE can create problems even for a trained professional (Nitko, 1983, p. 361). Knowing which forms and levels of a test to use is problematic for many adult educators (Kutner et al., 1996). Interpreting the wide variety of derived scores requires training and experience as well.

When administered by properly trained staff, all the assessments mentioned above can be used to satisfy the accountability requirements of the NRS (with the exception, perhaps, of the DAR, which has only one form). With more training and experience in selecting and using the right combination of tests, practitioners can use these tools to inform instruction. Scale scores and GEs can be used to help guide instruction, for example, but it is important to know that different tests construct these scores in different ways, and that the way in which they are constructed can affect interpretation.

IMPLICATIONS FOR PRACTICE, RESEARCH, AND POLICY

How well do common adult literacy assessments align with views of literacy in adult basic education, particularly along the dimensions of practice, context, and ability? First of all, none of the formal assessments discussed here were designed to assess literacy practices. Second, some of the commonly used adult literacy assessment instruments use content from multiple adult contexts, although none, of course, are able to provide information about all contexts. Third, the most commonly used standardized tests in adult education each measure just one or two components of the reading process and only a few of many aspects of the writing process.

The NRS requires just one assessment of any one aspect of basic literacy ability in virtually any context, however, so any of the commonly used tests could be used for federal accountability purposes. Adult literacy programs are not required by the NRS to measure literacy practices, but those focusing on family literacy are encouraged to measure literacy practices related to parents' interaction with their children. For this reason, instruments or procedures for measuring practices that have been validated through research or extensive use are needed. Literacy practices have been investigated throughout the history of adult basic education (Kaestle et al., 1991), and some of this research may serve as a starting point (for example, Purcell-Gates, Degener, Jacobson, & Soler, 2000; Mikulecky & Lloyd, 1997; Sticht, 1995).

Literacy assessment should not be used solely to satisfy requirements for accountability but should be fully integrated into instruction (Askov et al., 1997; Askov, 2000; Joint Task Force on Assessment, 1994; Joint Committee on Standards, 1999). How well do the most common adult literacy assessments support instructional models? For those programs that construct profiles of student strengths and weaknesses to provide guidance in the selection of instructional methods and materials (Chall, 1994; Chall & Curtis, 1992; Curtis, 1999), even a combination of the tests commonly used in adult literacy is insufficient (Strucker, 1997b; Chall, 1994; Snow & Strucker, 2000). Reading specialists have used combinations of other standardized norm-referenced and criterion-referenced tests to construct complete profiles (Chall, 1994; Chall & Curtis, 1992; Strucker, 1997b; Curtis, 1999). Using the ABLE, GORT, and WRAT together during assessment, for example, would provide information about all aspects of the reading process except word analysis. There are also single, standardized assessments that provide measures of many aspects of reading and writing (for example, the Woodcock and DAR).

Even for adult literacy programs that focus most of their energies on only one aspect of reading, such as reading comprehension, a single norm-referenced or criterion-referenced test may not be adequate. For some, the use of multiple-choice or short-answer formats, as opposed to extended, constructed responses (Martinez, 1999), is seen as a real limitation (Merrifield, 1998; Garcia & Pearson, 1991). These formats do not directly measure some comprehension abilities, such as comprehension monitoring and strategy use. Performance assessments are capable of directly measuring a wider range of comprehension abilities because they do not rely on short-answer formats (Martinez, 1999). These have probably been used by some of the 31 percent of programs that construct their own assessments (Kutner et al., 1996), although no research on the types of performance assessments actually used in adult literacy programs is available.

Related to the use of assessment for instruction is the issue of the use of standardized scores from norm-referenced tests to gauge learner strengths and weaknesses in literacy (for example, Chall & Curtis, 1992; Strucker, 1997b). The NRS uses scale scores and grade equivalent scores (GEs) from common adult literacy tests to help describe levels in the development of adults' literacy abilities (DAEL, 2000, p. 14). Norm-referenced scores are used primarily to compare the performance of a learner with that of a norm group. Using them to describe literacy development requires extensive experience in teaching and assessing literacy ability. An experienced diagnostician can presumably interpret a GE on a test, for example, because the diagnostician is familiar with the test, what it measures, and the psychometric use of GEs and also knows that even though different tests may use these same terms, GEs and scale scores may be derived from raw scores in different ways. Many recommend that GEs and scale scores be interpreted cautiously by those without this knowledge. The meaning of scale scores is not intuitive, and GEs may be overinterpreted because everyone is familiar with the concept of grade levels.

The use of standardized norm- and criterion-referenced scores for virtually any purpose has been questioned, usually in comparison with performance assessments. Questions about these tests come from within the field of adult literacy (for example, Beder, 1999; Merrifield, 1998; Padak & Padak, 1994) and among educators generally (for example, Pelligrino, Baxter, & Glaser, 1999). Common complaints include the following: standardized tests do not measure what has been learned, they focus on isolated skills, and they often fail to measure more complex reasoning and problem-solving abilities. Performance assessments can potentially do all of this because they are extremely flexible and can be designed by a particular program's practitioners to fit specific program needs.

As Merrifield (1998) states, the dilemma is that standardized tests do not adequately measure what is learned, while performance assessments, because of their ad hoc, informal nature, are not reliable enough for the comparisons across individuals and programs that policymakers require. As noted, however, some performance assessments, such as writing assessments, are becoming more standardized while some standardized assessments are becoming more flexible. The development of performance assessments seems to be a continuation of a series of innovations in assessment, such as those that brought criterion-referenced testing in the 1960s, that will add to the tools that can be used rather than supplant all others. Data derived from the NRS, which encourages the use of both performance and norm- and criterion-referenced tests, may help spur the development of reliable performance assessments and help to determine whether or not they will provide information that is sufficiently valid for policymakers' decisions.

Another, more intransigent dilemma in ABE is related to the issue of teacher training. Lack of resources, reliance on part-time staff, and the extensive use of volunteers means that adult literacy teachers on average have less experience and training than teachers at the K–12 level. Greater accountability, however, through the use of formal assessments, means that adult literacy teachers will be expected to do more (Merrifield, 1998; Beder, 1999). The use of assessment for accountability and instruction requires a greater degree of sophistication in the teaching of reading than recent evaluations of adult literacy programs suggest current staff have (Kutner et al., 1996; Calfee & Hiebert, 1991).

Although this dilemma is not one that will be easy to remedy, focusing on assessment during the training of adult literacy staff may actually have direct beneficial effects. If an adult literacy assessment instrument or system truly represents the domain of behaviors to be addressed during instruction, learning about the assessment will provide teachers with knowledge about adult literacy. Learning about a word analysis or reading comprehension assessment, for example, should provide information about what is expected of adults in these two domains. For instructional models that rely on assessment, assessment is a natural place to begin focusing training. Adult literacy instructors, and volunteers in particular, need to know about what reading is and how it develops (Wasik, 1998). This knowledge may be presented naturally as practitioners learn about and practice effective assessment procedures.

Practice

In the current environment, with its increased demands for accountability and the new National Reporting System, adult literacy programs cannot avoid formal assessment, as some in the past have managed to do. Assuming also that assessment should be integrated with instruction, the model described by Askov (Askov et al., 1997) and many others should be used: assess student needs, provide instruction based on assessment results, and assess students periodically to adjust instruction and determine whether or not instruction is leading to gains in literacy ability. For those programs that focus on providing direct, explicit instruction in all aspects or components of the reading process (for example, Chall, 1994; Curtis & Longo, 1997), assessment should include profiling adults' strengths and needs across components, and the assessment instruments chosen should be capable of doing this. Other models are possible, of course. For those programs that focus on one particular aspect of reading, or that view reading as a unitary process, for example, the instrument chosen may assess only this one aspect of reading, such as reading comprehension. Other programs may focus narrowly on one literacy context, such as health, the family, or the workplace, and assessments in these programs may rely more on instruments that have appropriate content.

Training in assessment is key at this point for adult literacy practitioners in local programs. As Calfee and others have noted (Calfee & Hiebert, 1991), teachers must have extensive knowledge of and practice with assessment to integrate teacher-based assessment effectively and reliably. How training is delivered as well as the content of any training are both important considerations. Training methods need to take into account the high turnover among adult literacy staff, many of whom are part-time or volunteer tutors. One-shot training workshops, for example, will not be effective. Ongoing and on-demand training programs that can be offered as new staff enter would seem to be a more appropriate model. Training program content will need to include instruction in administering assessments and interpreting their results, and it will need to be presented in a way that is understandable to those with the least amount of experience in a program, including volunteers.

Reliable and valid measures should be used by practitioners. This is an NRS requirement for accountability, but it is also important for instruction. Reliable measures provide better support for instruction. Guidelines provided by professional organizations for the selection and use of assessments should be used (such as Joint Committee on Standards, 1999; Joint Task Force on Assessment, 1994). The NRS requires states to audit local program assessment procedures to help insure reliability. Local programs should also attempt to assess or monitor instructors' assessment and instruction abilities. Assessing teacher knowledge should be just as important as assessing student knowledge.

Research

Research that evaluates whether and how various approaches to assessment in ABE lead to gains in literacy ability is needed. While the recommendation that assessment be used to guide instruction and to evaluate program effectiveness seems to be sound policy (for example, DAEL, 2000; Joint Committee on Standards, 1999; Joint Task Force on Assessment, 1994), research that links assessment to ABE students' gains in literacy ability is missing. Closely related to this is research that will support the training of ABE staff in the best approaches to assessment. This includes research on effective training methods and research on the abilities and needs of adult literacy staff. What do they know about what literacy is and how it develops? How reliably do they use assessment instruments?

Research is also needed on the most neglected aspects of adult literacy assessment. Formal measures for motivation and for specific literacy practices need to be developed. More formal measures and procedures for performance assessment are needed, as is research that will establish and measure their reliability. This could include broader, comparative research that looks at validity across various types of adult literacy assessment instruments.

More research is needed on the effects of context on literacy ability. Does the content or context of a literacy program—the degree to which it is functional, for example—affect gain in literacy ability (for example, Sticht & McDonald, 1992)? Do profiles change as content reflecting different contexts changes?

Finally, more research is needed on the best ways to measure various aspects of reading and writing processes to obtain useful profiles of adult literacy learners' strengths and needs. Research is being conducted by NCSALL, for example, that is identifying specific types of learner profiles (Strucker, 1997b; Snow & Strucker, 2000). How to best integrate profiles that result from the assessment of specific abilities into instruction is another area in which research is needed.

Policy

Policymakers need to provide adequate resources for the research described here as well as for the development, purchase, and use of assessments, including training. Although adult education has been, essentially, level-funded (or worse) since its inception in the 1960s

(Sticht, 1998), demands for program accountability have steadily increased.

Ways in which to evaluate the reliability of data being collected for the NRS should be specified. The NRS currently relies on states to collect reliability information through program audits. At a minimum, common guidelines or standards for auditing programs should be provided. Assessment data from the NRS will be used to measure the effectiveness of ABE programs. Because states and individual programs may use different criteria to determine adults' beginning and ending literacy levels, results will be open to the criticism that they are not reliable. A truly reliable assessment of effectiveness can come only from the consistent administration of a common assessment. This might be accomplished best through stratified random sampling of a large number of adults by a third party.

With this in mind, it is important to anticipate and guard against the NRS becoming exclusively a high-stakes system. High-stakes assessment for an instructional program occurs when the results of a single test are used as a basis for delivering consequences, such as funding incentives, or when test results are released publicly so that comparisons can be made across programs (Joint Task Force on Assessment, 1994; International Reading Association, 1999). Although the NRS does not rely on a single measure or test to evaluate program performance, it does provide states with performance incentives, requires them to publish assessment results, and requires them to evaluate and provide incentives for local programs (DAEL, 2000; PL-105–220, Workforce Investment Act, Title II, Chapter 1, Section 212).

Though the NRS collects data from many measures as opposed to just one, the way in which the system is structured will probably lead at least some states to use a single measure to evaluate many local programs, unless specific evaluation guidelines are provided that encourage the use of multiple measures. The central measure in the NRS system is gain in literacy ability, and this measure may be obtained by administering a standardized test at the beginning and end of an instructional cycle. Although this is not the only way in which gain may be measured, many states will select it because it is efficient and cost-effective.

Potential problems associated with high-stakes testing include, among others, a narrowing of the curriculum through teaching to the test and focusing attention on those students most likely to show gain on the test being used. To take an extreme example of curriculum narrowing, if the WRAT, a simple measure of word recognition, were the test selected to measure gain, teachers might be tempted to focus on word recognition and neglect other aspects of the reading process during instruction. High-stakes testing can also tempt a program to focus on a specific subset of students most likely to succeed—a practice called *creaming*—which has occurred in at least one federal program using performance standards (Condelli & Kutner, 1997). This is a potential problem for ABE programs, where so many students may have a reading disability (Snow & Strucker, 2000), and where programs may not assess extremely poor readers until they are "ready" (that is, they read at a higher level) (Kutner et al., 1996). Although Condelli and Kutner mention several ways to minimize the negative effects of high-stakes testing, such as setting reasonable, obtainable objectives, matching performance measures with program goals, and training and monitoring staff, the most effective approach is probably to require that funding decisions be based on evaluations that use multiple measures.

There is an inherent tension between high-stakes testing and established procedures for assessment within a program. High-stakes tests may be viewed as time-consuming add-ons or as replacements for existing assessment procedures. When a program lacks clear goals and adequate assessment practices, however, even strong opponents of externally mandated testing state that it may "fill a vacuum" and serve as a catalyst for needed change (Calfee & Hiebert, 1991). As the evaluations of adult literacy programs discussed in this chapter indicate, this seems to be the case for many adult literacy programs. Assuming that the training provided for states through the AEFLA is adequate, and that the states in turn provide adequate training for local programs, a high-stakes assessment implemented through the NRS may in some cases be beneficial. Whatever the outcomes, effective research is needed to describe and understand them. Discussion of any lessons learned should be based on a solid foundation that includes reliable research data.

Note

1. There are two editions of the TABE, the *TABE Forms 5 & 6*, published in 1987, and the *TABE Forms 7 & 8*, published in 1994. To distinguish between the two, the most recent TABE will be referred to simply as "the TABE" and the earlier edition will be referred to as "the 1987

TABE." The major difference between them is that the 1987 TABE provides separate reading comprehension and vocabulary scores while the most recent TABE provides only a reading comprehension score (vocabulary is measured as a part of reading comprehension).

References

Adams, M. J. (1990). *Beginning to read: Thinking and learning about print.* Cambridge, MA: MIT Press.

Adams, M. J. (1998). *Phonemic awareness in young children.* Baltimore: Brookes Publishing.

Alvermann, D., Young, J., Green, C., & Wisenbaker, J. (1999). Adolescents' perceptions and negotiations of literacy practices in after-school read and talk clubs. *American Educational Research Journal, 36*(2), 221–264.

American Council on Education. (1993). *The Tests of General Educational Development: Technical manual.* Washington, DC: American Council on Education.

Anderson, R. C. (1984). Role of the reader's schema in comprehension, learning, and memory. In H. Singer & R. B. Ruddell (Eds.), *Theoretical models and processes of reading* (3rd ed., pp. 372–384). Newark, DE: International Reading Association.

Askov, E. N. (2000). Adult literacy. In A. L. Wilson & E. R. Hayes (Eds.), *Handbook of adult and continuing education* (pp. 247–262). San Francisco: Jossey-Bass.

Askov, E., Van Horn, B., & Carman, P. (1997). Assessment in adult basic education programs. In A. Rose & M. Leahy (Eds.), *Assessing adult learning in diverse settings: Current issues and approaches* (Fall, pp. 65–74). San Francisco: Jossey-Bass.

Au, K. H. (1997). Ownership, literacy achievement, and students of diverse cultural backgrounds. In J. T. Guthrie & A. Wigfield (Eds.), *Reading engagement: Motivating readers through integrated instruction* (pp. 168–182). Newark, DE: International Reading Association.

Baker, L., Dreher, M. J., & Guthrie, J. T. (Eds.). (2000). *Engaging young readers: Promoting achievement and motivation.* New York: Guilford Press.

Beder, H. (1990). Motivational profiles of adult basic education students. *Adult Education Quarterly, 40*(2), 78–94.

Beder, H. (1999). *The outcomes and impacts of adult literacy education in the United States* (NCSALL Reports #6). Cambridge, MA: The National Center for the Study of Adult Learning and Literacy.

Bereiter, C. (1980). A framework for a cognitive theory of writing. In L. Gregg & E. R. Steinberg (Eds.), *Cognitive processes in writing* (pp. 73–93). Hillsdale, NJ: Erlbaum.

Brookfield, S. (1997, Fall). Assessing critical thinking. In A. Rose & M. Leahy (Eds.), *Assessing adult learning in diverse settings: Current issues and approaches* (pp. 17–30). San Francisco: Jossey-Bass.

Calfee, R., & Hiebert, E. (1991). Classroom assessment of reading. In R. Barr, M. L. Kamil, P. B. Mosenthal, & P. D. Pearson (Eds.), *Handbook of reading research* (Vol. 2, pp. 281–309). New York: Longman.

Carr, T. H., & Levy, B. A. (1990). *Reading and its development: Component skills approaches.* San Diego: Academic Press.

CASAS. (1989). *CASAS: Comprehensive Adult Student Assessment System.* San Diego: Author.

Chall, J. S. (1994). Patterns of adult reading. *Learning Disabilities, 5*(1), 29–33.

Chall, J. S. (1996). *Stages of reading development.* New York: Harcourt.

Chall, J. S., & Curtis, M. E. (1987). What clinical diagnosis tells us about children's reading. *Reading Teacher, 40,* 784–788.

Chall, J. S., & Curtis, M. E. (1990). Diagnostic achievement testing in reading. In C. Reynolds & R. Kamphaus (Eds.), *Handbook of psychological and educational assessment of children.* New York: Guilford Press.

Chall, J. S., & Curtis, M. E. (1992). Teaching the disabled or below-average reader. In S. J. Samuels & A. E. Farstrup (Eds.), *What research has to say about reading instruction* (pp. 253–276). Newark, DE: International Reading Association.

Collins, A., & Gentner, D. (1980). A framework for a cognitive theory of writing. In L. Gregg & E. R. Steinberg (Eds.), *Cognitive processes in writing* (pp. 51–72). Hillsdale, NJ: Erlbaum.

Colvin, R., & Root, J. (1982). *READ—Reading Evaluation Adult Diagnosis: A test for assessing adult student reading needs and progress* (Rev. ed.). Syracuse, NY: Literacy Volunteers of America.

Comings, J. P., Parrella, A., & Soricone, L. (1999). Persistence among adult basic education students in pre-GED classes (NCSALL Reports #12). Cambridge, MA: National Center for the Study of Adult Learning and Literacy, Harvard Graduate School of Education.

Condelli, L. (1996). *Evaluation systems in the adult education program: The role of quality indicators.* Washington, DC: Pelavin Research Institute.

Condelli, L., & Kutner, M. (1997). *Developing a national outcome reporting system for the adult education program.* Washington, DC: Pelavin Research Institute.

Condelli, L., Padilla, V., & Angeles, J. (1999). *Report on the pilot test for the National Reporting System.* Washington, DC: Office of Vocational and Adult Education, Division of Adult Education and Literacy.

Cramer, E. H., & Castle, M. (1994). *Fostering the love of reading: The affective domain in reading education.* Newark, DE: International Reading Association.

CTB/McGraw-Hill. (1987). *TABE Forms 5 & 6: Tests of Adult Basic Education.* Monterey, CA: Author.

CTB/McGraw-Hill. (1994a). *TABE Forms 7 & 8: Tests of Adult Basic Education.* Monterey, CA: Author.

CTB/McGraw-Hill. (1994b). *TABE Work-Related Foundation Skills.* Monterey, CA: Author.

Curtis, M. E. (1980). Development of components of reading skill. *Journal of Educational Psychology, 72*(5), 656–669.

Curtis, M. E. (1990). *Developing literacy in children and adults: Are there differences?* Paper presented at the Annual Meeting of the International Reading Association, Atlanta, GA.

Curtis, M. E. (1999). *When adolescents can't read: Methods and materials that work.* Cambridge, MA: Brookline Books.

Curtis, M. E., & Chmelka, M. B. (1994). Modifying the "Laubach Way to Reading" program for use with adolescents with learning disabilities. *Learning Disabilities Research and Practice, 9*(1), 38–43.

Curtis, M. E., & Longo, A. M. (1997). Reversing reading failure in young adults. *Focus On Basics, 1*(B), 18–22.

Davis, T. C., Crouch, M. A., & Long, S. (1992). *REALM: Rapid Estimate of Adult Literacy in Medicine.* Shreveport, LA: School of Medicine, Louisiana State University.

Diehl, W., & Mikulecky, L. (1980). The nature of reading at work. *Journal of Reading, 24,* 221–228.

Division of Adult Education and Literacy (DAEL). (2000). *Measures and methods for the National Reporting System for adult education: Implementation guidelines.* Washington, DC: Office of Vocational and Adult Education, U.S. Department of Education.

Dochy, F., Segers, M., & Buehl, M. M. (1999). The relation between assessment practices and outcomes of studies: The case of research on prior knowledge. *Review of Educational Research, 69*(2), 145–186.

Dunn, L. M., & Dunn, L. M. (1997). *Peabody Picture Vocabulary Test—Third Edition (PPVT-III).* Circle Pines, MN: American Guidance Service.

Educational Testing Service. (1991). *Tests of Applied Literacy Skills.* New York: Simon & Schuster.

Ehringhaus, C. (1990). Functional literacy assessment: Issues of interpretation. *Adult Education Quarterly, 40*(4), 187–196.

Ehringhaus, C. (1991). Teachers' perceptions of testing in adult basic education. *Adult Basic Education, 1*(3), 138–154.

Fehring, H., & Green, P. (2001). Critical literacy: A collection of articles from the Australian Literacy Educators' Association. Newark, DE: International Reading Association.

Fingeret, H. A. (1993). *It belongs to me: A guide to portfolio assessment in adult education programs.* Durham, NC: Literacy South.

Flower, L., & Hayes, J. (1981, December). A cognitive process theory of writing. *College Composition and Communication,* pp. 365–387.

Freire, P., & Macedo, D. (1987). *Literacy: Reading the word and the world.* South Hadley, MA: Bergin & Garvey.

Garcia, G. E., & Pearson, P. D. (1991). The role of assessment in a diverse society. In E. H. Hiebert (Ed.), *Literacy for a diverse society: Perspectives, practices, and policies* (pp. 253–278). New York: Teachers College Press.

Garner, B. (1999). Nationwide accountability: The National Reporting System. *Focus on Basics, 3*(B).

GED Testing Service. (1997). *Tests of General Educational Development: Official practice tests.* Washington, DC: American Council on Education.

General Accounting Office. (1975). *The adult basic education program: Progress in reducing illiteracy and improvements needed.* Washington, DC: U.S. Office of Education.

General Accounting Office. (1995). *Adult education: Measuring program results has been challenging* (GAO/HEHS-95–153). Washington, DC: U.S. General Accounting Office.

Goodman, Y. M. (1999). Revaluing readers while readers revalue themselves: Retrospective miscue analysis. In S. Barrentine (Ed.), *Reading assessment: Principles and practices for elementary teachers* (pp. 140–151). Newark, DE: International Reading Association.

Goodman, Y. M., & Burke, C. L. (1972). *Reading Miscue Inventory: Manual and procedures for diagnosis and evaluation.* New York: Macmillan.

Goodman, Y. M., Watson, D., & Burke, C. L. (1987). *Reading Miscue Inventory: Alternative procedures.* Katonah, NY: Owen.

Gregg, L. W., & Steinberg, E. R. (Eds.). (1980). *Cognitive processes in writing.* Hillsdale, NJ: Erlbaum.

Guthrie, J. T., & Greaney, V. (1991). *Literacy acts.* In R. Barr, M. L. Kamil, P. B. Mosenthal, & P. D. Pearson (Eds.), *Handbook of reading research* (Vol. 2, pp. 68–96). New York: Longman.

Guthrie, J. T., & Wigfield, A. (Eds.). (1997). *Reading engagement: Motivating readers through integrated instruction.* Newark, DE: International Reading Association.

Hammill, D., & Larsen, S. (1996). *TOWL: Tests of Written Language* (3rd ed.). Austin, TX: PRO-ED.

Harris, T., & Hodges, R. (1995). *The literacy dictionary.* Newark, DE: International Reading Association.

Hayes, J. R. (1996). A new framework for understanding cognition and affect in writing. In C. M. Levy & S. Ransdell (Eds.), *The science of writing: Theories, methods, individual differences, and applications* (pp. 1–27). Mahwah, NJ: Erlbaum.

Hiebert, E. H. (1991). *Literacy for a diverse society.* New York: Teachers College Press.

International Reading Association. (1999). High-stakes assessments in reading: A position statement of the International Reading Association. *Journal of Adolescent and Adult Literacy, 43*(3), 305–312.

Joint Committee on Standards for Educational and Psychological Testing of the American Educational Research Association and American Psychological Association and National Council on Measurement in Education. (1999). *Standards for educational and psychological testing.* Washington, DC: American Educational Research Association.

Joint Task Force on Assessment. (1994). *Standards for the assessment of reading and writing.* Newark, DE: International Reading Association and National Council of Teachers of English.

Kaestle, C. F., Damon-Moore, H., Stedman, L. C., Tinsley, K., & Trollinger, W. V., Jr. (1991). *Literacy in the United States: Readers and reading since 1880.* New Haven, CT: Yale University Press.

Karlsen, B., & Gardner, E. (1986). *ABLE: Adult Basic Learning Examination.* New York: The Psychological Corporation, Harcourt.

Kasworm, C., & Marienau, C. (1997, Fall). Principles for assessment of adult learning. In A. Rose & M. Leahy (Eds.), *Assessing adult learning in diverse settings: Current issues and approaches* (pp. 5–16). San Francisco: Jossey-Bass.

Kintsch, W. (1994). The role of knowledge in discourse comprehension: A construction-integration model. In R. B. Ruddell, M. R. Ruddell, & H. Singer (Eds.), *Theoretical models and processes of reading* (4th ed.). Newark, DE: International Reading Association. (Original work published in 1988)

Kirsch, I., & Jungeblut, A. (1986). *Literacy: Profiles of America's young adults* (Report No. 16-PL-02). Princeton, NJ: National Assessment of Educational Progress, Educational Testing Service.

Kirsch, I. S., Jungeblut, A., Jenkins, L., & Kolstad, A. (1993). *Adult literacy in America: A first look at the findings of the National Adult Literacy Survey.* Washington, DC: National Center for Education Statistics, U.S. Department of Education.

Kruidenier, J. R. (1990). Objectives and content of a course for professional and volunteer teachers of adults. Paper presented at the Annual Conference of the International Reading Association, Atlanta, GA.

Kruidenier, J. R. (1991). Planning and production processes in the written language of skilled and less-skilled writers. Unpublished doctoral dissertation, Harvard University, Cambridge, MA.

Kruidenier, J. R. (1993). Sentence planning processes in a writing-after-reading task. Paper presented at the American Education Research Association Annual Meeting, Atlanta, GA.

Kutner, M., Webb, L., & Matheson, N. (1996). *A review of statewide learner competency and assessment systems.* Washington, DC: Pelavin Research Institute.

Leipzig, D. H., & Afflerbach, P. (2000). Determining the suitability of assessments: Using the CURRV framework. In L. Baker, M. J. Dreher, & J. T. Guthrie (Eds.), *Engaging young readers: Promoting achievement and motivation.* New York: Guilford Press.

Lesgold, A. M., Roth, S. F., & Curtis, M. E. (1979). Foregrounding effects in discourse comprehension. *Journal of Verbal Learning & Verbal Behavior, 18*(3), 291–308.

Levy, M. C., & Ransdell, S. (Eds.). (1997). *The science of writing: Theories, methods, individual differences, and applications.* Hillsdale, NJ: Erlbaum.

Linn, R. L. (2000). Assessments and accountability. *Educational Researcher, 29*(2), 4–16.

Martinez, M. E. (1999). Cognition and the question of test item format. *Educational Psychologist, 34*(4), 207–218.

Merrifield, J. (1998). *Contested ground: Performance and accountability in adult basic education* (NCSALL Reports 1). Cambridge, MA: National Center for the Study of Adult Learning and Literacy.

Mikulecky, L., & Drew, R. (1991). Basic literacy skills in the workplace. In R. Barr, M. L. Kamil, P. B. Mosenthal, & P. D. Pearson (Eds.), *Handbook of reading research* (Vol. 2). New York: Longman.

Mikulecky, L., & Lloyd, P. (1997). Evaluation of workplace literacy programs: A profile of effective instructional practices. *Journal of Literacy Research, 29*(29), 555–585.

Murphy, P., Davis, T. C., Long, S. W., Jackson, R. H., & Decker, B. C. (1994). Rapid Estimate of Adult Literacy in Medicine (REALM): A quick reading test for patients. In M. C. Radencich (Ed.), *Adult literacy: A compendium of articles from the Journal of Reading* (pp. 79–86). Newark, DE: International Reading Association.

National Center for Family Literacy. (1996). *Outcomes and measures in family literacy programs.* Louisville, KY: Author.

National Reading Panel. (2000). *Teaching children to read: An evidence-based assessment of the scientific research literature on reading and its implications for reading instruction.* Washington, DC: National Institute of Child Health and Human Development.

Nitko, A. J. (1983). *Educational tests and measurement: An introduction.* New York: Harcourt.

Nitko, A. J. (1996). *Educational assessment of students.* Upper Saddle River, NJ: Prentice Hall.

Nurss, J., Parker, R., Williams, M., & Baker, D. (1995). *TOFHLA: Test of Functional Health Literacy.* Atlanta: Emory University.

Padak, N. D., Davidson, J. L., & Padak, G. M. (1994). Exploring reading with adult beginning readers. In M. C. Radencich (Ed.), *Adult literacy: A compendium of articles from the Journal of Reading* (pp. 56–60). Newark, DE: International Reading Association.

Padak, N. D., & Padak, G. M. (1994). What works: Adult literacy program evaluation. In M. C. Radencich (Ed.), *Adult literacy: A compendium of articles from the Journal of Reading* (pp. 86–93). Newark, DE: International Reading Association.

Paris, S. G. (1999). Portfolio assessment for young readers. In S. Barrentine (Ed.), *Reading assessment: Principles and practices for elementary teachers* (pp. 131–134). Newark, DE: International Reading Association.

Paris, S. G., Calfee, R. C., Filby, N., Hiebert, E. H., Pearson, P. D., Valencia, S. W., & Wolf, K. P. (1999). A framework for authentic literacy assessment. In S. Barrentine (Ed.), *Reading assessment: Prin-*

ciples and practices for elementary teachers (pp. 30–43). Newark, DE: International Reading Association.

Pelligrino, J., Baxter, G. P., & Glaser, R. (1999). Addressing the "Two Disciplines" problem: Linking theories of cognition and learning with assessment and instructional practice. In A. Iran-Nejad & P. D. Pearson (Eds.), *Review of research in education* (Vol. 24, pp. 307–354). Washington, DC: American Educational Research Association.

Perfetti, C. A. (1985). *Reading ability.* New York: Oxford University Press.

Perfetti, C., & Curtis, M. E. (1987). Reading. In R. F. Dillon & R. J. Sternberg (Eds.), *Cognition and instruction* (pp. 13–57). New York: Academic Press.

Pressley, M. (1998). *Reading instruction that works: The case for balanced teaching.* New York: Guilford Press.

Purcell-Gates, V., Degener, S., Jacobson, E., & Soler, M. (2000). Affecting change in literacy practices of adult learners: Impact of two dimensions of instruction (Report #17). Cambridge, MA: The National Center for the Study of Adult Learning and Literacy, Harvard Graduate School of Education.

Reder, S. (1994). Practice engagement theory: A sociocultural approach to literacy across languages and cultures. In B. M. Ferdman, R. M. Weber, & A. G. Ramírez (Eds.), *Literacy across languages and cultures.* Albany, NY: State University of New York Press.

Resnick, D. P., & Resnick, L. B. (1977). The nature of literacy: An historical explanation. *Harvard Educational Review, 47*(3).

Rosner, J. (1979). TAAS: Test of Auditory Analysis Skills. In J. Rosner, *Helping children overcome learning disabilities.* Novato, CA: Academic Therapy Publications.

Roswell, F., & Chall, J. S. (1992). *DARTTS: Diagnostic Assessments of Reading and Trial Teaching Strategies.* Chicago: Riverside.

Roswell, F. G., & Chall, J. S. (1994). *Creating successful readers: A practical guide to testing and teaching at all age levels.* Chicago: Riverside.

Roswell, F., & Natchez, G. (1979). *Reading disability: A human approach to evaluation and treatment of reading and writing difficulties* (4th ed.). New York: Basic Books.

Secretary's Commission on Achieving Necessary Skills (SCANS). (1991). *What work requires of schools: A SCANS report for America 2000.* Washington, DC: U.S. Department of Labor.

Sheehan-Holt, J. K., & Smith, M. C. (2000). Does basic skills education affect adults' literacy proficiencies and reading practices? *Reading Research Quarterly, 35*(2), 226–243.

Slosson, R. L., & Nicholson, C. L. (1990). *Slosson Oral Reading Test, Revised.* East Aurora, NY: Slosson Educational Publications.

Smith, M. C. (1990). The development and use of an instrument for assessing adults' attitudes toward reading. *Journal of Research and Development in Education, 23*(3), 156–161.

Smith, M. C. (1995). Differences in adults' reading practices and literacy proficiencies. *Reading Research Quarterly, 31*(2), 196–219.

Smith, M. C. (2000). The real-world reading practices of adults. *Journal of Literacy Research, 32*(1), 25–52.

Snow, C., Burns, S. M., & Griffin, P. (1998). *Preventing reading difficulties in young children: A report of the National Research Panel.* Washington, DC: National Academy Press.

Snow, C. E., & Strucker, J. (2000). Lessons from *Preventing reading difficulties in young children for adult learning and literacy.* In J. Comings, B. Garner, & C. Smith (Eds.), *Annual review of adult learning and literacy: A project of the National Center for the Study of Adult Learning and Literacy* (Vol. 1, pp. 25–73). San Francisco: Jossey-Bass.

Stahl, S. (1999). Why innovations come and go (and mostly go): The case of whole language. *Educational Researcher, 28*(8), 13–22.

Steck-Vaughn Company. (1997). *AMES: Adult Measure of Essential Skills.* Austin, TX: Author.

Stein, S. G. (1997). *Equipped for the future: A reform agenda for adult literacy and lifelong learning.* Washington, DC: National Institute for Literacy.

Sticht, T. (1972). Determination of adult functional literacy skill levels. *Reading Research Quarterly, 7*(3), 424–465.

Sticht, T. (1990). *Testing and assessment in adult basic education and English as a second language programs.* San Diego: Applied Behavioral & Cognitive Sciences.

Sticht, T. (1995). *The military experience and workplace literacy: A review and synthesis for policy and practice.* Philadelphia: National Center on Adult Literacy.

Sticht, T. (1998). *Beyond 2000: Future directions for adult education.* Washington, DC: Office of Vocational and Adult Education.

Sticht, T. G., Hofstetter, C. R., & Hofstetter, C. H. (1996). Assessing adult literacy by telephone. *Journal of Literacy Research, 28*(4), 525–559.

Sticht, T. G., & McDonald, B. A. (1992). Teaching adults to read. In S. J. Samuels & A. E. Farstrup (Eds.), *What research has to say about reading instruction* (pp. 314–334). Newark, DE: International Reading Association.

Strucker, J. (1992). Patterns of reading in Adult Basic Education. Unpublished doctoral dissertation, Harvard University Graduate School of Education, Cambridge, MA.

Strucker, J. (1997a). *The reading components approach.* Cambridge, MA: National Center for the Study of Adult Literacy and Learning, Harvard University Graduate School of Education.

Strucker, J. (1997b). What silent reading tests alone can't tell you: Two case studies in adult reading differences. *Focus on Basics, 40*(B), 13–17.

Torgesen, J., Wagner, R., & Rashotte, C. (1999). *Test of Word Reading Efficiency.* Austin, TX: PRO-ED.

Torrance, M., & Jeffery, G. C. (Eds.). (1999). *The cognitive demands of writing: Processing capacity and working memory in text production.* Amsterdam: Amsterdam University Press.

van Dijk, T., & Kintsch, W. (1983). *Strategies of discourse comprehension.* New York: Academic Press.

Venezky, R. L. (1991). The development of literacy in the industrialized nations of the West. In R. Barr, M. L. Kamil, P. B. Mosenthal, & P. D. Pearson (Eds.), *Handbook of reading research* (Vol. 2, pp. 46–67). New York: Longman.

Wagner, R., Torgesen, J., & Rashotte, C. (1999). *Comprehensive Test of Phonological Awareness.* Austin, TX: PRO-ED.

Warden, M. R., & Hutchinson, T. A. (1992). *Writing Process Test.* Chicago: Riverside.

Wasik, B. (1998). Volunteer tutoring programs in reading. *Reading Research Quarterly, 33*(3).

Weiderholt, J. L., & Bryant, B. R. (1992). *GORT-3: Gray Oral Reading Test: Third Edition.* Austin, TX: PRO-ED.

Wilkinson, G. S. (1993). *WRAT3: The Wide Range Achievement Test, 1993 Edition.* Wilmington, DE: Wide Range.

Woodcock, R. W. (1997). *Woodcock-Johnson Diagnostic Reading Battery.* Itasca, IL: Riverside.

Woodcock, R. W., & Johnson, M. B. (1989). *Woodcock Johnson Tests of Achievement.* Itasca, IL: Riverside.

Wrigley, H. S. (1998). Knowledge in action: The promise of project-based learning. *Focus on Basics, 2*(D), 13–18.

Young, M. B., Fitzgerald, N., & Fleischman, H. (1994). *National evaluation of adult education programs: Draft final report.* Arlington, VA: Development Associates.

CHAPTER FIVE

The Inclusion of Numeracy in Adult Basic Education

Dave Tout
Mary Jane Schmitt

N umeracy is an essential skill. In the United States, it may be the cognitive skill that most highly correlates with economic success (Murnane, Willet, & Levy, 1995). It is thus troubling that some segments of the population have been found to be much less numerate than others, limiting their potential to fully participate in and benefit from what society has to offer. The U.S. adult basic education (ABE) system has yet to sufficiently address the gap between those who are less numerate and those who are more numerate. Research on numeracy is minimal. Instructional practice is often constrained by commercial publications and standardized tests and often operates from an outdated notion of what constitutes "basic math." Policy has yet to recognize numeracy as an essential part of being "literate" enough to negotiate the demands of the contemporary workplace and modern life.

Even so, this is also a particularly active, promising time in the developmental trajectory of adult numeracy education. In 2000, two compendia concerned with how adults use and learn mathematics were published. Numeracy is treated as a distinct domain in the international Adult Literacy and Lifeskills (ALL) assessment survey to be conducted in 2002; the National Science Foundation (NSF) has for the first time funded a major mathematics curriculum project for adults enrolled in adult basic and adult secondary education programs; and in July 2000 a conference was held that brought together researchers and practitioners from twelve countries to discuss a wide range of emergent issues in the field of adult numeracy. The time thus seems ripe to examine just how far the field of adult numeracy has come, how far it yet needs to go, and where it might look for models of progress and accomplishment.

NUMERACY VERSUS MATH

Before we can consider research, examine practice, or describe and evaluate policy, we must define and understand the object of research, instruction, and policy. We are only beginning to develop an understanding and consensus around the meaning of the term *numeracy.*

Whether it is to interpret information in a political television ad, make a deal when buying a car, or follow the instructions in a diagram at work, most people today need a range of mathematical skills to negotiate the demands of our information-intensive culture. That set of necessary skills involves much more than being able to add, subtract, multiply, and divide with numbers. It includes the ability to manage and solve problems using measurements, space, data, and numbers in a variety of formats and for a variety of purposes. What do we call this type of skill, in which mathematics is applied to real life? Is it numeracy? Or is it mathematics? Today there exists neither a universally accepted definition of numeracy nor an agreement about its relationship to mathematics. In fact, in the United States, the term has only recently been added to the vernacular (Gal & Schmitt, 1994; Curry, Schmitt, & Waldron, 1996).

Numeracy has often been cast as the pretender, the junior, inferior partner to mathematics, because it is considered to deal only with numbers and the four basic arithmetic operations of addition, subtraction, multiplication, and division. It conjures the image of doing computation with pencil and paper. Many people—in education, the media, government, and the general public—still take this view (see Harris, 1997, pp. x, 161, 197). Perhaps because numeracy has long been thought of as a lesser academic discipline, many ABE teachers prefer to speak of mathematics. But the term *mathematics* also has its naysayers, especially among many adult numeracy students who associate it with the vagaries of secondary school "math classes." These ABE students most likely failed mathematics in the secondary school system, and they return to math as adults with much trepidation. They associate "math" with feelings of failure, stupidity, and powerlessness. Such negative feelings toward math are often collectively referred to as *math anxiety* (Frankenstein, 1989; Tobias, 1978; Zaslavsky, 1994b). Mathematics has also been used as a social divider, a marker that sets apart those who can "do" math from those who can't—a gatekeeper rather than a gateway. Mathematics has also been something of a nemesis to women. Traditionally, math is a subject in which girls have received little encouragement and a professional field in which they have had few role models (Barnes, 1988; Walkerdine, 1989; Willis, 1989; Secada, Fennema, & Adajian, 1995; Harris, 1997).

The first known use of the term numeracy appeared in a British publication in 1959, in which it is described as the mirror image of literacy (Crowther Report, 1959). One of the first attempts to fully define numeracy—in this case, the word used was numerate—appeared in another British publication in 1982: "We would wish the word 'numerate' to imply the possession of two attributes. The first is an 'at homeness' with numbers and an ability to make use of the mathematical skills which enable an individual to cope with the practical demands of . . . everyday life. The second is an ability to have some appreciation and understanding of information which is presented in mathematical terms, for instance in graphs, charts or tables or by reference to percentage increase or decrease. Taken together these imply that a numerate person should be expected to be able to appreciate and understand some of the ways in which mathematics can be used as a means of communication" (Cockcroft, 1982, paragraph 39).

"Most important of all," the authors of the report said, "is the need to have sufficient confidence to make effective use of whatever mathematical skill and understanding is possessed, whether this be little or much" (paragraph 34).

Some later definitions are more expansive. Here is an example from the Queensland, Australia, Department of Education in 1994: "Numeracy involves abilities that include interpreting, applying and communicating mathematical information in commonly encountered situations to enable full, critical and effective participation in a wide range of life roles" (quoted in Gal, van Groenstijn, Manly, Schmitt, & Tout, 1999, p. 10). What appears in most definitions of numeracy from the 1980s and 1990s is the use of mathematics in real-life situations and the idea that it can be used in a goal-oriented way, depending on the needs and interests of the individual in a given context (home, community, workplace). These definitions also incorporate the ability to communicate about math. Collectively, they suggest that numeracy refers not just to the ability to perform basic calculations but to the ability to perform a wider range of math skills, such as making measurements, interpreting statistical information, and giving and following directions.

In recent years, especially in Australia, much discussion and debate in the ABE community has focused on defining the relationship between mathematics and numeracy and on coming to terms with the concept of critical numeracy, or the use of mathematics for purposes of meaningful engagement with one's community. As Johnston (1994) argues, "To be numerate is more than being able to manipulate numbers, or even being able to 'succeed' in school or university mathematics. Numeracy is a critical awareness which builds bridges between mathematics and the real world, with all its diversity. . . . In this sense . . . there is no particular 'level' of mathematics associated with [numeracy]: it is as important for an engineer to be numerate as it is for a primary school child, a parent, a car driver or a gardener. The different contexts will require different mathematics to be activated and engaged in" (p. 34). Essential to the concept of critical numeracy is the view that mathematics is a vital tool in today's society—a bridge between school-based, or traditional, mathematics and the real world—and a tool that should be accessible to all members of society, not just a few "brainy" mathematicians.

This wider view of the concept of numeracy is also evident in the planned 2002 redesign of the 1992 International Adult Literacy Survey (IALS), a large-scale comparative survey. Like the IALS, the Adult Literacy and Lifeskills (ALL) survey is intended to assess the distribution of basic skills in the adult populations of participating countries and to analyze the possible relationship of those skills to various economic indicators, but ALL is expanding the domains assessed. It will include an assessment of numeracy skills, and thus represents the first instance of international cooperation in the effort to develop numeracy as a theoretical and research-supported domain. The authors of an ALL working paper (Gal et al., 1999) have arrived at a definition of adult "numerate behavior," the observable characteristics of numeracy: "Numerate behavior is observed when people manage a situation or solve a problem in a real context;[1] it involves responding to information about mathematical ideas that may be represented in a range of ways; it requires the activation of a range of enabling knowledge, behaviors, and processes" (p. 11).

Exhibit 5.1 presents the ALL numeracy team's description of numerate behavior. It distinguishes five facets (context, response, mathematical ideas, mathematical representation, and enabling knowledge and behaviors), each of which has several components. In the ALL

Numerate behavior involves:

Managing a situation or solving a problem in a real context
everyday life
work
societal
further learning

by responding
identifying or locating
acting upon*
interpreting
communicating about

to information about mathematical ideas
quantity and number
dimension and shape
pattern and relationships
data and chance
change

that is represented in a range of ways
objects and pictures
numbers and symbols
formulas
diagrams and maps
graphs
tables
texts

and requires activation of a range of enabling
knowledge, behaviors, and processes.
mathematical knowledge and understanding
mathematical problem-solving skills
literacy skills
beliefs and attitudes

Exhibit 5.1. Numerate Behavior and Its Facets.

Acting upon would include ordering or sorting, counting, estimating, computing, measuring, modeling.

Source: Adapted from Gal et al., 1999, p. 12.

framework, numeracy involves much more than the "quantitative literacy" described in the IALS. Numeracy has to do not only with quantity and number but also with dimension and shape; patterns and relationships (such as being able to generalize and represent the relationship between where one lives and the cost of housing); data and chance (such as being able to understand how polls are based on sampling); and the mathematics of change (such as being able to represent how prices fluctuate and populations vary). The ALL team argues that people need to identify, interpret, act upon, and communicate about mathematical information, and the framework details the ways mathematical information can be represented; it also recognizes that to be numerate, adults need not only mathematical skills but also literacy and problem-solving skills. In this view, numeracy is also dependent on disposition, such as anxiety or self-confidence, which affects how one responds in situations requiring use of numeracy skills.

In this new light, numeracy is seen as the bridge between math and the real world. It is an umbrella term that expands both the breadth of the mathematics that is considered and the contexts in which adults use that mathematics. Numeracy is about making meaning of mathematics, at whatever level of mathematical skill, and mathematics is a tool to be used in a variety of applications in both education and life. "Numeracy is not less than mathematics, but more" (Johnston & Tout, 1995, p. xiii).

In further explaining the concept of numeracy, it is helpful to contrast the way in which the new numeracy might be taught with the way math tends to be taught in a traditional classroom. Very generally, when teachers teach math, students use a textbook or workbook and do lots of repetitive practice, they prepare for tests and exams, and they learn formal rules, often by rote, with little consideration of why and how the skills they are expected to learn can be put to use in the real world. When teachers teach numeracy, they are more likely to teach math from a more authentic, contextual point of view, one in which math is derived from some actual or modeled activity, in which investigations and projects are used as vehicles for learning. Teachers of numeracy are also more likely to take into account the students' various informal ways of doing math, allowing the understandings and strategies amassed in and out of school to serve as valid resources.

This essential difference between the teaching of math and the teaching of numeracy is the reason why terminology is important. And it is the reason why the term numeracy, as described above, should be used to indicate what it is we do when we teach math in ABE. It is a way forward. As Schmitt (2000) writes: "Adult basic education and GED [General Educational Development] mathematics instruction should be less concerned with school mathematics and more concerned with the mathematical demands of the lived-in world: the demands that adults meet in their roles as workers, family members, and community members. Therefore we need to view this new term numeracy not as a synonym for mathematics but as a new discipline defined as the bridge that links mathematics and the real world" (p. 4).

NUMERACY IN U.S.
ADULT BASIC EDUCATION

We began our search for the state of adult numeracy education in the United States by sampling two bodies of literature: the general literature on adult basic education and literacy,[2] including federal and state government policy documents, reference documents, and research reports,[3] and the literature that directly addresses adult numeracy or mathematics in ABE.[4] Our search of the general literature confirmed the findings of researchers in the mid-1990s that scant reference is made to numeracy or mathematics in such sources (Gal, 1993; Nesbit, 1996). Our search of the more focused literature suggests that information on numeracy and math is easy to find in practitioner writings and field-initiated studies (Gal, 1993; Mullinix, 1994; Leonelli, Merson, & Schmitt, 1994; Beder, 1999). In terms of research, however, there is little to report.

Research

Research in U.S. adult numeracy education appears at the intersection of two fields: mathematics education and adult basic education. The former concerns the development of mathematical knowledge in individuals and, more recently, in groups (primarily children), the latter the development of basic skills among adults. (For the purposes of this chapter our definition of ABE includes adult secondary and GED instruction.) Our survey of the literature on adult numeracy education revealed a dramatic absence of attention to the development of mathematics skills in adults enrolled in basic education courses. Almost ten thousand articles in the ERIC (Educational Resources Information Center) database, all of which were published between 1980 and 2001, concern mathematics education, and about six thousand relate to ABE, but only seventeen relate to both. When we limited our search to articles published in the United States, we found that an equal number concern each field (approximately three thousand to four thousand each), while only nine deal with the mathematics education of adults in basic education.

Literature surveys conducted by other researchers produced comparable results. From 1982 to 1998, more than three thousand articles in forty-eight education research journals dealt with mathematics education research where ethnicity, gender, social class, or disabilities were also considered. Of those, only 0.2 percent (five) concerned ABE (Lubienski, 1999). This figure sits in stark contrast with the 79 percent that examined K–12 mathematics education or a subset thereof and the 18 percent that concerned math education on the postsecondary level. Safford-Ramus (2000) identified and examined 113 U.S. dissertations listed in the databases of Dissertation Abstracts from 1980 to 2000 dealing with adult mathematics education, 34 of which addressed ABE.

Does this small body of research on ABE mathematics education say anything of value to the field? While we yearn for more research, the existing articles do reveal two interesting trends. First, unlike the research in mathematics education for children, research on mathematics education for adults for the most part does not address cognition or learning (student achievement). In the ERIC documents, Ginsburg and Gal's (1995) study of adults' informal and formal knowledge of percentages stands alone as a study of how adults think mathematically. Safford-Ramus (2000) found little attention paid to cognition when looking at adult mathematics education research: most of the work published in doctoral dissertations and journals concerned topics such as math anxiety. Outside of ABE, however, "the majority of mathematics education research focused on student cognition and outcomes, with relatively little attention to contextual or cultural issues" (Lubienski, 1999, p. 1).

Some attempts are being made to set the stage for more research. The National Center on Adult Literacy (NCAL) has published technical reports (Gal, 1993; Gal & Schmitt, 1994) that lay out the need for a research program, and the National Center for the Study of Adult Learning and Literacy (NCSALL) took a major step in connecting with international research efforts by hosting Adults Learning Mathematics—A Research Forum (ALM7 Conference) in July 2000. The topics discussed at the forum exemplify the field's emergent issues: assessment, frameworks, and standards, contexts in which adults practice mathematics, instructional approaches, parents as co-learners, research into practice, teacher knowledge, theoretical frameworks for adults learning mathematics, adults' understandings of mathematical concepts, and the use of mathematics in the workplace.

Practice

The dearth of material on adult numeracy education in research is not reflected in practice. Gal (1993, 2000) observed that while official reports, such as state reports on ABE provision and the outcomes of test results, convey the impression that little adult mathematics instruction takes place, numeracy activity is evident in publishers' materials and in surveys of adult education centers. A survey of 650 ABE programs in fifteen states indicated that more than 80 percent of adults enrolled received some math-related instruction (Gal & Schuh, 1994). Numeracy skills have also been identified alongside literacy skills as being important to successful employment, training and workplace practices, helping to establish numeracy training as part of workplace basic skills programs (Secretary's Commission on Achieving Necessary Skills [SCANS], 1991, 1992; Mikulecky, 1994; Bynner & Parsons, 1997). Despite the scant attention paid outside the classroom, mathematics teaching and learning does appear to be going on inside the classroom.

TEACHING STAFF AND PROFESSIONAL DEVELOPMENT. The most complete picture of the teachers who provide ABE math instruction can be found in two state-focused studies that were the subjects of dissertations. One was conducted in Massachusetts (Mullinix, 1994) and the other in Arkansas (Ward, 2000). In her survey of 167 Arkansas GED teachers, Ward profiled the typical GED teacher as one who teaches all subjects (including math) (96 percent) and has a bachelor's degree in elementary education (64 percent). An Arkansas GED teacher is almost certain to prefer teaching math with individualized instruction (95 percent) and to use repeated practice as the method of choice (99 percent). The Mullinix survey of 141 Massachusetts ABE math teachers found that over half of them came to be math instructors either "by accident" (36 percent) or as "part of the program package" (24 percent)—that is, math was included in the subjects they must teach. At least 55 percent reported having no training in mathematics pedagogy. In another estimate, fewer than 5 percent of teachers in programs providing numeracy education were found to be certified to teach mathematics (Gal & Schuh, 1994).

Although it may not have been noticed by policymakers or government, the need for teacher support and professional development made evident by Ward and Mullinix has not gone unnoticed by teachers. In recent years several practitioner groups have emerged to create opportunities for themselves and others to increase their knowledge of both mathematics content and pedagogy. The Massachusetts ABE Math Team in 1994 formed a collective of sixteen teachers to study the standards developed for K–12 students by the National Council of Teachers of Mathematics (NCTM), the U.S.-based professional organization for mathematics educators. The Massachusetts team then published a set of standards adapted for adults in ABE and GED programs (Leonelli & Schwendeman, 1994; Leonelli, Merson, & Schmitt, 1994). The Math Exchange Group (MEG) in New York City meets regularly to work on math problems and to promote their own and their students' understanding of math.

Ohio, Maine, Oregon, Illinois, and Pennsylvania have teachers and staff developers who lead workshops for their colleagues. Most of these teachers are founding members of the Adult Numeracy Network (ANN is now an at-large NCTM affiliate that meets during the annual NCTM conference).[5] ANN has reached out to hundreds of ABE teachers through its newsletter, the *Math Practitioner,* and has engaged many teachers in conversation about math through its numeracy electronic discussion list.[6] ANN also published the *Framework for Adult Numeracy Standards* (Curry et al., 1996). These curriculum standards consolidate several perspectives, mainly those supported by the NCTM, the Secretary's Commission on Achieving Necessary Skills (SCANS, 1991), and the ABE Mathematics Team in Massachusetts as well as those of adult learners, numeracy teachers, and employers. The aim of the standards is to present a framework which would form a comprehensive basis for states to develop their own numeracy curriculum standards. It is based on seven themes—three about the processes of learning math (relevance and connections, problem solving and reasoning, and communication) and four that are content-based (number and number sense, data, geometry, and algebra).

Various members of ANN continue to take leading roles in significant projects. Two members run the new LINCS Science and Numeracy Collection, and others have received a grant from the National Science Foundation to adapt three standards-based K–12 curricula to ABE environments. This effort—called the Extending Mathematical

Power (EMPower) project—is being developed at TERC in Massachusetts. The impact of these practitioner groups can also be seen in the growing number of sessions focused on math at state and regional ABE conferences.

These valuable efforts notwithstanding, no organized or structured form of professional support exists to meet the ongoing needs of those ABE practitioners who teach math. No government-sponsored programs or initiatives such as "family literacy" or "workplace education" have been developed, and no universities offer formal courses in adult numeracy or adult mathematics education.

CURRICULUM, INSTRUCTION, AND ASSESSMENT. At present, the two primary drivers of the math curriculum in ABE are the GED exam and commercially published workbooks. The 1988 version of the GED mathematics test, which is being revised for 2002, is a prime motivator for including math in instruction. The test consists largely of multiple-choice word problems presented in adult contexts that are classified as 50 percent arithmetic, 30 percent algebra, and 20 percent geometry. Many GED and pre-GED mathematics workbooks reflect this breakdown, and, in general, present computational routines, with opportunities for repeated practice of these routines in direct preparation for the test. Teachers looking for something more often turn to materials that emphasize cooperative problem solving and visualization. Although such materials were developed for middle or secondary school students, they are full of ideas suitable for teaching adults. Examples include EQUALS Project materials (for example, *Family Math* and *Get It Together*), the Visual Math Materials (Foreman & Bennett, 1995), the NCTM addenda series (for example, Burton, 1993; Del Grande, 1993), and some of the Australian adult numeracy materials (*Strength in Numbers; Mathematics: A New Beginning; Numeracy on the Line*).

Unfortunately, as the Arkansas teachers reported in Ward's survey, much math teaching is based on practicing routine procedures with students using workbooks (Schmitt, 2000; Kloosterman, Hassan, & Wiest, 2000). Workbooks, if used as the sole source of math instruction, discourage intuitive approaches and promote a mathematics that comes from an outside authority rather than a personal mathematics that can be applied in many situations. This style of math instruction has largely been discredited in the field of children's mathematics education, where a range of different strategies are recommended (see Grouws & Cebulla, 2000).

Although the GED is the high-stakes assessment of choice, ABE programs are often required to demonstrate student progress through standardized tests. The Tests of Adult Basic Education (TABE), which is reportedly used in 80 percent of all U.S. adult literacy programs (Gal & Schuh, 1994), is another major influence on the teaching of adult numeracy. The TABE includes two math sections, Computation and Concepts/Applications, and it is in many ways similar to the GED except that it more specifically diagnoses skills. Another driver of the curriculum will undoubtedly be the National Reporting System (NRS), which at present suggests that the TABE, the Comprehensive Adult Student Assessment System (CASAS), and the Adult Measure of Essential Skills (AMES) be used to assess student progress. The possible danger with a nationally directed assessment scheme like the NRS is that it can promote teaching that is focused predominantly on raising standardized test scores. Adults who may want classroom learning to address the mathematical demands of their daily life, to prepare them for further education, or for specific work or employment purposes may find themselves in competition with the program's need to demonstrate progress against the assessment scheme.

Policy

Each year more than 4 million adults attend federal- and state-funded ABE programs in the United States. In 1997, 39 percent of these adults enrolled in classes in English for speakers of other languages (ESOL), 38 percent attended classes in literacy and basic skills instruction (ABE), and 23 percent entered classes in adult secondary education (ASE) (U.S. Department of Education, 1997).[7] In each of the three instructional groupings, the need for literacy—the ability to read and write—is accepted by policymakers and practitioners alike. Similarly, few would question the need for newcomers to the United States to become fluent speakers of English. Periodically, other types of knowledge or skill are added to the agenda of ABE, ASE, and ESOL services. For example, at various times funders have decided that ABE programs should include instruction on citizenship, health, parenting, or technology.[8] However, literacy and language learning and improvement remain the focus of ABE.[9]

Public relations and advocacy play an important role in shaping and promoting government educational policy. For more than a decade, advocates for ABE have campaigned hard to make sure that literacy becomes a national priority. The fruits of their efforts are evident in the titles of the major organizational structures created in the 1990s to advance the cause of ABE: the National Center for the Study of Adult Learning and Literacy, the National Center on Literacy, the National Institute for Literacy, the Division of Adult Education and Literacy (prior to 1991, the Division of Adult Education). Likewise, the titles of major legislative actions and documents authorizing and regulating adult basic skills provision have come to stress the importance of "literacy." The Adult Basic Education section of the Economic Opportunity Act of 1964 and the Adult Education Act of 1966 have been replaced by the National Literacy Act of 1991 and the Adult Education and Family Literacy Act of the Workforce Investment Act of 1998. Looking beyond the titles for evidence that numeracy is on policymakers' radar screen is revealing as well. Numeracy—whether sought in terms of its most restrictive definition (as merely "computation"), in terms of a commonly used less restrictive definition (as "computation and problem solving"), or in terms of the comprehensive definition supported in this chapter—appears only sporadically in the text of major policy and public relations documents aimed at expanding and improving ABE.

Numeracy is sometimes omitted entirely. One example is the widely promulgated document *From the Margins to the Mainstream: An Action Agenda for Literacy,* which was one result of the National Literacy Summit 2000. According to the National Institute for Literacy (NIFL), "Hundreds of individuals and organizations across the country have contributed to the Summit document, which can guide the field's work over the next decade" (NIFL, 2000). Yet in this important paper the only mention of "computation," "mathematics," or "numeracy" appears in a sidebar quoting the definition of literacy from the Adult Education Act of 1991. One might surmise that when the term literacy is used in the document it is intended to include numeracy, but this may not be the case, as is evident in the definition of literacy on the cover as "the quality or state of being literate" and of literate as "one who can read and write" (National Literacy Summit 2000 Steering Committee, 2000).

Some policy documents do include numeracy. The National Reporting System (NRS) for Adult Education is an outcomes-based reporting system for state-administered, federally funded adult education programs. It holds states' ABE programs accountable for tracking student progress. Across the NRS's six levels of educational gain in numeracy skills, mathematical progress is described primarily in terms of increases in students' decontextualized computational skills with whole numbers, fractions, decimals, and percents. In the NRS Implementation Guidelines (U.S. Department of Education, 2000b), Level 1, Beginning ABE Literacy, addresses number recognition, counting, and addition and subtraction of single-digit numbers; Level 2, Beginning Basic Education, expands to three-digit addition and subtraction, multiplication tables through twelve, and simple fractions; Level 3, Low Intermediate Basic Education, includes the four operations with three-digit whole numbers; and Level 4, High Intermediate Basic Education, sets expectations for all operations on whole numbers and fractions as well as fraction and decimal conversion. Any instruction that goes beyond computation is reserved for the two higher levels of learners. It is not until Level 5, Low Adult Secondary Education, that operations with decimals, simple algebraic equations, tables and graphs, and "use of math in business transactions" are inserted. Finally, the description of High Adult Secondary Education, Level 6, requires that the "individual can make estimates of time and space and can apply principles of geometry to measure angles, lines, and surfaces; can also apply trigonometric functions" (p. 16). The message here is that context is not important and that adult education programs are accountable to get computation out of the way in the first four levels, and introduce concepts and skills around space, geometry and measurement, data, statistics, and graphs, and algebra only after number skills are developed.

Thus, while the NRS does make use of the term *numeracy,* it is not used in the same way the term is understood in this chapter, where adult context and various math content areas are integrated at all levels of progress. The Adult Literacy and Lifeskills Survey's facets of numerate behavior, the NCTM Principles and Standards, and the ANN Framework for Adult Numeracy Standards are consistent in the perspective that context and the four domains of mathematics are critical to all stages of a person's mathematical development.

Another policy document starts from contexts that are real and important for adults. *Equipped for the Future [EFF] Content Standards: What Adults Need to Know for the Twenty-First Century* (Stein, 2000) is grounded in data gathered from adults on their roles as workers, parents, and community members. As such it attempts to holistically describe the core skills adults need to carry out their roles effectively as parents, citizens, and workers. However, of the sixteen EFF standards, only one specifically addresses numeracy or mathematics. This one is under the banner of Decision-Making Skills and is called Use Math to Solve Problems and Communicate. In our view, this perspective is more adult-appropriate than the NRS perspective because it starts from the position of adults' using a range of purposeful skills to participate effectively in society. Even so, the EFF standards could go further to explicate the mathematics and skills within those contexts. While many of the other sixteen standards could incorporate some math skills and understanding, or could be integrated with the math standard, this is not made explicit in any way. In the section of EFF that illustrates how the EFF might work in practice, there are no examples of applying the math standard. Without this explication and support to teachers, it is possible that numeracy practice will not be enhanced or encouraged by this major program of the National Institute for Literacy.

LESSONS FROM K–12

Given the short history of adult numeracy education, ABE might make use of the research, practice, and policy in mathematics education that is not directly focused on adults. Surely some characteristics of sound teaching practice can cross such boundaries.

Research in mathematics education is explicitly driven and practice and policy implicitly driven by underlying epistemologies about the nature of thinking and knowledge acquisition. Over the last few decades, great interest has been stirred in the mathematics education community over alternatives to the traditional perspectives on what it means to learn and know mathematics. The discussion has centered largely on the concept of constructivism as opposed to transmissionism and its many variations and interpretations.

In the transmissionist model, teachers act as the experts, and their role is to transmit their knowledge directly to their students. The knowledge is seen as objective, and the learning is about receiving the information handed down, absorbing the facts, and reproducing them. Constructivists see learning as a form of understanding constructed by the learner, and they focus on the ways in which the individual learner makes sense of mathematics. In social constructivism, an offshoot of constructivism, learning is seen as an activity in which shared mathematical meanings are constructed with others and drawn from the environment. Recent cognitive theories hold that knowledge is constructed and restructured under a variety of constraints or conditions that either facilitate or limit the range of what can be learned. Here are some interpretations of the key implications of constructivism for classroom practice, paraphrased from Hatano (1996, pp. 211–213):

- Mathematical knowledge is acquired by construction; therefore, students should be given the opportunity to actively participate in the learning process rather than be forced to swallow large amounts of information.

- Cognitive restructuring is necessary to advance mathematical knowledge; to that end, instruction should induce successive restructurings of mathematical knowledge.

- Mathematical knowledge is constrained by internal factors (cognitive, such as innate and early understandings and previous knowledge) and external factors (sociocultural, situated in contexts, such as peers, teachers, tools, and artifacts); it follows that each collection of factors may either facilitate or limit mathematical learning.

Because constructivism is a theory about the nature of learning, it does not directly address classroom practice. Nevertheless, constructivist research has highlighted the many shortcomings of traditional mathematics education, which is rooted in transmissionism, and has raised awareness of the different theories and philosophies behind mathematics and mathematics education. (Key players in these discussions and debates have included Piaget, Vygotsky, Mellin-Olsen, von Glaserfield, Cobb, Noss, Ernest, Wittgenstein, and Lakatos. Some useful readings on constructivism and related debates include Davis, Maher, & Noddings, 1990; Ernest, 1989, 1998; Mellin-Olsen, 1987; and Malone & Taylor, 1993.)

Research

Considerable research has been conducted on how children learn math. Profoundly influenced by Piaget's theories of genetic epistemology and developmental psychology, research in mathematical thinking and learning has focused on the psychology of the individual and the personal construction of knowledge. More recently, social and cultural aspects of mathematical activity have been included in theories of mathematical learning.

In a summary of the significant findings in international K–12 mathematics research, Grouws and Cebulla (2000) outline the implications for teaching as follows:

- *Opportunity to learn:* The extent of the students' opportunity to learn mathematics content bears directly and decisively on student mathematics achievement (p. 10).

- *Focus on meaning:* Focusing instruction on the meaningful development of important mathematical ideas increases the level of student learning (p. 13).

- *Learning while solving problems:* Students can learn both concepts and skills by solving problems (p. 15).

- *Opportunity for both invention and practice:* Giving students opportunities to discover and invent new knowledge and to practice what they have learned improves student achievement (p. 17).

- *Openness to student solution methods and student interaction:* Teaching that incorporates students' intuitive methods of solving problems can increase student learning, especially when combined with opportunities for student interaction and discussion (p. 19).

- *Small group learning:* Letting students work in small groups on activities, problems, and assignments can increase student mathematics achievement (p. 21).

- *Whole-class discussion:* Whole-class discussion following individual and group work improves student achievement (p. 23).

- *Number sense:* Teaching mathematics with a focus on number sense encourages students to become problem solvers in a wide variety of situations and to view mathematics as a discipline in which thinking is important (p. 25).

- *Concrete materials:* Long-term use of concrete materials is positively related to increases in student mathematics achievement and improved attitudes toward mathematics (p. 27).

• *Use of calculators:* Using calculators in the learning of mathematics can result in increased achievement and improved student attitudes (p. 29).

In our view, all of these strategies and approaches can be applied to teaching mathematics at any level, including ABE.

Two areas of research in K–12 math education that are especially relevant to adult mathematics education are ethnomathematics, a relatively new term for a field of study that has captured the interest of educators throughout the twentieth century, and gender.

ETHNOMATHEMATICS AND FUNCTIONAL MATH. Sometimes called street math, ethnomathematics is concerned with how mathematics is used in different cultures and in social and work situations outside the classroom—that is, in real life. Bishop (1994) writes that mathematics has generally been "assumed to be culture-free and value-free knowledge; explanations of 'failure' and 'difficulty' in relation to school mathematics were sought either in terms of the learner's cognitive attributes or in terms of the quality of the teaching . . . received . . . 'social' and 'cultural' issues in mathematics education research were rarely considered" (p. 15). In the late 1970s and early 1980s, interest in the social and cultural aspects of mathematics and mathematics education increased. According to Gerdes (1994), it is during this period that D'Ambrosio proposed his "ethnomathematical program" as a means of tracking and analyzing the processes of generalization, transmission, diffusion, and institutionalization of [mathematical] knowledge in diverse cultural systems" (p. 19).

Ethnomathematics can inform mathematics education. Zaslavsky (1994a) stated the following:

> Why is it important to introduce ethnomathematical perspectives into the mathematics curriculum? Students should recognize that mathematical practices and ideas arose out of the real needs and interests of human beings. . . .
>
> Students should learn how mathematics impacts on other subject areas—social studies, language arts, fine arts, science. Most important, they should have the opportunity to see the relevance of mathematics to their own lives and to their community, to research their own ethnomathematics. [p. 6]

Zaslavsky goes on to recommend how an ethnomathematical perspective could be incorporated into a mathematics curriculum:

> The entire mathematics curriculum must be restructured so that mathematical concepts and ethnomathematical aspects are synthesized. Rather than a curriculum emphasizing hundreds of isolated skills, mathematics education will embody real-life applications in the form of projects based on themes and mathematical concepts.
>
> Teachers at all levels must be well grounded in mathematics and at the same time be familiar with the interface between mathematics and other subject areas. [p. 7]

Much research on the ways people use math every day does in fact focus on adults rather than children, looking at how adults perform mathematical tasks in their daily lives, and as such is relevant to adult numeracy practices. Three main messages to adult educators seem to emerge from this research. One is the acknowledgment that formal, or school-based, math is not the only math. A person's mathematical knowledge has probably been acquired via both formal and informal learning. The second message is that informal learning is as valuable as formal, school-based learning. The third is that students should be encouraged to build on this range of real-life mathematics experiences while also learning the practices of formal math.[10]

A related view of how to improve school mathematics instruction, especially at the high school level, concerns functional math, wherein the instruction and the curriculum are connected to real-world applications. Forman and Steen (1999) describe and promote the need for a functional math curriculum:

> Any mathematics curriculum designed on functional grounds . . . will emphasize authentic applications from everyday life and work. . . . By highlighting the rich mathematics embedded in everyday tasks, this approach . . . can dispel both minimalist views about the mathematics required for work and elitist views of academic mathematics as an area with little to learn from work-based problems.
>
> Neither traditional college-preparatory mathematics curricula nor the newer standards-inspired curricula were designed specifically to meet either the technical and problem solving needs of the contemporary workforce or the modern demands of active citizenship. [p. vi]

Forman and Steen then proceed to explain why and how such a functional mathematics curriculum could work to cater to both the traditional and reformist views of mathematics while at the same time making the learning of mathematics relevant and meaningful to all students.

Functional math has much in common with ethnomathematics. Both argue for an approach that covers a wide range of math skills embedded within social contexts and purposes and that values personal ways of doing math. Both sit comfortably alongside the view of numeracy advocated in this chapter.[11]

GENDER STUDIES. Much has been written about girls and mathematics (Walkerdine, 1989; Willis, 1989; Secada et al., 1995; Harris, 1997), and much of the research in this area is linked with the ethnomathematics movement. A quote from a U.K. report by Harris (1997) demonstrates how these fields overlap in their view that informal, real-life mathematical knowledge is as valuable as that gained through formal instruction: "Throughout the world it is women and girls who underachieve in mathematics. Mathematics is the study above all others that denotes the heights of intellect. Throughout the world, the activity that most clearly denotes the work of women, in both the unpaid, domestic sphere and in paid employment, is work with cloth. Work with cloth symbolizes women as empty-headed and trivial. Yet constructing cloth, decorating it during construction and converting it into garments, is work that cannot be done without involving spatial and numerical concepts that are the foundations of mathematics" (p. 191).

In the United States, much work has been done to promote the success of girls in mathematics, most notably by the Lawrence Hall of Science in Berkeley, California, through the EQUALS project, which since 1977 has been developing programs that promote equity for underrepresented groups in mathematics. These approaches to teaching have challenged the traditionally male-dominated domain of math education and promoted alternatives that in many cases are attractive not only to girls but to the many boys who struggle with learning mathematics in a traditional classroom. Such approaches include working cooperatively, promoting discussion and idea sharing, and using hands-on materials. They have much in common with the approaches to learning math promoted by ethnomathematicians and social constructivists.

Practice

For some time now there has been evidence of dissatisfaction with what children are learning—or not learning—in math class. In 1990, in a national publication about mathematics education, Davis, Maher, and Noddings (1990) described the situation as follows:

> By now nearly everyone has probably read, or at least heard of, the recent spate of reports showing that students in the United States are not doing very well in mathematics. . . . This leaves the United States with what might be called a war on two fronts. There is first, the fact of unsatisfactory results. But the second front is perhaps even more threatening: there is major disagreement on how to proceed in order to make things better. One school of thought would argue for "more" and "more explicit." That is to say, they would argue that the United States needs more days of school per year, or more hours of mathematics instruction per week, or more homework, or all of the above, together with a highly explicit identification of the knowledge that we want students to acquire, and a sharply directed emphasis on precisely this knowledge. Prescriptions in this direction usually suggest more frequent testing, and making more—perhaps even teachers' salaries—dependent on the outcome of this testing.
>
> A different diagnosis and prescription might be said to tend in nearly the opposite direction. . . . These recommendations argue for making mathematics more natural, fitting it better into the context of children's lives, conceivably even moving toward less testing. [p. 1]

Nearly ten years later, Forman and Steen (1999) expressed similar sentiments:

> Despite mathematics' reputation as an ancient subject consisting of indisputable facts, mathematics education has recently become the source of passionate debate. At stake is nothing less than the fundamental nature of school mathematics: its content (what should be taught), pedagogy (how it should be taught), and assessment (what should be expected). At times these "math wars" have become so heated that [U.S.] Education Secretary Richard Riley has issued a public call for a truce.
>
> At the risk of oversimplifying, this debate can be characterized as a clash between "traditionalists," who expect schools to provide the kind

of well-focused mathematics curriculum that colleges have historically expected, and "reformers," who espouse a broader curriculum that incorporates uses of technology, data analysis, and modern applications of mathematics. The reform approach is championed by the National Council of Teachers of Mathematics, whose standards advocate a robust eleven-year core curriculum for all students. [p. 2]

What seems to be a universal point of agreement is that current and past methods of teaching math to children have not been entirely successful. Researchers have attempted to determine why this is the case, and their efforts have resulted in some of the debates and recommendations just described. So far, the research seems to have had little impact on the outcome of mathematics education—that is, on student abilities. But this isn't to say that progress has not been made. Studies of student performance, such as those conducted through the National Assessment of Educational Progress (NAEP), indicate that student performance is rising, albeit slowly (Dossey & Usiskin, 2000, pp. 20–22).

Probably the strongest influence in terms of school practice has been the standards established by the National Council of Teachers of Mathematics. Building on recommendations from the mathematics education community at large, NCTM went through a long process culminating in the production of three standards documents on curricula and evaluation: *Curriculum and Evaluation Standards for School Mathematics* (NCTM, 1989), *Professional Standards for Teaching Mathematics* (NCTM, 1991), and *Assessment Standards for School Mathematics* (NCTM, 1995). Based on research findings and generally supportive of the constructivist view of learning mathematics, these standards drove the reform agenda in school math education through the 1990s. The NCTM standards influenced state standards and curriculum frameworks, instructional materials, teacher education, and classroom practice (NCTM, 2000). In 2000, NCTM published a revised version called *Principles and Standards for School Mathematics*. Despite the apparent value of the NCTM standards and knowledge about constructivism and ethnomathematics, great unrest about teaching practice and student outcomes continues to exist. Tradition in the way math is taught in the classroom is deeply entrenched, and no effort as yet has appeared capable of initiating fundamental change in teaching practice. Changing and developing new curriculum standards, writing new teaching materials, and the like appear only to chip away at the edges. Tradition is often the barrier to progress.

What mathematics teachers seem to do in their classrooms is teach in much the same way that they themselves were taught; what they experienced themselves as successful mathematics students is what they hand on to their own students. An Australian educator stated the problem as follows: "While teachers operate at an intuitive level as pragmatists, not articulating to themselves the present theory which drives their practice, they are effectively paralyzed in terms of their capacity to change radically. The non-theorized practitioner is a kind of well-intentioned misguided or unguided missile in the classroom, likely to take up a new idea and add it to the repertoire but unable to generate infinite practice for new contexts" (Boomer, 1986/1994, p. 68).

Another issue is the focus on computation. In a recent commentary on the similarities and differences between adult and K–12 mathematics teaching, Kloosterman, Hassan, and Wiest (2000) said, "One explanation for the gap between mathematical experiences in school and workplace or everyday mathematics is tradition. The curriculum has always been focused on computation, so that is what is expected in mathematics classrooms" (p. 52). Grouws and Cebulla (2000) report the following: "Data from the Third International Mathematics and Science Study (TIMSS) video study show that over 90 percent of mathematics class time in the United States eighth grade classrooms is spent practicing routine procedures, with the remainder of the time generally spent applying procedures in new situations. . . . In contrast, students at the same grade level in typical Japanese classrooms spend approximately 40 percent of instructional time practicing routine procedures, 15 percent applying procedures in new situations, and 45 percent inventing new procedures and analyzing new situations (p. 17).

As we have stated a number of times, it does appear that practice in the traditional math classroom may focus on calculations and routine procedures to the detriment of other recommended activities and strategies, such as those listed earlier by Grouws and Cebulla. These include constructivist-based strategies such as encouraging students to discover their own, personal, and invented procedures and applying them to new situations, which as noted earlier seems to be more the case in Japan than in the United States.

Other initiatives in practice have been in the development of classroom teaching resources: textbooks and workbooks. But it is estimated that only about 10–15 percent of elementary schools are using one of the newer, more conceptually based series of mathematics texts, most of which are the result of projects supported by the National Science Foundation. At the middle school level (grades 6–8) and the high school level (9–12), newer resources emanating from other NSF-supported projects are becoming more widespread (Dossey & Usiskin, 2000). In all states except Iowa, state-level education authorities set curriculum guidelines, and this often determines which textbooks will be adopted by local school districts. Most of these books take a conservative pencil-and-paper approach to teaching in which students are shown one approach to problem solving.

Policy

Dissatisfaction with student performance in mathematics has driven major policy initiatives for K–12 mathematics education at the federal, state, and local levels. In K–12 education, unlike ABE, the national political dialogue has focused fairly equally on literacy and numeracy. This was true when the National Educational Goals (U.S. Department of Education, 1989) were put in place during the administration of President George H. W. Bush and remained so in 1997 when the first two of President Bill Clinton's seven educational priorities were stated as follows: "All students will read independently and well by the end of 3rd grade," and "All students will master challenging mathematics, including the foundations of algebra and geometry, by the end of 8th grade" (Clinton, 1997). Following these announcements, a presidential directive was issued to the U.S. Department of Education and the National Science Foundation that resulted in America Counts, an initiative focusing on six strategic areas in math and science education: teacher preparation, increased learning time for students, research into best practices, public understanding of today's mathematics, challenging and engaging curriculum, and coordinated federal, state, and local efforts (U.S. Department of Education, 1998). In *Before It's Too Late: A Report to the Nation from the National Commission on Mathematics and Science Teaching for the Twenty-First Century,* the authors point to four enduring reasons why the nation should take action to improve children's education in the arenas of math and science: to address the rapid pace of change in the global economy and the workplace, to facilitate everyday decision making, to bolster national security, and to acknowledge the intrinsic cultural value of mathematic and scientific knowledge (U.S. Department of Education, 2000a). This initiative may have a chance of being more than a rhetorical vehicle for politicians—it has struck a chord with the educational leadership of the NCTM and the National Science Foundation as well as with community, business, and political leaders.

As is the case in practice, probably the most significant recent influence on mathematics education policy in the United States has been the standards developed by the NCTM. A new, revised set of standards was released in April 2000 under the title *Principles and Standards for School Mathematics* (NCTM, 2000). The standards are guided by six principles:

1. *Equity:* Excellence in mathematics education requires equity—high expectations and strong support for all students.

2. *Curriculum:* A curriculum is more than a collection of activities. It must be coherent, focused on important mathematics, and well articulated across grade levels.

3. *Teaching:* Effective mathematics teaching requires understanding what students know and need to learn and then challenging and supporting them to learn it well.

4. *Learning:* Students must learn mathematics with understanding, actively building new knowledge from experience and prior knowledge.

5. *Assessment:* Assessment should support the learning of important mathematics and furnish useful information to both teachers and students.

6. *Technology:* Technology is essential in teaching and learning mathematics; it influences the mathematics that is taught and enhances student learning.

At each of four grade levels—pre-K–2, 3–5, 6–8, and 9–12—the *Principles and Standards* contains a comprehensive body of mathematical understandings and competencies organized into five content areas—number and operation, algebra, geometry, measurement, and data analysis and probability—and five ways of acquiring and using that content—problem solving, reasoning and proof, communication, connections, and representation. Despite its potential for influencing policy and practice, the *Principles and Standards* is only a resource and guide; it carries no legal weight. Still, previous NCTM standards had a major influence on state curriculum and policy, and it is expected that the 2000 standards will have a similar impact.

LESSONS FROM ABROAD

America is not alone in its need to face up to the problem of "innumeracy." A quick analysis of ERIC documents on adult numeracy gives a broad indication of the state of adult numeracy education in other English-speaking countries relative to the United States. Of 412 documents found as the result of a Boolean search for the words *adult* and *numeracy* where the country of origin could be identified, 29 percent originated in the United States, compared with 30 percent in Australia, 22 percent in the United Kingdom, and 8 percent in Canada. We will take a fairly close look at some of the numeracy activity in Australia and touch on some of the significant work done in other countries that may be of interest to ABE educators in considering future approaches to adult numeracy provision in the United States.

In the late 1970s, the time at which adult numeracy practice was more or less officially recognized in the United States and abroad, the country with the most activity was the United Kingdom. In 1981, the United Kingdom undertook what was probably the first large-scale assessment of the numeracy skills of a general adult population, basing it on interviews with 2,890 individuals (Advisory Council for Adult and Continuing Education, 1982). It was there, in 1982, that the Cockcroft report, a very important document in the history of adult numeracy education, was completed. The United Kingdom continued to be active in researching adult numeracy, and a study and consequent report, *Does Numeracy Matter?* (Bynner & Parsons, 1997), found that poor numeracy skills did have a major impact on an adult's life, compounding the problems that can result from poor literacy skills: "People without numeracy skills suffered worse disadvantage in employment than those with poor literacy skills alone. They left school early, frequently without qualifications, and had more difficulty in getting and maintaining full-time employment. The jobs entered were generally low grade with limited training opportunities and poor pay prospects. Women with numeracy difficulties appeared especially vulnerable to exclusion from the clerical and sales jobs to which they aspired" (p. 27).

A number of reports and articles have described the development of adult numeracy research and practice in the United Kingdom, including Coben (2000) and Benn (1997). The United Kingdom has also recently launched *Skills for Life—The National Strategy for Improving Adult Literacy and Numeracy Skills* (Department for Education and Employment, 2001). Indeed, the decades of work by British numeracy practitioners have made numeracy a solid partner with literacy in policy as well as practice.

Elsewhere, including in the Netherlands, Australia, and Canada, the late 1970s and early 1980s saw the gradual emergence of adult numeracy practice, usually following and modeled on adult literacy teaching practice. It was not until the 1990s that recognition of the need for numeracy education became a subject of significant interest to education providers, writers, and researchers. There seem to be a couple of reasons for this. One was International Literacy Year in 1990, which stirred many countries to put more money into adult literacy provision, some of which undoubtedly flowed into numeracy provision. The other significant influence was the interest in workplace reform and the provision of workplace basic skills training, where numeracy skills were recognized as being as important as literacy and communication skills (for example, the Essential Skills Research Project in Canada and the Workplace English Language and Literacy [WELL] program in Australia).

Research

A few attempts have been made to review research in the area of adult numeracy (Adult Literacy and Basic Skills Unit, 1994; Brooks et al., 2001; Coben, 2000; Gal, 1993), but these reports indicate that little research has been completed. However, adult numeracy interest groups have been developed, either in their own right or as part of other, larger organizations. Conferences have been held to bring together researchers and experienced practitioners within countries and from around the world. One example of this kind of activity is a UNESCO international seminar on adult numeracy held in Paris in 1993. Another was the development in 1994 of the research group Adults Learning Mathematics—A Research Forum. This group, initially a U.K.-based interest group, drew the interest of other countries and is now international in scope. An annual conference is held, and the proceedings of each have been published. In 2000, the group held its first ever conference outside of Europe, in Boston. In addition, two successful working groups were held as part of the large quadrennial International Congresses on Mathematical Education in Sevilla, Spain, in 1996 (ICME 8; see FitzSimons, 1997), and in Tokyo, Japan, in 2000 (ICME 9; see Fujita, 2000). Taken together, the proceedings from these conferences are a rich resource on current thinking about adult numeracy education.

Almost as a direct consequence of these activities, two new international compilations of research and study into adult numeracy have been published: in the United States, *Adult Numeracy Development: Theory, Research, Practice* (Gal, 2000), and in the United Kingdom, *Perspectives on Adults Learning Mathematics: Research and Practice* (Coben, O'Donoghue, & FitzSimons, 2000). Most of the articles in both date from 1995 or 1996. Together the two books represent the first major commercially published, internationally based collections of writings about adult numeracy, including chapters or sections that review current research. The U.S. publication, edited by Iddo Gal, is more practical in its focus and is of particular interest to an American audience in that a number of the authors write about practices in the United States. The book has four parts: perspectives on numeracy, approaches to instruction, reflecting on practice and learning, and assessment. The U.K. publication is more research-oriented and has a more international flavor. The section titled "Perspectives on Research on Adults Learning" brings together probably the most comprehensive analysis of research in this area to date. There is some overlap between the two books, with many authors in common, but they provide a solid base of reflection and research on which to move forward.

Another significant publication on theory and research in adult numeracy education, this one from the United Kingdom, is Roseanne Benn's *Adults Count Too: Mathematics for Empowerment* (1997). Benn locates numeracy practice within the wider sphere of ABE, describes and discusses relevant theories such as constructivism and fields of research such as ethnomathematics, and looks at the meaning of numeracy and implications for teaching, curriculum, and professional development.

In Australia, a number of projects were launched in the mid-1990s focusing on areas of research such as the pedagogical relationship between adult literacy and numeracy (Lee, Chapman, & Roe, 1993). One research project, called *Numeracy in Practice* (Johnston, Baynham, Kelly, Barlow, & Marks, 1997), looked at teaching numeracy to young unemployed people. A major influence in Australian numeracy research and development has been the work of Betty Johnston and her colleague, Keiko Yasukawa, who have argued for a critical constructivist approach to adult numeracy teaching (see Johnston, 1994). This approach was the basis for a substantial adult numeracy teaching training program (discussed later in this chapter) and has also influenced teaching practice and curriculum development across Australia.

Practice

In the area of practice, developments abroad have paralleled those in the United States, taking place in curriculum or standards frameworks, associated assessment practices, and professional development and training.

CURRICULUM AND INSTRUCTION. For most of its history here and abroad, ABE has been an informal, student-focused form of education with no formal accreditation process or systemwide curriculum. But in the 1990s the pressure for competency-based education and training pushed the field to develop an accredited curriculum built on competency-based learning outcomes. While many countries have adopted a school-based and traditional transmissionist model in developing curriculum standards for adult numeracy (Ciancone & Tout, 2001; Tout, 2000), there are examples of constructivist approaches to curriculum development. Following are two such examples, one from the Netherlands and one from Australia.

Realistic Mathematics Education (RME) was developed in the Netherlands during the 1970s.[12] It was developed primarily for schools but has also formed the basis of adult numeracy practice in the Netherlands, and the provision of adult numeracy education coincided with the development of RME. RME starts from the assumption that students should be given the opportunity to reinvent mathematics for themselves and that the subject matter should be "real" for them. This concept of the student reinventing and conceptualizing a personal mathematics is central to RME and is called *mathematizing*. It has much in common with the concept of social constructivism.

Building on RME, adult numeracy provision in the Netherlands focuses on functional contexts and applications, values problem solving, and encourages interactions between students, thereby making communication an important aspect of mathematics education. RME values individual, informal approaches to problem solving; in this it is unlike many other approaches to mathematics education (Gravemeijer, 1994;

Matthijsse, 2000). This is taken into account in assessment as well, as discussed later in this chapter (van Groenestijn, 2000).

A range of work has been done in Australia to create standards and a hierarchy of numeracy skill development for adult basic education that is not based on school mathematics. As in the United States, individual Australian states can develop their own curriculum. The most widely adopted approach is the Certificates in General Education for Adults (CGEA) (Kindler, Kenrick, Marr, Tout, & Wignall, 1996), a nationally accredited, competency-based curriculum framework. The CGEA takes the view that numeracy is about making meaning of mathematics and has developed a set of learning outcomes in keeping with this view.

Rather than organizing learning outcomes in the traditional fashion (in accordance with the five standard areas of school math education—number and operation, geometry, data analysis and probability, measurement, and algebra—as described, for example, in the NCTM standards), the CGEA organizes outcomes around the purpose and use of mathematics in social contexts. These outcomes are organized into four different categories, or domains (referred to as different numeracies), across four different levels of student development:

- *Numeracy for practical purposes* concerns aspects of the physical world that have to do with designing, making, and measuring. There are two learning outcomes: design (for example, recognizing and using shapes in packaging, buildings, and art) and measurement (for example, in cooking and making furniture).

- *Numeracy for interpreting society* concerns interpreting and reflecting on numerical and graphical or statistical information of relevance to self, work, or community. The two learning outcomes are data (for example, graphs and statistics of consumer prices or sporting event scores) and numerical information (for example, information on financial transactions from banks or newspaper articles).

- *Numeracy for personal organization* focuses on personal situations and interactions involving money, time, and travel. There are two learning outcomes, one dealing with money and time, the other with location and direction.

• *Numeracy for knowledge* is introduced only at level 3 of the four-level CGEA curriculum framework and deals with the skills needed for further study in mathematics or in other areas of study that require an understanding of math. Learning outcomes focus on problem solving and algebraic and graphical techniques. At this level adults begin to learn (or relearn) the formal aspects of mathematics.

Within the individual CGEA learning outcomes themselves, the assessment criteria that need to be met by students are broken down into three subcategories: mathematical knowledge and techniques, language, and interpretation. Even at this level of detail the emphasis is not only on mathematical skills but on the skills of communicating about the mathematics involved in problems and interpreting the solutions.

Consequences follow from this way of designing curriculum standards. First is the actual importance of mathematics. The CGEA states that numeracy is about using math for some particular social purpose within a certain context, and the implication is that mathematics is an important, useful, and vital tool in contemporary society. It also acknowledges that formal mathematics has its place, at least as a pathway to further study, through the fourth category of learning outcomes, "numeracy for knowledge." Second, the CGEA encourages the teaching of numeracy in a holistic, integrated way, and literacy and numeracy are often taught together. For numeracy teachers who do not have formal training in math, the CGEA learning outcomes are easier to understand and work with than the traditional school-based mathematics curriculum (Ciancone & Tout, 2001).

In both the RME approach of the Netherlands and the CGEA in Australia, the curriculum is based on teaching in a context. In such environments, teaching becomes task-oriented—that is, it involves engaging students in problem solving via investigations or projects involving real-life mathematics. Teachers develop realistic tasks or investigations that are of interest to the students, and students then go about solving the problems posed. The mathematics skills that are taught arise out of the tasks being investigated. One consequence of this arrangement is that classes engage in whole group, small group, and individual work, and this is also how the math skills are learned and practiced. Another consequence is that conventional textbooks do not really suit this approach. The learning involved requires students to work actively on projects or investigations, not to work their way through a sequence of sums or word problems in a book. As discussed further later in this chapter, the assessment that tends to follow from this approach is not test-based.

A range of teaching resources have been developed in Australia that model a constructivist approach to what is considered to be good adult numeracy teaching practice (Marr & Helme, 1990; Goddard, Marr, & Martin, 1991). These resources are grounded in a method of teaching adult numeracy that does the following:

- Encourages and uses familiar and relevant language in the classroom

- Encourages students to work cooperatively to encourage interaction and discussion and to help them learn from each other

- Encourages enjoyment and success

- Uses practical and "hands-on" materials

- Tries to place learning in a context that students know and understand, drawing on their backgrounds, interests, and experiences

- Helps students learn through understanding, not by relying on memorization

ASSESSMENT. To match the philosophy and approach of their RME framework, adult educators in the Netherlands developed a comprehensive assessment scheme called the Supermarket Strategy (van Groenestijn, Matthijsse, & van Amersfoort, 1992). The Supermarket Strategy is designed to evaluate not only students' success or failure in solving mathematics problems but also the strategies they use to do so. To be consistent with the RME approach, assessment items and processes consist of functional problems from everyday life that students can solve by means of their own methods. A mock advertising leaflet is used to provide a realistic stimulus for sets of supermarket-related problems. Observation of the ways in which the students solve the problems are the source of profiles of their "capabilities that combine both qualitative and quantitative elements, rather than a single summary 'standardized score' or a 'grade level' as often used in other countries" (van Groenestijn, 2000, p. 342).

In Australia, most assessments in ABE (for both literacy and numeracy) are based on a range of different options through which teachers create a portfolio of evidence by collecting samples of student work, recording their observations of student activities, and collecting student self-assessments or journal entries. The nature of the portfolio that is developed depends on the curriculum being followed. Neither national nor state-based tests are used. Standards are maintained and kept consistent by having teachers moderate student work with other teachers—that is, teachers from different providers meet to discuss and come to a general agreement about the proficiency scope and level of samples of student work.

On a national level, the Australian government instituted a scheme of assessment that all nationally funded programs in adult literacy or ESOL are required to use. Because the federal government runs a number of labor market programs and workplace education programs, along with migrant education programs, this scheme, called the National Reporting System (NRS), has become a major assessment tool in ABE across the country (Coates, Fitzpatrick, McKenna, & Makin, 1995). A team of adult numeracy practitioners was recruited to write the numeracy components of the NRS, and this group, working within a very tight time frame, developed an assessment scheme that attempted to support a constructivist view of numeracy education. Student performance is assessed on the basis of four criteria, which are described somewhat differently for each of the five levels of the NRS. Generally, the criteria can be described in terms of the ability to

- Identify the mathematical information and relationships in the task
- Perform the mathematics required to carry out the task
- Reflect on the effect of the use of the mathematics for the task, including interpreting results and commenting on the appropriateness of the mathematics for the circumstances
- Use informal and formal language, symbolic notation, and the conventions of mathematics needed to carry out and report on the task

These indicators are then supported in detail by such criteria as mathematical knowledge, conditions of performance, problem-solving strategies, mathematical representation, and meaning-making strategies.

The NRS has not resulted in the development of standardized tests, either for placement or for formative or summative assessment. Teachers and programs are encouraged to develop tools for assessment that are suited to the needs of their programs and students. In recent years, as use of the NRS has increased, inexperienced teachers have wanted to use students' pages of sums to assess numeracy. Doing sums does not meet the requirements of the NRS—to meet the four criteria, students need to undertake some form of problem solving that involves a range of skills (identification, communication, reflection, and so on), not just computation.

TEACHER SUPPORT AND PROFESSIONAL DEVELOPMENT. As in the United States, countries such as the United Kingdom and Australia have begun to recognize the need for adequate training and support of adult numeracy practitioners. Coben and Chanda (1997) describe the ad hoc nature of adult numeracy training in the United Kingdom and list a range of reasons why this training is unpopular with practitioners: lack of experienced or qualified numeracy staff to act as leaders or mentors, lack of funding, lack of well-developed training materials—all of which reflect numeracy's somewhat second-class status in ABE when compared with literacy. The authors believe that a program for teacher training in numeracy should be developed that is based on articulated theory and research: "The accreditation framework for numeracy teachers has developed largely without benefit of research and underpinning theory. There has been no involvement of universities, which are, after all, institutions where educational research is undertaken" (p. 386). The authors go on to recommend a program for teacher training developed in Australia in 1995 by the ABE faculty at a university. Called *Adult Numeracy Teaching: Making Meaning in Mathematics* (Johnston & Tout 1995), the published program was designed to establish a link between theory, research, and practice.

Adult Numeracy Teaching (ANT) is an eighty-four-hour training program developed as a continuation of other available numeracy training programs (such as *Breaking the Maths Barrier* [Marr & Helme, 1991]) and as a pathway to postgraduate courses in ABE at universities. In discussing professional development courses in Australia, Tout and Marr (1997) cite the need to develop "four models of adult numeracy professional development and training. These can be described loosely under the categories (a) conference sessions and workshops, (b) short-term in-service programs, (c) long-term in-service programs, and (d) postgraduate study" (p. 149). The third and fourth of these are needed, the authors argue, because "substantial change in teaching practice requires extensive attention to teacher attitudes and hidden theories upon which their current teaching is based. Thus the need has emerged for even more substantial, theoretically based, professional development programs, which provide opportunities for participants to reflect seriously on their current practice and the inner beliefs which guide such practice" (p. 150). Out of this perceived need, the ANT course was developed. A number of universities across Australia have given ANT advanced credit status, such that completing the course makes practitioners eligible for credit toward subjects in postgraduate ABE teacher training courses.

The ANT program is designed to help practitioners develop a critical appreciation of the role mathematics plays in society and espouses a constructivist approach to teaching and learning, calling for practitioners to do some mathematics themselves. The idea that "to teach numeracy you must know how to do mathematics" (p. x) is clearly communicated.

Policy

As in the United States, adult numeracy provision in other countries is often the poor relation to literacy. In Australia, federal policy initiatives refer largely to "literacy," although somewhere in a document a clause may be added stating that literacy includes numeracy or some more minor form of numeracy, such as recognition of numbers. In other countries numeracy is often included under the label "basic skills."

All the same, numeracy is alive and well in both Australia and the Netherlands because it is now embedded in curriculum and assessment frameworks and instructional materials. One way to ensure proper acknowledgment of numeracy in policy is to involve numeracy educators in the development of curriculum frameworks, assessment schemes, and teaching materials. Once numeracy is written into such frameworks on an equal footing with literacy, students and teachers will expect numeracy education to be provided. This expectation can then lead to policy development. In Australia, for example, all ABE and adult ESOL curriculum documents now incorporate a substantial numeracy stream. Its inclusion began when a number of ABE programs made numeracy an equal partner to literacy. The NRS followed suit, and now the ESOL curriculum, which had been concerned mainly with oral communication, has been extended to include numeracy skills.

IMPLICATIONS FOR RESEARCH, PRACTICE, AND POLICY

Numeracy, not just literacy and language, should be considered a central focus of adult basic education. If this goal is to be realized, adult numeracy education must be supported by research, embraced in practice, and clearly communicated in policy at federal, state, and local levels.

As a first step toward significantly improving numeracy education for adults, those in the ABE field might consider the strategies for improving math and science education for K–12 students recommended in *An Action Strategy for Improving Achievement in Mathematics and Science* (U.S. Department of Education, 1998). These strategies correspond with those identified at the Conference on Adult Mathematical Literacy (Gal & Schmitt, 1994) and published in the ensuing *Framework for Adult Numeracy Standards* sponsored by the Adult Numeracy Network (Curry et al., 1996). From these recommendations, we emphasize the following:

- Conduct research into how adults learn mathematics.
- Improve teacher preparation.
- Create challenging and engaging curricula.
- Improve public understanding of today's mathematics.
- Coordinate federal, state, and local efforts.

This coherent list of strategies could provide a strong foundation from which the field can plan to proceed. We have used them as such to formulate our specific recommendations for improving research, practice, and policy in adult numeracy education.

Research

Research in adult numeracy in the United States is thin. We need to develop a research culture. Research should focus on issues of cognition and attempt to ask questions about both the numeracy demands of society and the ways in which adults can develop numerate thinking to meet those demands. We need to know more about how adults think mathematically, what resources they bring to bear in approaching and solving problems, and what instructional interventions support the development of adult numerate thinking. Research also needs to be conducted about adult students' inherent attitudes toward math—about math anxiety and the effect it has on students' ability to learn. Research centers such as NCSALL, NCAL, and NIFL should join with collaboratives such as the Adult Numeracy Network and Adults Learning Mathematics to develop a strategic research agenda that connects research with practice and policy. Practitioner research such as that described by Meader (2001) or that conducted by the Massachusetts ABE Math Team is a good model for moving forward in this respect. But other lines of research need to be developed as well.

There is no doubt that the research in K–12 mathematics education has much to offer ABE. Methods and findings from studies on children's and teachers' mathematical understandings published in the NCTM's *Journal for Research in Mathematics Education,* for example, can serve as models for research into the adult learners and their teachers. Gender studies conducted in K–12 math education are particularly relevant to adult numeracy practice because the majority of ABE students are women, as are their teachers. There are also lessons from the research into instruction that has produced the recommendations promoted by Grouws and Cebulla (2000), the functional math curriculum for schools, and the standards described by the NCTM. The outcomes of such K–12 research should be adapted and used in teaching adult numeracy.

However, it must also be acknowledged that adult numeracy educators are faced with a set of circumstances quite different from those of K–12 educators. In his preface to *Perspectives on Adults Learning Mathematics,* Bishop (2000) argues, for instance, that research in adult mathematics education is a much more complex endeavor than research in K–12 mathematics education. In many ways, he says, practice in the former is less circumscribed, its goals less explicit, the location and time more varied, materials and assessments less publicly available, and teachers less recognized and, by many accounts, uncertified. These differences suggest that school mathematics' theoretical paradigms in research, practice, and policy must be carefully scrutinized for appropriateness to ABE.

Consequently, it is also important to learn from overseas research on adult numeracy. The proceedings from the annual conferences of Adults Learning Mathematics—A Research Forum (to date, seven volumes) and the recent compendia edited by Gal (2000) and Coben et al. (2000) are books that must become part of the knowledge base of U.S. practitioners and policymakers as well as researchers.

Practice

Improvements in practice will depend on improvements in teacher preparation and in curriculum, instruction, and assessment.

TEACHER PREPARATION. Adult numeracy personnel in the United States seem to be in need of more teacher support and professional development. A large segment of ABE teachers lacks pedagogical and content knowledge adequate to teach adults mathematics. Any change in practice needs to begin by equipping ABE teachers with both pedagogical and content knowledge of numeracy as well as with good instruction techniques, instructional materials, curriculum frameworks, and assessment instruments. A range of substantial and innovative professional development and training programs can support this knowledge acquisition. These programs should be built on the broad definition of numeracy described in this chapter and on what is known from K–12 mathematics research, from fields such as ethnomathematics, and from overseas numeracy practices in these areas.

Toward these ends, ABE should consider using some of the Australian adult numeracy teacher training materials as a basis for developing a similar range of training and professional development materials in the United States. Once these materials have been developed, state and regional adult literacy resource centers and state departments of education should provide teachers and volunteer tutors with the training, and universities should be encouraged to offer courses in adult numeracy or adult mathematics education. The creation of state and local teams of teachers who come together over a period of years to implement change in their classrooms is as important as the development of training materials. This team approach has proven to be an essential factor in making progress in this area, as is seen in the teams in New York City and Massachusetts.

CHALLENGING AND ENGAGING CURRICULUM, INSTRUCTION, AND ASSESSMENT. Another crucial aspect of improving practice is the writing of innovative curriculum. Cohesive, comprehensive curricula are needed that will provide students with opportunities for problem solving and communication and that connect with real and important issues in their lives. One good U.S. curriculum guide is *A Framework for Adult Numeracy Standards* (Curry et al., 1996). These curriculum standards consolidate several perspectives, mainly those supported by the NCTM, the Secretary's Commission on Achieving Necessary Skills (SCANS, 1991), and the ABE Mathematics Team in Massachusetts (Leonelli & Schwendeman, 1994) but also those of adult learners, numeracy teachers, and employers. The *Framework for Adult Numeracy Standards* is organized into seven broad themes or areas:

- Relevance and connections to real-life situations
- Problem solving, reasoning, and decision making
- Communication of mathematical ideas and processes
- Number and number sense
- Data
- Geometry: spatial sense and measurement
- Algebra: patterns and functions

The first three themes concern processes of being numerate, while the latter four cover key content areas of mathematics. This model supports the view that numeracy is about making meaning of mathematics. It should be promoted and used in more states in the development of ABE curriculum. More documentation of good practice in adult numeracy curriculum and instruction is already starting to appear through organizations such as ANN and Adults Learning Mathematics. Other, more recent articles that promote good practice in teaching numeracy (such as Ginsburg & Gal, 2000; Kloosterman et al., 2000) need to be disseminated and their recommended approaches actively promoted to teachers and instructors.

Curriculum developers should look further afield than to those materials now available commercially. They should examine the reform curriculum in K–12 that emphasizes problem solving and investigation over formulaic approaches. The EMPower Project currently in development at TERC has been funded by the National Science Foundation to do just that. Guided by the ANN framework, the project is adapting three K–12 reform curricula to ABE settings.

The field might also consider using some of the ideas behind the Australian Certificates in General Education for Adults (Kindler et al., 1996). In instruction, curriculum, and assessment, both the Netherlands and Australia have developed frameworks (for example, RME, the CGEA, and the Australian NRS) and related teaching approaches and materials that appear to be consistent with recommendations and approaches developed for U.S. K–12 math education, including ethnomathematics and functional math. It also appears that Australia has developed a comprehensive range of numeracy teacher preparation programs (*Breaking the Maths Barrier* and *Adult Numeracy Teaching*). Although all these frameworks and approaches cannot simply be transported and directly applied to ABE in the United States, it would be worthwhile to consider how they might be adapted and utilized in developing similar schemes here.

An analysis of good adult numeracy practice overseas (for example, the activities in both the Netherlands and Australia) and in K–12 mathematics education (for example, the NCTM standards) shows that those in the best position to improve numeracy education in ABE are practitioners, especially experienced practitioners. These practitioners need to become involved in developing curriculum standards, assessment tools, training programs for other teachers, and instructional materials for students. There are signs of such activity already. The Adult Numeracy Network and citywide and statewide teams of practitioners have become involved with developing curriculum frameworks, and the EMPower Project at TERC is developing teaching materials.

Similarly, any assessment or testing systems used should be aligned with and support these new types of curriculum and instruction. Improvement in curriculum will have little effect if assessment practices conflict with teaching practices. Morale and practice can suffer, and assessment practices can end up driving instructional and materials development. Assessment practices based on NCTM approaches such as the ANN framework and on overseas adult numeracy practices, such as those in the Netherlands and Australia, should be considered. For the U.S. assessment systems now being used, such as the GED, CASAS, TABE, ABLE, and AMES, it would be useful to have numeracy practitioners and researchers work with test developers to institute strategies and resources that will support teachers in introducing good assessment practices.

Policy

Why has literacy upstaged numeracy in the language of policymaking? One obvious reason is that leadership and advocacy for ABE comes from practitioners and researchers with backgrounds in language and literacy. They are the ones who have helped their respective fields mature, developed theoretical frameworks, and conducted research to advance the body of knowledge about how adults come to acquire another language and learn to read. They are the ones who have influenced policy. Experienced numeracy practitioners and researchers—and they do exist—need to be included and supported in the development of any ABE policy.

PUBLIC UNDERSTANDING OF TODAY'S MATHEMATICS. The public needs to see the importance of numeracy—not simply mathematics—as a personal resource that can benefit the community at large. A campaign promoting the idea that all adults can and should improve their numeracy skills could be the backdrop for the involvement of ABE. Numeracy campaigns should stress the need for all adults to expand their repertoire of math skills in interpreting and manipulating numerical information and concepts. We've been a population ridden with math fear and math avoidance. A campaign to educate the public about the importance of numeracy must address these issues. ABE needs to join forces with K–12 as well as international adult numeracy experts to develop a successful public relations campaign.

COORDINATED FEDERAL, STATE, AND LOCAL EFFORTS. Changes at the policy level often flow from the work undertaken by practitioners, as can be illustrated by the stable and established state of numeracy practices in the Netherlands, the United Kingdom, and Australia, where over a number of years practitioners successfully developed the curriculum standards, assessment tools, training programs, and instructional materials. All the strategies outlined here in the sections on research and practice, if pursued over a period of time, will eventually filter through at the policy level. But, again, experienced teachers must become involved to argue the adult numeracy case—not only with the policymakers but with their literacy and ABE, ASE, and ESOL colleagues. Other practitioners must be convinced that numeracy should be an equal and valid part of service provision. The National

Council of Teachers of Mathematics, the National Science Foundation, and the U.S. Department of Education should be lobbied to launch a campaign to improve adult numeracy. In addition, the National Reporting System and the Equipped for the Future initiative should establish links with the Adult Numeracy Network and Adults Learning Mathematics—A Research Forum to open up the lines of communication between practitioners and policymakers.

Two documents have the potential to serve as unifying guides for efforts at all levels: the Adult Literacy and Lifeskills Survey's *Numeracy Framework,* which defines numeracy and numerate behavior, and the ANN framework, which targets the curricular areas to be developed.

CONCLUSION

Numeracy, as defined in this paper, should be viewed as part of the core skill base of any literate individual. ABE advocates need to share that view as well, and this new "language, literacy, and numeracy" perspective should be clearly articulated in federal, state, and local policy and public relations documents. Only then will policy documents and the necessary teacher training programs and curriculum and assessment practices provide a platform from which comprehensive and successful numeracy instructional programs can be developed. Without the emphasis on numeracy as a core essential skill, one that is critical for adults in society, ABE will be unable to fulfill its promise as a second chance for all the adults who choose to participate. Numeracy needs to be brought to the fore.

Notes

1. The authors make a distinction between the words *real* and *realistic.* The former refers to real adults managing real situations in the real world, whereas the latter implies adults operating within someone's simulation or approximation of the real world. A word problem from a math book about unit pricing would be an example of "realistic" math, whereas the shopper's activity while making decisions in the supermarket would be a "real" situation.
2. Since *literacy* is sometimes used as a synonym for adult basic education, we include in this first grouping the body of literature about literacy programs and the practice of literacy instruction.

3. For these we drew from the Division of Adult Education and Literacy Clearinghouse Bibliography of Resource Materials 1998 because it lists the major U.S. policy and advocacy documents published from 1989 to 1998 and from other major documents published from 1998 to 2000 (for example, *From the Margins to the Mainstream, EFF Content Standards*).

4. For this we referred to the results of an ERIC search of the Boolean logic on keywords *adult basic education* and *mathematics education*, with the United States as the geographic source. We also consulted dissertation abstracts (1980–2000) that deal with math in U.S. ABE and GED settings, publishers' catalogs for 1999–2000 on adult education instructional and assessment materials, and a sampling of practitioner-published work on the issue of ABE/GED mathematics instruction.

5. ANN was founded in 1994 at the Conference on Adult Mathematical Literacy, sponsored by the National Center on Adult Literacy, the National Council of Teachers of Mathematics, and the U.S. Department of Education.

6. To subscribe to the *Math Practitioner* discussion list, send an e-mail message to majordomo@world.std.com. Type *subscribe numeracy* in the message area.

7. Although this number comes from participation data directly reported by ABE, ASE, and ESOL programs to federal and state government agencies, it is interesting to note its close approximation to findings from the 1999 National Household Education Survey. From this survey, it was estimated that 46 percent of the U.S. adult population, or 90 million adults, participated in some form of adult education. Adult basic education participants (ABE, GED, and ESOL) accounted for about 5 percent of adults who participate in some form of adult education. According to this report, more than 50 percent of those adults with less than a high school diploma who participate in any adult education activity reported being enrolled in ABE, GED, or ESOL (NCES, 1999).

8. In the Division of Adult Education and Literacy Clearinghouse Bibliography of Resource Materials 1998 (http://www.ed.gov/offices/OVAE/bib98.html), a list of special populations and areas of interest included adults with disabilities/special learning needs; correctional education; English as a second language (ESL); family literacy; health literacy; homeless, welfare reform; older persons; staff development; technology, volunteers, and workplace/workforce literacy; skill standards; adult education program management; competency based education; evaluation/assessment; GED; and life skills.

9. In the Division of Adult Education and Literacy Clearinghouse Bibliography of Resource Materials 1998, a manual search found the word *math* or *mathematics* or *numeracy* listed in the titles of 5 documents, whereas the term *literacy* was listed 213 times.

10. For more information about ethnomathematics, see Ascher, 1991; Harris, 1991; Nelson, Joseph, & William, 1993; Powell & Frankenstein, 1997.

11. For more information on ethnomathematics research with adults, see Harris, 1991, 1997, 2000; Knijnik, 1997, 2000; Nunes, Schliemann, & Carraher, 1993; and Schliemann, 1998.

12. For interpretations in terms of adult numeracy see van Groenestijn, 2000, and Matthijsse, 2000.

References

Adult Literacy and Basic Skills Unit. (1994). *Basic skills research: Bibliography of research in adult literacy and basic skills.* London: Author.

Advisory Council for Adult and Continuing Education. (1982). *Adults' mathematical ability and performance.* Leicester, UK: Author.

Ascher, M. (1991). *Ethnomathematics: A multicultural view of mathematical ideas.* New York: Chapman & Hall.

Barnes, M. (1988). Mathematics: A barrier for women? In B. Caine, M. de Lepervach, & E. Grosz (Eds.), *Crossing boundaries.* Sydney: Allen & Unwin.

Beder, H. (1999). *The outcomes and impacts of adult literacy education in the United States* (NCSALL Report #6.). Cambridge, MA: National Center for the Study of Adult Learning and Literacy.

Benn, R. (1997). *Adults count too: Mathematics for empowerment.* Leicester, UK: National Institute of Adult Continuing Education (NIACE).

Bishop, A. (1994). Cultural conflicts in mathematics education: Developing a research agenda. *For the Learning of Mathematics, 14*(2).

Bishop, A. (2000). Overcoming obstacles to the democratization of mathematics education. In H. Fujita (Ed.), *Abstracts of plenary lectures and regular lectures, ICME 9.* Japan: International Congress on Mathematical Education.

Boomer, G. (1994). From catechism to communication: Language, learning and mathematics. In D. Bell & S. Guthrie (Eds.), *An integrated approach to teaching literacy and numeracy.* Sydney: NSW TAFE Commission. (Original work published 1986)

Brooks, G., Giles, K., Harman, J., Kendall, S., Rees, F., & Whittaker, S. (2001). *Assembling the fragments: A review of research on adult basic skills.* (Research Report No. 220). Norwich, UK: DfEE Publications.

Burton, G. M. (1993). *Curriculum and evaluation standards for school mathematics.* Addenda series, grades K–6: Number sense and operations. Reston, VA: National Council of Teachers of Mathematics.

Bynner, J., & Parsons, S. (1997). *Does numeracy matter? Evidence from the National Child Development Study on the impact of poor numeracy on adult life.* London: Basic Skills Agency.

Ciancone, T., & Tout, D. (2001). Learning outcomes: Skills or function? In K. Safford-Ramus & M. J. Schmitt (Eds.), *A conversation between researchers ιd practitioners: Proceedings of the Seventh Annual Conference on Adults Learning Mathematics—ALM7.* Cambridge, MA: National Center for the Study of Adult Learning and Literacy.

Clinton, W. J. (1997, March 6). Preparing students to meet national standards of excellence in eighth grade math and improving math and science education. Presidential Memo for the Secretary of Education and the Director of the National Science Foundation.

Coates, S., Fitzpatrick, L., McKenna, A., & Makin, A. (1995). *National Reporting System.* Melbourne, Australia: Adult, Community and Further Education Board.

Coben, D. (2000). Numeracy, mathematics and adult learning practice. In I. Gal (Ed.), *Adult numeracy development: Theory, research, practice.* Cresskill, NJ: Hampton Press.

Coben, D., & Chanda, N. (1997). Teaching "not less than maths, but more": An overview of recent developments in adult numeracy teacher development in England, with a sidelong glance at Australia. *Teacher Development, 1*(3), 375–392.

Coben, D., O'Donoghue, J., & FitzSimons, G. E. (Eds.). (2000). *Perspectives on adults learning mathematics: Research and practice.* Dordrecht, Netherlands: Kluwer.

Cockcroft, W. H. (1982). *Mathematics counts.* London: HMSO.

Crowther Report. (1959). 15–18: Report of the Central Advisory Council of Education (England). Vol. 1, London: HMSO.

Curry, D., Schmitt, M. J., & Waldron, S. (1996). *A framework for adult numeracy standards: The mathematical skills and abilities adults need to be equipped for the future.* Boston: World Education.

Davis, R., Maher, C., & Noddings, N. (Eds.). (1990). *Constructivist views on the teaching and learning of mathematics.* Reston, VA: National Council of Teachers of Mathematics.

Del Grande, J. (1993). *Curriculum and evaluation standards for school mathematics.* Addenda series, grades K–6: Geometry and spatial sense. Reston, VA: National Council of Teachers of Mathematics.

Department for Education and Employment. (2001). *Skills for life: The national strategy for improving adult literacy and numeracy skills.* Nottingham, UK: DfEE Publications.

Department of Education, Queensland. (1994). *Literacy and numeracy strategy, 1994–98.* Brisbane, Australia: Author.

Dossey, J., & Usiskin, Z. (2000). *Mathematics education in the United States 2000.* Reston, VA: National Council of Teachers of Mathematics.

EQUALS (1986). *Get it together.* Berkeley, CA: Lawrence Hall of Science, University of California.

Ernest, P. (Ed.). (1989). *Mathematics teaching: The state of the art.* Barcombe, UK: Falmer Press.

Ernest, P. (1998). *Social constructivism as a philosophy of mathematics.* Albany, NY: State University of New York Press.

FitzSimons, G. E. (Ed.). (1997). *Adults returning to study mathematics: Papers from working group 18 at the 8th International Congress on Mathematical Education (ICME 8), Sevilla, Spain.* Adelaide: Australian Association of Mathematics Teachers (AAMT).

Foreman, L., & Bennett, A. (1995). *Visual mathematics.* Salem, OR: Math Learning Center.

Forman, S. L., & Steen, L. A. (1999). *Beyond eighth grade: Functional mathematics for life and work.* Berkeley, CA: National Center for Research in Vocational Education, University of California.

Frankenstein, M. (1989). *Relearning mathematics: A different third R—radical maths.* London: Free Association Books.

Fujita, H. (Ed.). (2000). *Abstracts of plenary lectures and regular lectures, ICME 9.* Japan: International Congress on Mathematical Education.

Gal, I. (1993). *Issues and challenges in adult numeracy.* Philadelphia: National Center on Adult Literacy, University of Pennsylvania.

Gal, I. (Ed.). (2000). *Adult numeracy development: Theory, research, practice.* Cresskill, NJ: Hampton Press.

Gal, I., & Schmitt, M. J. (Eds.). (1994). *Proceedings: Conference on Adult Mathematical Literacy.* Philadelphia: National Center on Adult Literacy, University of Pennsylvania.

Gal, I., & Schuh, A. (1994). *Who counts in adult literacy programs? A national survey of numeracy education.* (Technical Report No. TR94–09). Philadelphia: National Center on Adult Literacy, University of Pennsylvania.

Gal, I., & Stoudt, A. (1997–98, Winter). Numeracy: Becoming literate with numbers. *Adult Learning, 9*(2).

Gal, I., van Groenestijn, M., Manly, M., Schmitt, M. J., & Tout, D. (1999). *Numeracy conceptual framework for the international Adult Literacy and Lifeskills (ALL) Survey.* Ottawa: National Center for Educational Statistics and Statistics Canada.

Gerdes, P. (1994, June). Reflections on ethnomathematics. *For the Learning of Mathematics, 14*(2).

Ginsburg, L., & Gal, I. (1995, October 21–24). Linking formal and informal skills: The case of percents. Paper presented at the 17th annual meeting of the North American chapter of the International Group for the Psychology of Mathematics Education, Columbus, OH.

Ginsburg, L. & Gal, I. (2000). Instructional strategies for adult numeracy education. In I. Gal (Ed.), *Adult numeracy development: Theory, research, practice.* Cresskill, NJ: Hampton Press.

Goddard, R., Marr, B., & Martin, J. (1991). *Strength in numbers.* Melbourne, Australia: Adult, Community and Further Education Board.

Gravemeijer, K.P.E. (1994). *Developing realistic mathematics instruction.* Utrecht, Netherlands: Freudenthal Institute.

Grouws, D. A., & Cebulla, K. J. (2000). *Improving student achievement in mathematics.* Brussels: International Academy of Education and International Bureau of Education.

Harris, M. (1991). *Schools, mathematics and work.* Basingstoke, UK: Falmer Press.

Harris, M. (1997). *Common threads: Women, mathematics and work.* Stoke on Trent, Staffordshire: Trentham Books.

Harris, M. (2000). Women, mathematics and work. In D. Coben, J. O'Donoghue, & G. E. FitzSimons (Eds.), *Perspectives on adults learning mathematics: Research and practice.* Dordrecht, Netherlands: Kluwer.

Hatano, G. (1996). A conception of knowledge acquisition and its implication for mathematics education. In L. Steffe & P. Nesher (Eds.), *Theories of mathematical learning.* Mahwah, NJ: Erlbaum.

Johnston, B. (1994, Summer). Critical numeracy. *FinePrint, 16*(4). Melbourne, Australia: VALBEC.

Johnston, B., Baynham, M., Kelly, S., Barlow, K., & Marks, G. (1997). *Numeracy in practice: Effective pedagogy in numeracy for unemployed young people.* Sydney: University of Technology.

Johnston, B., & Tout, D. (1995). *Adult numeracy teaching: Making meaning in mathematics.* Melbourne, Australia: National Staff Development Committee.

Kindler, J., Kenrick, R., Marr, B., Tout, D., & Wignall, L. (1996). *Certificates in general education for adults.* Melbourne, Australia: Adult, Community and Further Education Board.

Kloosterman, P., Hassan, M. A., & Wiest, L. (2000). Building a problem-solving environment for teaching mathematics. In I. Gal (Ed.), *Adult numeracy development: Theory, research, practice.* Cresskill, NJ: Hampton Press.

Knijnik, G. (1997). Mathematics education and the struggle for land in Brazil. In G. E. FitzSimons (Ed.), *Adults returning to study mathematics: Papers from working group 18 at the 8th International Congress on Mathematical Education (ICME 8), Sevilla, Spain.* Adelaide: Australian Association of Mathematics Teachers (AAMT).

Knijnik, G. (2000). Ethnomathematics and political struggles. In D. Coben, J. O'Donoghue, & G. E. FitzSimons (Eds.), *Perspectives on adults learning mathematics: Research and practice.* Dordrecht, Netherlands: Kluwer.

Lee, A., Chapman, A., & Roe, P. (1993). *Report on the pedagogical relationships between adult literacy and numeracy.* Canberra, Australia: Department of Employment, Education and Training.

Leonelli, E., Merson, M. W., & Schmitt, M. J. (Eds.). (1994). *The ABE math standards project.* Vol. 2: *Implementing the Massachusetts adult basic education math standards: Our research stories.* Holyoke, MA: SABES, Holyoke Community College.

Leonelli, E., & Schwendeman, R. (Eds.). (1994). *The ABE math standards project.* Vol. 1: *The Massachusetts adult basic education math standards.* Holyoke, MA: SABES, Holyoke Community College.

Lubienski, S. T. (1999). What's hot? What's not? A survey of mathematics education research 1982–1998. Paper presented at the American Education Research Association Meeting, Montreal.

Malone, J., & Taylor, P. (Eds.). (1993). *Constructivist interpretations of teaching and learning mathematics.* Perth, Australia: National Key Center for School Science and Mathematics, Curtin University of Technology.

Marr, B., & Helme, S. (1990). Mathematical literacy. In D. Tout & J. Kindler, *Working together: New directions in adult basic education.* Melbourne, Australia: Division of Further Education.

Marr, B., & Helme, S. (1991). *Breaking the maths barrier.* Canberra, Australia: Department of Employment, Education and Training.

Matthijsse, W. (2000). Adult numeracy at the elementary level: Addition and subtraction up to 100. In I. Gal (Ed.), *Adult numeracy development: Theory, research, practice.* Cresskill, NJ: Hampton Press.

Meader, P. (2001). A teacher's transformation into teacher-researcher. In K. Safford-Ramus & M. J. Schmitt (Eds.), *A conversation between researchers and practitioners: Proceedings of the Seventh Annual Conference on Adults Learning Mathematics—ALM7*. Boston: National Center for the Study of Adult Learning and Literacy.

Mellin-Olsen, S. (1987). *The politics of mathematics education*. Reidel: Dordrecht.

Mikulecky, L. (1994). Needed skills and skill gaps: Adult numeracy demands, abilities, and instruction. In I. Gal & M. J. Schmitt (Eds.), *Proceedings: Conference on Adult Mathematical Literacy*. Philadelphia: National Center on Adult Literacy, University of Pennsylvania.

Mullinix, B. (1994). *Exploring what counts: Mathematics instruction in adult basic education*. Boston: World Education.

Murnane, R., Willet, J., & Levy, F. (1995, March). The growing importance of cognitive skills in wage determination. (Working Paper No. 50–76). Cambridge, MA: National Bureau of Economic Research.

National Center for Education Statistics (NCES). (1999). National Household Education Survey (NHES), Adult Education Component. Available online: http://www.nces.ed.gov/surveys/nsopf. Access date: April 4, 2000.

National Council of Teachers of Mathematics (NCTM). (1989). *Curriculum and evaluation standards for school mathematics*. Reston, VA: Author.

National Council of Teachers of Mathematics (NCTM). (1991). *Professional standards for teaching mathematics*. Reston, VA: Author.

National Council of Teachers of Mathematics (NCTM). (1995). *Assessment standards for school mathematics*. Reston, VA: Author.

National Council of Teachers of Mathematics (NCTM). (2000). *Principles and standards for school mathematics*. Reston, VA: Author.

National Institute for Literacy. (2000). NIFL Web site, http://www.nifl.gov. Accessed October 2001.

National Literacy Summit 2000 Steering Committee. (2000). *From the margins to the mainstream: An action agenda for literacy*. Washington, DC: Author. Available online: http://www.natcoalitionliteracy.org/. Accessed October 2001.

Nelson, D., Joseph, G. G., & William, J. (1993). *Multicultural mathematics: Teaching mathematics from a global perspective*. Oxford, UK: Oxford University Press.

Nesbit, T. (1996, Summer). What counts? Mathematics education for adults. *Adult Basic Education, 6,* 69–83.

Nunes, T., Schliemann, A., & Carraher, D. (1993). *Street mathematics and school mathematics.* Cambridge, UK: Cambridge University Press.

Powell, A. B., & Frankenstein, M. (Eds.). (1997). *Ethnomathematics: Challenging Eurocentrism in mathematics education.* Albany, NY: State University of New York Press.

Safford-Ramus, K. (2000). A review and summary of research on adult mathematics education in North America (1980–2000). In Hiroshi Fujita (Ed.), *Abstracts of Plenary Lectures and Regular Lectures, ICME 9.* Japan: International Congress on Mathematical Education.

Schliemann, A. D. (1998). Everyday mathematics and adult mathematics education. In M. van Groenestijn and D. Coben, Eds. *Mathematics as part of lifelong learning.* Proceedings of the fifth international conference of "Adults Learning Maths—A Research Forum." London: Goldsmiths College.

Schmitt, M. J. (2000, September). Developing adults' numerate thinking: Getting out from under the workbooks. *Focus on Basics, 4*(B).

Secada, W., Fennema, E., & Adajian, L. (Eds.). (1995). *New directions for equity in mathematics education.* Cambridge, UK: Cambridge University Press.

Secretary's Commission on Achieving Necessary Skills (SCANS). (1991). *What work requires of schools: A SCANS report for America 2000.* Washington, DC: U.S. Department of Labor.

Secretary's Commission on Achieving Necessary Skills (SCANS). (1992). *Learning a living: A blueprint for high performance.* Washington, DC: U.S. Department of Labor.

Stein, S. (2000). *Equipped for the Future content standards: What adults need to know and be able to do in the twenty-first century.* (ED Pubs document EX0099P.) Washington, DC: National Institute for Literacy.

Tobias, S. (1978). *Overcoming math anxiety.* New York: Norton.

Tout, D. (2000, September). A Global numeracy? Does it exist? Paper presented at "Lens on Literacy," the Australian Council for Adult Literacy National Conference, Perth, Australia.

Tout, D., & Marr, B. (1997). Changing practice: Adult numeracy professional development. In G. E. FitzSimons (Ed.), *Adults returning to study mathematics: Papers from working group 18 at the 8th International Congress on Mathematical Education (ICME 8), Sevilla, Spain.* Adelaide: Australian Association of Mathematics Teachers (AAMT).

U.S. Department of Education. (1989). Report of the National Educational Goals Panel. Washington, DC: U.S. Department of Education.

U.S. Department of Education. (1997). *Statistical performance tables.* Washington, DC: Author.

U.S. Department of Education. (1998). *An action strategy for improving achievement in mathematics and science.* Washington, DC: Author.

U.S. Department of Education. (2000a). *Before it's too late.* A report to the nation from the National Commission on Mathematics and Science Teaching for the 21st Century [The Glenn Commission Report]. Washington, DC: Author.

U.S. Department of Education. (2000b, June). *National reporting system for adult education: Implementation guidelines.* Washington, DC: Author.

van Groenestijn, M. (2000). Assessment of adult students' mathematical strategies. In I. Gal (Ed.), *Adult numeracy development: Theory, research, practice.* Cresskill, NJ: Hampton Press.

van Groenestijn, M., Matthijsse, W., & van Amersfoort, J. (1992). *Supermarktstrategie, een procedure voor niveaubepalen bij rekenen in de basiseducatie* [Supermarket strategy: A procedure to determine the level of numeracy in adult basic education]. Utrecht, Netherlands: Stichting IDEE.

Walkerdine, V. (1989). *Counting girls out.* London: Virago Education and University of London Institute of Education.

Ward, J. E. (2000). Arkansas GED mathematics instruction: History repeating itself. In K. Safford-Ramus & M. J. Schmitt (Eds.), *Proceedings of the Seventh Annual Adult Learning Mathematics Conference—ALM7.* Cambridge, MA: National Center for the Study of Adult Learning and Literacy.

Willis, S. (1989). *Real girls don't do math: Gender and the construction of privilege.* Geelong, Australia: Deakin University Press.

Zaslavsky, C. (1994a). "Africa Counts" and ethnomathematics. In *For the Learning of Mathematics, 14*(2).

Zaslavsky, C. (1994b). *Fear of math: How to get over it and get on with your life.* New Brunswick, NJ: Rutgers University Press.

CHAPTER SIX

Professionalization and Certification for Teachers in Adult Basic Education

John P. Sabatini
Lynda Ginsburg
Mary Russell

M any factors have converged over the past decade to steadily accelerate the drive for professionalization in the field of adult literacy. In a number of states, professional development support and infrastructures have become well established, and efforts to codify these efforts in systems of certification are under way (Belzer, Drennon, & Smith, 2001; National Institute for Literacy, 2000). The U.S. Department of Education's development of a National Reporting System (NRS) and the accountability requirements contained in Title II (the Adult and Family Literacy Act) of the Workforce Investment Act (WIA) of 1998 have reinforced this trend. By the first quarter of 2000, dozens of states were initiating and implementing standards and accountability systems to better monitor the effectiveness of adult basic education (ABE) programs. Programs will be held to higher standards for student outcomes and to stronger indicators of program quality. One such indicator is the existence of ongoing staff development processes and program planning processes (Office of Vocational and Adult Education, 1992).

Legislative mandates are not the only nor perhaps even the main force sustaining professionalization efforts, however. ABE professional organizations, researchers, and service providers have long debated, advocated, and experimented with models for certification (Galbraith & Gilley, 1986). The National Literacy Summit convened more than twenty-five meetings across the country, bringing together instructors, tutors, service providers, learners, businesspeople, and policymakers to inform the priorities of its national action agenda. *From the Margins to the Mainstream: An Action Agenda for Literacy,* the report from the National Literacy Summit (2000), includes a number of proposals aimed at creating a comprehensive, high-quality delivery system for adult learners by improving the quality of instruction available to them. This action agenda asks all states to "establish a certification process for instructional staff based on standards that value both academic knowledge and life experience" and "to include alternative [teacher] assessment methods such as portfolios."

What kinds of professionalization efforts are being advocated? Webb (1997) answers this question succinctly: "Many states are seeking to establish standards or criteria that distinguish adult educators as professionals and that reflect what these educators need to know to successfully teach adults." The rationale is to advance professionalism in a mostly part-time field in a way that distinguishes it from K–12. Many believe that K–12 standards for professionalism do not necessarily translate into ABE standards.

Yet there is a definition of the term *professionalization* that can be applied not only to both K–12 and ABE but to numerous other professions, from medicine to law. Essentially, *professionalization* is the movement in any field toward some standards of educational preparation and competency. Professionalization is a movement to apply the following measures (Shanahan, Meehan, & Mogge, 1994, p. 1):

• Use education or training to improve the quality of practice.

• Standardize professional responses.[1]

• Better define a collection of persons as representing a field of endeavor.

• Enhance communication within that field.

Shanahan, Meehan, and Mogge (1994) define *professionalization* as "the process of using education and certification to enhance the quality of performance of those within an occupational field" (p. iii). *Certification* is defined by Galbraith and Gilley (1985) as "the process by which a professional organization or an independent external agency recognizes the competence of individual practitioners" (p. 12). These definitions reflect our understanding of the two terms as we use them in this chapter.

In reviewing processes of certification across professions, Galbraith and Gilley (1986) concluded that the primary purpose was to promote professional competencies of members. Secondary purposes included promoting professionalism and public prestige through the identification of an agreed-upon body of knowledge, a set of competencies, and a regulatory mechanism that evaluates proficiency of practitioners before they can achieve professional status. The restrictive nature of regulatory mechanisms (self-imposed by the professional community) communicates the importance of the knowledge and competencies, as well as defining and stabilizing group membership as unique and distinct. The motives for certification are many, including the desire for self-improvement, increased status, and control of access to and level of competency in the profession. There is also concern that requirements will be imposed on the field by state and federal legislators if it does not take action itself. Certification helps practitioners by providing a structure that clearly communicates the expectations of the profession, allowing practitioners to measure themselves and develop plans of self-improvement against established standards.

Galbraith and Gilley (1985, 1986) emphasized the importance of a program of certification being developed voluntarily by a professional organization (as opposed to being mandated by legislative bodies) that represents the interests and needs of the profession (as opposed to the interests of political bodies), and they predicate their program model on this distinction. In the absence of a single, strong national organization speaking and representing the profession of adult literacy educators, state-level professional organizations, coalitions, and advocacy groups, often working in tandem with the state agencies that administer ABE, have taken on the role of moving and shaping certification programs and processes.

To advance professionalization for teachers of adult literacy, with their particular needs and concerns, Webb (1997) proposes action in the following areas:

• Promote professional growth that is "valid and distinct" to ABE and is recognized or affirmed by school boards, employers of adult educators, and the local community.

• Develop teaching certificates that are tied directly to ABE curricula and learner needs.

• Establish criteria to distinguish a "professional" adult literacy educator from a volunteer in a field in which the vast majority of practitioners are part-time and many are volunteers.

• Examine the impact of certification standards on teacher performance in the classroom, with concern for balancing the need to establish and maintain professional standards with the need to avoid screening out good but noncredentialed teachers.

When Shanahan, Meehan, and Mogge (1994) reviewed the issue of professionalization, they characterized previous discussions and debates as controversial, negative, and heated, marked more by discord than unity. A key point of disagreement was whether or under what conditions certification could be considered necessary or desirable. They found only two points of consensus: the desire to improve the quality of teaching and the recognition of how difficult it would be to establish a process to improve it. The fieldwork we conducted for this report has led us to a more optimistic forecast. Although some unresolved concerns remain and recent changes in federal legislation have left the field somewhat uneasy, a common desire for consensus appears to be emerging. In this chapter, we identify and discuss the forces at work in this more positive atmosphere and review the concerns that continue to arise when the processes of teacher professionalization and certification are implemented.

WHAT ABE CAN LEARN
FROM THE K–12 EXPERIENCE

Adult basic education has long been in the shadow of the K–12 education system, sharing or adapting its curriculum and standards, classrooms, means of assessment, resources, and teachers. In a survey of over four hundred full-time and part-time adult basic educators, Sabatini and colleagues (2000) found that only 20 percent had taught solely in adult literacy, with most beginning their careers as elementary or secondary school teachers. To professionalize their field, adult literacy educators must step out from the shadow of the K–12 system and recognize themselves as an allied but unique professional community. In doing so, however, it would be wise to learn from the successes and failures of the K–12 system. Of particular interest to the field is the attention now being paid to the quality of K–12 teachers and teacher preparation programs. A new emphasis on higher student achievement, demands for greater accountability, and research demonstrating the importance of teacher quality on student achievement (American Federation of Teachers, 2000) have all raised the stakes for K–12 teachers.

A reform model has emerged as a driving force in the K–12 arena: what the learner needs to know is expressed in the form of content and curriculum standards, which in turn inform teaching competencies, which in turn inform teacher certification and professional development. Content standards also form the basis for the development of student achievement and outcome assessments—a key accountability tool for evaluating teacher, program, and school effectiveness. Reviewing this model as it works in the K–12 arena is useful for evaluating the extent to which adult literacy educators may or may not want to adopt K–12 initiatives.

Content Standards

Content standards are increasingly the driving force behind efforts to reform teacher standards, certification, professional development, and accountability in the K–12 system. Learners, teachers, schools, and school systems are held accountable for learner outcomes based on assessments aligned with content standards. These standards indicate what is of value to learn and to know. They provide a framework for the content and pedagogical knowledge a teacher is expected to have mastered. K–12 standards typically have credibility among K–12 teachers because they are developed and issued by consortia of national councils, boards of teachers, and content experts—that is, the professional organizations of the teaching profession (for example, National Council for the Social Studies, 1994; National Council of Teachers of Mathematics, 2000; National Research Council, 1996).

Content standards are also used as a foundation for the development of teaching standards or competencies (for the purposes of this chapter, we consider the terms *teaching standards* and *competencies* to be interchangeable; the former tends to be the term used in K–12 education, the latter the term used in ABE). For example, the National

Committee on Science Education uses the phrase "professional development standards" to describe its expectations of science teachers, describing them as a "vision for the development of professional knowledge and skill among teachers" (National Research Council, 1996, p. 4). Teaching standards or competencies form the basis for developing indicators and assessments of teaching quality, just as content standards form the basis for student outcome assessments. When teaching standards are adopted, evidence of proficiency need not be indirectly certified in the form of completed coursework or a score on a standardized exam but rather through a competency-based system using performance assessments (for example, National Board for Professional Teaching Standards Certification).

Certification

States offer many levels and types of certification, specifying the grade levels, subjects, and conditions under which a teacher may teach. Early childhood (ages one to five), elementary, middle, secondary, and special education are typical certification types. Many states have requirements for professional development to maintain initial and second-stage certificate validity. States offer separate certifications for teachers, administrators, and other support specialists such as librarians, counselors, and reading specialists.

Closely linked to certification is a state's process for evaluating and approving teacher preparation programs. The purpose of such approval or accreditation is to ensure a common curriculum framework and professional standards so that the state's teacher education programs produce graduates who meet the state's certification requirements. Most states use the standards developed by the National Council for Accreditation of Teacher Education (NCATE) (ERIC Digest, 1986).

The preparation of teachers as professionals is routinely the culmination of an undergraduate, four-year program that includes seven steps: (1) liberal arts and sciences course requirements, (2) entry standards for acceptance into teacher education programs, (3) courses in pedagogy, (4) academic subject major (for most), (5) clinical experience, (6) exit and licensure requirements, and (7) an induction period (American Federation of Teachers, 2000). Initial K–12 teacher certification requirements typically include the following:

- Graduation from an accredited higher education institution that has a state-approved teacher education program. This includes a minimum grade-point average on coursework and successful completion of a field-based clinical experience. Some states accept completion of out-of-state teacher preparation programs approved by the NCATE.

- Review of college transcripts and other evidence to ensure that specific coursework and other state requirements have been met.

- Satisfactory scores on licensing exams. Currently, forty states require basic skills exams, thirty require subject-matter exams, and twenty-five require "knowledge of teaching" exams. There are nineteen general knowledge exams and thirteen assessments of teaching performance. Only six states require no examination for initial teacher certification.

In most cases, certification must be renewed or updated regularly. There are typically requirements for periodic maintenance activities to ensure that teachers keep current (such as completion of additional coursework or in-service activities) and that higher levels of proficiency be attained within a specified time (such as earning an M.A.). Completion of requirements in an area of specialization may be a requirement or an option, leading in some states to what is known as a certificate endorsement. Endorsements are typically add-ons to, not substitutes for, certification. For instance, a secondary education teacher might have endorsements in specific subject areas. Adding an endorsement to an existing certification type is one way to introduce change and flexibility to a certification process that is well established, highly specific, and not otherwise susceptible to change by outsiders.

State-funded K–12 school systems and some state community college systems (California, North Carolina, and Iowa at present) have regulations that include certifications in hiring requirements. Non-state-funded educational entities, such as private K–12 schools, while not governed by these regulations, in many cases choose to require certifications when making hiring decisions. Alternative systems exist to certify individuals with expertise or experience who have not completed a four-year program. Emergency waivers are issued when the demand for teachers exceeds the supply.

Governance and Stakeholders

Governance and stakeholders in the K–12 system are consistent across states and include state legislatures, state departments of education, local school boards, professional education organizations, teachers' unions, school administrators, teachers, and families. The state legislature writes laws for educational policies that may specify regulations regarding content standards, state assessments of learner outcomes, and certification requirements. A state department of education or affiliated agency administers state policies concerning certification of teachers and accrediting of teacher preparation programs, often via a licensing board or council. National or state professional organizations and teaching unions may advocate and influence certification rules and regulations. Local school boards govern local school systems, although they are bound by state rules when hiring teachers.

Teacher Training and Professional Development

Accountability and *incentives* are key words in K–12 teaching today. Increasingly, districts, schools, and teachers are being held accountable for the learning outcomes of their students.[2] When students perform poorly, attention is often directed at the quality of the teaching. The suggested remedy is to improve the quality and accountability of teacher preparation programs and professional development opportunities, requiring new and more rigorous teacher examinations and creating more direct measures of specific teaching proficiencies. However, raising the standards for initial teaching certification is especially difficult given the forecast of significant K–12 teacher shortages projected nationwide. Mandatory requirements for maintaining certification remain the primary mechanism for enhancing teacher competency.

Merit-based systems that reward teachers for student outcomes are a less punitive approach to accountability often advocated by legislators and administrators, but how merit is to be measured and the system implemented raises many complex issues with regard to the structure of teachers' contracts. Hence, teacher union support or resistance is critical to the adoption of merit-based systems. Incentives to engage in professional development or to enhance certification levels are another mechanism for improving teacher quality. Incentives may take the form of salary increases, release time, or recognition, but, again, most changes must be negotiated as part of teacher contract discussions.

The basis for K–12 certification via completion of an accredited teacher preparation program is the assumption that higher education courses (including clinical field experience) ensure a minimal standard of teacher quality and accountability. However, research has shown that even successful completion of a course of study—the "seat-time" model—is no guarantee that any theoretical knowledge and skills learned will translate into teaching competency in practice (McAninch, 1993). The only time a candidate teacher is authentically engaged in the professional practice of teaching is in the field-based clinical experience, and the quality of these experiences varies greatly from program to program. The same criticisms apply to in-service professional development used for maintenance of credentials. In general, critics have questioned the relevance, transfer, and applicability to increased competency of participation in graduate courses, workshops, or conferences.

One response to the criticism of the seat-time model has been to require licensing exams to ensure a minimal competency level. The requirement of licensing exams *at all* is a consequence of the fact that satisfactory completion of an accredited preparation program is not a sufficient guarantee that every candidate teacher will possess even the minimal basic skills, much less sufficient professional competency.

The completion of an accredited program of coursework and satisfactory performance on exams are still only indirect measures of teaching competency. Another alternative has been the development of teaching standards and competency-based credentialing systems, such as that developed by the National Board for Professional Teaching Standards (NBTPS). The movement of a number of states to accept NBTPS credentials, which are based on performance assessments, can be viewed as a more general response to the inadequacies of a seat-time or "seat-time plus exams" model.

The goal of improving K–12 teacher preparation and in-service professional development has received heightened attention in recent years (American Federation of Teachers, 2000). A U.S. Department of Education (2000) report identified a number of barriers to the improvement of teaching, including the following:

• Lack of rigor in many teacher education programs
• Lack of a set of standard qualifications for entering the profession
• Lack of accountability by higher education institutions for preparing teachers

- Little collaboration between institutions of higher education and K–12 educators
- Lack of consensus on a core curriculum
- Inadequate field experiences that come too late, are too short in duration, and are not focused on teachers' greatest needs
- Little incorporation of state K–12 student content and performance standards in teacher education core curricula
- Low and inappropriate standards for teacher certification that do not substantiate an ability to perform in the classroom (for example, certifying teachers via a norm-referenced exam with low cut scores)
- Complicated and restrictive state licensure systems

In short, the K–12 preparation system is far from ideal. This list of barriers to effective teacher preparation illustrates some of the specific pitfalls that an adult certification system might wish to avoid or to address.

WHAT IS THE ABE EXPERIENCE?

Despite its fallibility, the reform model that is driving change in the K–12 system does provide a framework for considering an ABE teaching certification system. Does the model of content standards aligned with outcome assessments, informing teaching standards, which in turn inform certification and professional development, fit the ABE experience? Is there an equivalent ABE system on the horizon? In this section, we address these questions and draw comparisons with the K–12 reform experience where helpful, but the focus is on the unique concerns of ABE.

Content Standards

Until recently, standards in ABE programs have typically been defined by the assessment instruments used. Adult secondary education students, for example, are most often preparing to take the tests of General Educational Development (GED), which are based on five high school subject areas. Although the new GED will be aligned with the new secondary-level content standards, a GED teacher continues to need a broad understanding of each subject, not necessarily a deep understanding of any one.[3] In some states and programs, student outcomes are assessed by means of a traditional basic skills test, such as the Test of Adult Basic Education (TABE), with subtests in categories such as vocabulary, reading comprehension, and mathematics.

The context of ABE content standards is changing, and the changes have implications for teacher standards and certification. Publication of the 1991 report by the Secretary's Commission on Achieving Necessary Skills (SCANS) served to jump-start the process of examining the extent to which ABE programs prepared learners to meet the expectations of the workplace. The SCANS Report acknowledged the importance of reading, writing, and arithmetic and mathematics as three of five "Basic Skills" (the others are listening and speaking). In addition, a person must be able to use these skills in meaningful contexts. Proficiency in all the Foundation Skills (which include the Basic Skills plus Thinking Skills and Personal Qualities) is necessary to develop and demonstrate workplace competencies. The SCANS Report pointed to the kinds of tasks adults have to perform in the workplace and defined levels of proficiency and performance benchmarks.

Because the SCANS Report was developed in adult workplace contexts and defined the competencies expected of adults, the ABE community embraced the concepts, the language, and the expanded set of competencies. The scope of ABE content began to be defined by how skills were to be used in adult settings other than a school setting.

A number of states have developed or are in the process of developing content standards for ABE learners and have correlated assessment instruments with these new standards (Kutner, Webb, & Matheson, 1996). In several instances, these standards are aligned with those in the Comprehensive Adult Student Assessment System (CASAS). CASAS tests are based on critical competencies and skill areas drawn from the workplace, community, and family. At the secondary education level, Pennsylvania is experimenting with methods for validating a diploma project as a credential option for learners. Learners need to demonstrate secondary-level performance capabilities to trained assessors.

In the K–12 arena, the expressed needs of learners are not typically part of the content standards development process. In developing content standards for adult learners, however, learner needs are an important starting point. The National Institute for Literacy's Equipped for the Future (EFF) initiative is to date the most comprehensive alternative approach to adult learning content standards. The EFF project applied a broad-based, consensus-building process, including surveys and focus groups of adult learners, to determine learners' goals and needs. The respondents identified four purposes for learning: to gain access to information to help them orient themselves in the world; to develop a voice—that is, to be able to express ideas and opinions with confidence; to take independent action to solve problems and make decisions on their own; and to build a bridge to the future in learning how to learn and keep up with a changing world (National Institute for Literacy, 1995). It was then determined what sorts of skills students would need to meet these ends. These included communication skills (in which one finds reading and writing), decision-making skills (in which one finds math concepts), interpersonal skills, and lifelong learning skills. In the EFF framework, adult skills are enlisted in the service of empowering learners, giving them the wherewithal to fulfill their roles as workers, family members, and community members. EFF standards can be characterized as a statement of what is valued in ABE instruction: what learners should know and be able to do. Integration of EFF standards with the National Reporting System—for example, establishing valid assessments or functional descriptive statements corresponding to the functional levels of the NRS—is an idea endorsed in the National Literacy Summit action agenda (2000). As yet, however, no performance assessments aligned with EFF standards have been constructed; neither have any EFF standards been accepted as national standards (although a process for doing so is under way).

Consequently, a unified approach to measuring adult achievement outcomes does not yet exist. The National Reporting System for Adult Education is a project that has developed core outcome measures that meet the requirements of the Workforce Investment Act of 1998 as well as state accountability requirements (Condelli, 2000). Students' educational gains are measured according to the degree to which they have advanced in educational functioning level. There are four levels of basic education, two of secondary education, and six levels of English for speakers of other languages (ESOL). To move to a new level, students must have mastered a certain set of skills and competencies in multiple literacy areas (for example, reading, numeracy, speaking). The descriptors for the skills and competencies required at each level can be aligned with standardized assessment instruments (tests or performance assessments). Outcomes are assessed by such measures as whether students have obtained employment, entered another program to further their education, or received a secondary school diploma or passed the GED tests.

The functional level descriptors of the NRS define achievement in a way that accommodates the diversity of ABE delivery systems and is compatible across related ABE and training programs. The NRS measures, standardizes, and codifies the use of a variety of assessment instruments for the purpose of aggregating student gains data. When ABE outcomes are based on assessment-driven standards such as these, however, it is not clear what relationship or implication K–12 standards have for the preparation or professionalization of adult educators. The functioning levels are guideposts that point the way for what teachers of adults must be able to do for learners. High-quality teachers should know how to move learners from one level to the next, whether it is in the context of preparing students for jobs, for higher education, or to pass the GED tests. The specifics of those teacher competencies are less well defined.

As in K–12, the better the articulation of adult content standards and their relationship to accountability systems, the better these standards are able to serve as a foundation for teaching standards and competencies. A significant issue that must be addressed by the ABE community is the extent to which a customer-driven set of standards such as EFF can be aligned with the kinds of content standards that are driving K–12 curriculum, assessment, and teacher standards, given the increased emphasis K–12 teacher preparation programs are placing on these standards. The relevance of K–12 certification would seem to hinge on the value placed by the ABE community on the teaching competencies that are derived from K–12 content standards.

Teacher Certification: To Be or Not to Be K–12-Certified

A range of possibilities is open to states as they consider how best to certify or credential adult literacy educators, from accepting any level of K–12 certification to creating a unique and separate certification for adult teachers. The current requirements (or lack thereof) for ABE teacher certification in the fifty states are listed in Table 6.1. This information is based on a report by Kutner et al. (1996) and a needs analysis conducted by the National Adult Education Professional Development Consortium (forthcoming). Seventeen states require that anyone hired to teach ABE full- or part-time be a certified K–12

1	No certification or credential required	AK, CO, FL, ID, IL, IA, ME, NE, OR, SD
1.1	No certification required but states encourage setting of some standards	GA, MD, MS, PA, RI, VT
1.2	No certification required, but most are certified teachers anyway	HI, MT, NH, ND
1.3	No certification required, but most are employed by higher ed institution that sets its own standards	NC, NM, WA, WY
2	State Elementary or Secondary Ed required	IN, KY, NJ, NY, OH, OK, SC, TN
2.1	State Elementary or Secondary Ed required, but may be waived for certain conditions	AZ, MA, UT, VA
2.2	State teaching license and special conditions	NV, MI, (TX)
3.0	Adult teaching certificate or credential	AR, CT, LA, DC, KS
3.1	State teaching license or adult basic education license	WV
3.2	Adult teaching certificate and State teaching license	AL, (TX), MN, MO
3.3	Adult teaching certificate with side conditions	DE, CA

Table 6.1. Certification or Credentialing Requirements and Systems in States.

teacher. At least four states provide waivers for special circumstances. Nine others require some form of adult certification. In three states, teacher certification and an adult certification or other requirements are requisite; in Washington State the requirement is either regular teacher certification or an adult teacher certification.

Four states do not require teacher certification, but the hiring practices or system administration of local educational agencies ensures that most adult educators are certified teachers. Four other states do not require teacher certification in part because administration is through institutions of higher education that have their own hiring guidelines. Even in states with no required certification, voluntary or optional certification or credentialing may exist and be encouraged. For example, hiring preferences or compensation levels may be influenced by whether the candidate has completed a state-accredited teacher preparation program or holds state teacher certification.

Sabatini et al. (2000) conducted a survey targeting full-time and part-time adult educators who spend a majority of their time teaching adults. Fewer than twenty of over four hundred respondents (less than 5 percent) possessed a degree in ABE. More than 80 percent had prior educational experience spread across elementary, secondary, community college, and training work. While 37 percent had been teaching adults for five years or fewer, 63 percent had been teaching adults for more than five years. About two-thirds were certified as elementary or secondary teachers, with about 40 percent indicating that the certification was required by the program or state.

At first glance, one might expect K–12 certification types in ABE to mirror those applied in K–12 education—that is,

- Elementary-level reading, writing, and mathematics certifications would apply to teachers of basic-level adult learners.

- Secondary education certifications and endorsements would apply to teachers of adult secondary education and preparation for the GED credential.

- Special education certification would apply to teachers of adults with special learning needs.

- Specializations in ESOL would apply to teachers of adult ESOL.

But the arrangement is not that simple. In the same survey (Sabatini et al., 2000), K–12 certification level was not a strong predictor of primary adult teaching assignment. That is, elementary teachers were only slightly more likely to teach basic-level adult students than teachers with other certification levels; secondary teachers were only slightly more likely to teach adult secondary or GED students.

Our search of the literature did not produce any research documenting the extent to which K–12 teacher preparation programs benefit adult educators. Teacher preparation programs that specialize in ABE are not common, though many schools and departments offer some coursework specific to ABE. In most states there is a university with a higher education program or department that offers M.A., M.Ed., Ed.D., or Ph.D. degrees in adult education (Evans & Sherman, 1999), but this is not necessarily synonymous with a focus on teacher preparation in ABE. Such graduate programs may include ABE, training, and human development, and their target audiences are administrators, researchers, trainers, and future higher education instructors; these programs do not necessarily prepare enrollees to teach adults basic skills. Even if more teacher preparation programs in ABE were available, so few states have been able to support adult literacy educators full time and offer them a stable career path (Arkansas being an exception) that demand for new graduate programs is unlikely. This seems especially true given the current and projected shortage of qualified K–12 teachers.

In the absence of an infrastructure supporting the flow of ABE teachers directly from traditional teacher preparation programs, the most common approach to certification for instructors hired as adult educators has taken the form of in-service requirements. Graduate-level courses are sanctioned by many of the states requiring or promoting an ABE certification or endorsement (for example, Arkansas and California).

There remain two problems with this approach. First, many states, especially large or rural states, are unable to give all adult educators access to higher education courses (for example, Mississippi, Minnesota, and Kansas). Second, as in the K–12 setting, the field questions how well the learning that takes place in a strictly seat-time, course-based system can be translated into the practical competencies of teaching adults. As a result, many states are implementing alternative approaches through which adult teachers can acquire the skills to meet teaching competencies.

On one hand, it is not unreasonable to suggest that being a professional teacher is a strong prerequisite for becoming a proficient adult basic educator. On the other, it has been argued that the presence of nontraditional teachers, including individuals who may not have completed a four-year undergraduate program or volunteers whose responsibilities evolve over time, is a strength of the current ABE service system because it increases local community participation and diversity. Any process that systematically screens out or discourages such individuals might prove controversial or unacceptable to many established providers (Perin, 1998–99; Webb, 1997).

As is the case with reforms of K–12 certification systems toward more direct assessment of teacher competencies via performance assessments such as portfolios, ABE certification processes are becoming increasingly innovative and flexible in their approach. A variety of professional development activities—such as professional presentations, action research, self-study, and institutes and conferences, with performance validated via portfolios, résumés, awards, and video cases—are being considered as means toward certification. Several states are developing flexible, tiered certification or parallel credentialing processes that allow teachers to design a course of study that is directly relevant to the needs of ABE programs and teachers. At the heart of this approach are teacher standards and competencies.

Teaching Competencies and Competency-Based Systems

Teaching competencies articulate what adult educators should know and be able to do. They can be used as a framework for developing needs assessments and training materials or activities. Performance indicators, measures, and assessment instruments can be developed to assess teacher competencies directly. A competency-based training and accountability system can be employed to provide flexibility at the program or state level, overcoming some criticisms of the seat-time teacher certification model. For example, performance assessments can be used to enhance and document the competencies of those adult educators already hired and working in the field.

Identifying and establishing a framework that targets competencies that are valid and distinct to adult educators is therefore a valuable step toward increased professionalization of the field. In the past, this has been an area of contention (Shanahan, Meehan, & Mogge, 1994). Identifying a core curriculum or set of teaching competencies (or standards) that define the profession of teaching has been a trouble spot for the improvement of K–12 teaching as well (American Federation of Teachers, 2000; U.S. Department of Education, 2000). The inability to define a core set of instructional and pedagogical practices and knowledge that are proven to be effective and fundamental to teaching reinforces the uneven quality of teacher preparation programs and weakens the credibility of teaching as a profession (American Federation of Teachers, 2000).

In the next sections, we describe an initiative toward establishing a framework for ABE professional teaching competencies. A format and process for establishing and using teaching competencies as a basis for certification has been developed by the National Board for Professional Teaching Standards.

PRO-NET'S COMPETENCIES. A set of instructor competencies has been articulated as part of the work of the Building Professional Development Partnerships for Adult Educators Project (PRO-NET) funded by the Division of Adult Education and Literacy of the U.S. Department of Education. Sherman, Tibbetts, Woodruff, and Wiedler (1999) compiled lists of competencies,[4] then used a multistate process to develop performance indicators aligned with the competencies. The authors conducted a field-based process utilizing input from more than three hundred ABE instructors and program administrators and reviewed the literature on instructional practices in ABE to inform the quality of their list. The result is a framework of three themes related to effective instruction:

- Keeping current in content area and in instructional strategies
- Communicating and collaborating with colleagues and learners to facilitate learning
- Working positively and nonjudgmentally with diverse populations

These themes are further defined in six categories of competency, wherein the teacher

- Maintains knowledge and pursues professional development
- Organizes and delivers instruction
- Manages instructional resources
- Continually assesses and monitors learning
- Manages program responsibilities and enhances program organization
- Provides learner guidance and referral

Within each category are specific competency statements, performance indicators, and recommendations that evidence be collected to assess, evaluate, and train teachers. Table 6.2 shows an example of a specific competency and corresponding indicators from the category "maintains knowledge and pursues professional development." The authors have not defined the specific evidence that would support the claim that a competency has been achieved, rather recommending that instructors and programmers develop their own evidence based on the content of individual programs.

The competencies are intended for a wide audience and can be used to achieve multiple goals (Sherman et al., 1999). At the state and program levels, the competencies can be used for the following purposes:

	Theme: Maintains Knowledge Base and Pursues Own Professionalism	
Competency	Indicator of Competency	Program-Specific Evidence
2. Develops and maintains an in-depth knowledge base in own content area and in other relevant areas	Maintains Knowledge Base: 2.1 Has professional preparation and or training in primary content area 2.2 Participates in professional development related to own or relevant areas . . . 2.3 Describes how content area knowledge can be transferred to the instructional setting	Authors of report recommend that this section be completed by instructors (as self-assessment) and program administrators based on the individual program.

Table 6.2. Competencies and Performance Indicators.
Source: Adapted from Sherman et al., 1999, p. 20.

• Support and complement state and program performance standards

• Build on existing competencies

• Foster the development of new competencies

• Provide a basis for instructor certification

• Develop guidelines for hiring and recruiting staff

• Provide a basis for an assessment of professional development needs

At the individual level, the authors recommend using the competencies to conduct self- and peer assessment and to prepare for certification.

The PRO-NET group advocates a range of professional development activities, including workshops, conferences, and study groups (Sherman et al., 1999; Webb, 1997). Traditionally, it has been hard to apply measures of accountability to such in-service formats except in terms of participation or seat-time. Specification of competencies can help to ensure a connection is made between training activities. As yet, the PRO-NET group has not taken the step of defining the evidence or attempting to design and validate measures of specific competencies or overall teacher competence. Such a process can be found in National Board Certification.

A NATIONAL BOARD FOR TEACHING COMPETENCIES. One model for developing certification based on professional competencies for ABE teachers in a field that has no infrastructure for teacher preparation might be the National Board for Professional Teaching Standards (NBPTS). The NBPTS has developed numerous frameworks for certification in education. There is significant overlap across frameworks in the general topic areas expected of teachers. The framework for "Early Adolescence Through Young Adulthood/Career and Technical Education" is provided as an example (see Exhibit 6.1). We selected this specific framework because the face validity of the themes and topics corresponds well with topics that might be covered in a body of professional standards for ABE teachers.

Teachers achieve certification after successfully completing a performance assessment process. The performance assessment takes into account varied aspects of teaching and consists of two parts: a portfolio and assessment center exercises. The portfolio is completed in the classroom and contains videotapes of classroom teaching, samples of student work, and written commentary. Portfolio requirements vary from assessment to assessment, but they are based on evidence of accomplished teaching practice with current classes and students. Portfolios generally require four or five classroom-based exercises, may ask for videotapes of classroom interactions or samples of student work, and require written analysis and reflections. Another part of the portfolio documents teachers' work outside the classroom with families, colleagues, and the community. Teachers are asked to show evidence of their accomplishments and comment on the importance of

---

Theme 1:   Creating a productive learning environment, knowledge of students, knowledge of subject matter, learning environment diversity

Theme 2:   Advancing student learning, advancing knowledge of career and technical subject matter

Theme 3:   Transition to work and adult roles, workplace readiness, managing and balancing multiple life roles, social development

Theme 4:   Professional development and outreach reflective of collaborative partnerships, contributions to the education profession, family and community partnerships

---

Exhibit 6.1. NBPTS Framework for Early Adolescence
Through Young Adulthood and Career and Technical Education.

those accomplishments. The goal of all these exercises is to document that teachers meet National Board standards. Teachers take an average of about 120 hours over four months, about a day a week, to complete their portfolios. A good portfolio both reflects the standards and gives a true picture of a teacher's level of accomplishment.

In the Assessment Center Exercises teacher candidates complete written tasks and exercises focused on pedagogical content and knowledge. The assessments ask candidates to respond to specific prompts, which may be based on materials sent to candidates well in advance. Exercises may be simulated situations to which teachers must respond, or they may be explorations of pedagogical issues.

Both the portfolio and assessment center approaches are applicable to the context of adult basic education. One possibility for the field to consider is working directly with the National Board to create a certificate for adult educators. Another possibility is for states to adopt elements of the process model used by the National Board as part of their certification process.[5]

SUMMARY. Because many ABE teachers have K–12 experience, determining the extent to which teaching competencies for adult educators overlap with the teaching standards of K–12 teachers is a critical issue. Many teachers will want to build on their current certification rather than start all over again. But the adult educator's professional responsibilities are different from those of the traditional K–12 teacher. First, in ABE there is less consensus on the need for and role of training and preparation in the traditional academic course areas. Second, ABE program missions have traditionally embraced broader purposes for literacy, including such areas as community and emancipatory education, family and parenting, life skills, and workforce preparation. In evaluating differences between ABE and K–12, one might conclude that the teaching demands in ABE are qualitatively different from those in K–12, so the training and preparation, to be effective, must be different as well, perhaps to the extent that no certification is necessary but that extensive in-service education is required. Or one might conclude that the demands of adult teaching are an extension of K–12 skills and warrant a separate ABE endorsement in addition to basic certification. Finally, one might conclude that teaching is no different, so K–12 certification alone is fine for adult educators (as it is now in seventeen states).

Governance and Stakeholders

The policymakers and administrators of the existing state K–12 certification boards are critical stakeholders in any initiatives or reforms
aimed at ABE; K–12 state educational agencies administer ABE in
forty-two states (solely in twenty-four states, jointly with postsecondary
agencies in eighteen states) (National Adult Education Professional Development Consortium, 1998). State boards for community colleges
administer ABE in four states (Mississippi, North Carolina, Oregon,
and Washington), a separate state vo-tech agency administers it in three
states (Arkansas, Georgia, and Wisconsin), and a workforce development cabinet administers it in one state (Kentucky). ABE staff are a
small percentage of state education staff. More than 80 percent of the
states have fewer than twenty state staff members working for ABE;
more than 50 percent have ten or fewer (National Adult Education Professional Development Consortium, 1998). ABE budgets are a small
fraction of state education spending. The relationship forged between
the ABE community and these other educational stakeholders determines the nature and form of ABE professionalization efforts.

Providers of adult literacy services may be local educational agencies, institutions of higher education, community-based organizations,
libraries, public or private nonprofits, public housing authorities, correctional agencies, family literacy providers, or consortia of for-profit
agencies. Furthermore, because funding of ABE by WIA block grants
may be supplemented at the state or program level by other special
grants or private foundation funding, overly rigid or mandatory certifications may not be workable or enforceable for all stakeholders.
Consequently, the viability or practicality of a teacher certification
process depends on negotiations between the stakeholders at the gov-
erning and service-delivery levels. Consortia of stakeholders and advocacy groups may need to develop strategic plans and visions to work
directly with legislatures and policymakers to reform and build new
systems that better fit the unique needs of ABE in the state.

At first glance, stakeholders put at risk by a movement toward increased professionalization sanctioned through mechanisms of licensing and certification would appear to be the following:

• Community-based programs that recruit staff from the area
  who may not have the educational background to achieve
  certification

- Volunteer organizations in which the volunteer is the learners' primary teacher
- Programs that rely on part-time staff who do not have the time or incentive to acquire credentials

The reality is that many states are sensitive to these needs and make special provisions to ensure that the entire field of adult literacy service providers is given the opportunity to pursue professional development. As Shanahan, Meehan, and Mogge (1994) point out, no one has ever debated the value and utility of volunteers, only the role they play, especially when tutors are assigned as the only instructor for the lowest-level learners. As for community-based, nontraditional staff, to the extent that a certification program follows the traditional K–12 teaching model (in which a bachelor's degree is a minimal requirement and additional higher education is often assumed), it could be a barrier to community-based recruits who may be effective with learners but are not in a position, financially or otherwise, to pursue a four-year degree. Legitimate alternate pathways can be created for such staff, however, with the ultimate goal of building into the system a pathway from volunteer to part-time to full-time professional.

Accountability and Incentives

Few topics raise as many strong opinions and feelings as accountability (see Merrifield, 1998). Much of the strong emotion is reserved for state and federal policymakers and legislators who would hold local programs and teachers accountable for student learning or other program-level requirements (for example, program evaluation and improvement indicators) without making provisions for the resources and training necessary to accomplish the tasks. The chronic instability of funding and unreliable career paths create a dual difficulty for programs that must recruit and retain both students and quality teachers. Demand too much from teachers and the already thin field of qualified candidates will become even thinner. Set the requirements too low and the field cannot achieve the level of professionalism it seeks to garner increased support and credibility.

The NRS was designed to create a national database of information and outcomes to demonstrate the overall effectiveness of the federally funded ABE program to meet WIA accountability requirements.

The outcomes data form the basis of federally awarded state incentive grants based on performance. States are also required to evaluate local program performance on these same indicators as one condition of local funding, although they are free to use other indicators as well. In addition to learner outcomes, states may choose to use the quality of instructional staff as a local program quality indicator. In lieu of making it mandatory to hire certified teachers, the number or proportion of state-certified teachers employed by programs could be a quality indicator, as could evidence of improved performance of staff on measures of competency (such as portfolios). The proper balance of incentives, sanctions, and mandatory requirements must be struck based on consideration of each state context.

CASE STUDIES: MASSACHUSETTS AND TEXAS

In summarizing the advantages and disadvantages of professionalization in adult literacy education, Perin (1998–99) notes that a key factor in securing field support is the perception of who is certifying that professionalization. Many professions are self-regulated through boards or councils made up of representatives of the profession who set standards for minimal competency and ongoing maintenance of professional status.

Central to the debate on the reform of teacher preparation and development in ABE is the method by which teacher competence will be evaluated. On one side of this issue are those who believe that what is needed is an increase in traditional requirements, such as coursework, testing, and in-service training. On the other are those who believe that the traditional system is hopelessly flawed and that the only way to ensure teacher competence is to provide alternative, performance-based measures. This is not an easy issue to resolve, and in ABE it is complicated by the lack of both traditional and performance-based measures that are applicable to a fragmented field.

To demonstrate the real-life process of developing certification systems, we present case studies of two states, Massachusetts and Texas. Both are working to change the systems they use both to deliver ABE services and to provide for the professional development that will be needed to implement that delivery. Although the specifics of the two states' policies and plans are different, their goal is the same: to improve the quality of teaching. Each state also acknowledges that though some concrete reform steps can and must be taken, the delivery system, infrastructure, and funding streams of ABE are not yet able to support the implementation of full-scale systems. We make no claim that these two cases are representative of the nation. However, they do address many of the issues facing all fifty states as they attempt to put systems for teacher certification in place. We have classified the direction of the changes taking place in these systems as follows:

- Changes that originate at the state level and are driven by changes in legislation (for example, the Workforce Investment Act) or policy. We have labeled these "top-down" changes.
- Changes that originate in the field and are driven by perceived problems in the delivery of services or the quality of the workforce. We have labeled these "bottom- up."
- Changes that are driven by a number of different forces, including pressure from federal or state legislation and the perception of unmet student needs within the existing system. We have labeled these "hybrid" changes.

In our discussion, we provide a snapshot of the progress in each state as it moves toward professionalization for ABE teachers. We do this by focusing on the state's previous history, where the impetus for change originated and how it developed, current plans for implementation, plans to measure success, and the present status of professionalization. In the summary, we briefly review the similarities and differences in the approaches of each state.

Massachusetts

Certification efforts for teachers of ABE in Massachusetts began in 1970 with the establishment of the State Committee on Adult Education. This group established the K–12 certification requirement for all ABE teachers and mandated an additional two courses in ABE for certification. This effort was not successful and was discontinued. For the next twenty-five years, Massachusetts struggled with certification issues. Overall, the state's certification history has included both the state and the field taking turns driving the process. The state's Department of Education lists the following points as key differences, concerns, and challenges among the various stakeholders:

- The most obvious divisions have been between adult educators employed by organizations that require a Department granted certification for employment (for example school districts and correctional facilities) and those that do not (for example institutions of higher education and community based organizations).

- Many of the 2500 adult educators who already possess from one to thirty years of experience in this field believe that certification must recognize the essential skills and abilities they already possess and they may not need to enroll in courses to fulfill ABE licensure standards.

- Adult students (and the practitioners who serve them) are confronted with substantially different circumstances from children trying to master the same skills: their pursuit of education is voluntary, not mandatory; they must balance competing priorities; and in some respects they learn differently from children.

- An estimated 70 percent of Massachusetts adult educators are employed part-time, without benefits, with incomes on average 20% below K–12 educators. [Department of Education, Commonwealth of Massachusetts, 2001]

To accommodate these concerns and challenges, the Massachusetts legislature established a task force consisting of representatives from the field to consider options for certification other than course requirements, called the Staff Development and Teacher Certification Task Force. On the recommendation of the task force, in 1991, the System for Adult Basic Education Support (SABES) was established with the support of funds separate from the K–12 system. Massachusetts is unusual in having established an infrastructure for the training and licensing of ABE teachers that is separate from the K–12 system in terms of both funding and operation. SABES was designated as the state's primary 353 (funding for professional development) grantee and was charged with creating a meaningful certification for teachers that would both accommodate the diverse needs of the students who enroll in ABE programs and recognize the special competency required of its teachers.

DIRECTION OF CHANGE. Having learned from previous experience, the state made an unusual effort to reject the top-down approach it had adopted in 1970, which mandated coursework for teachers. Instead, it empowered SABES to obtain support from the field by soliciting input from teachers and program directors in developing the requirements for certification. To inform practitioners and other interested persons and to provide a forum for discussion of diverse points of view, SABES invited practitioners from across the state to participate in a series of focus groups (called "certification road shows"). These groups identified what they perceived to be the components of an "ideal system" of certification. That system would

- Be based on meaningful competencies agreed upon by field representatives
- Recognize the prior experience, knowledge, and skills of teachers
- Require teachers to reflect on their teaching philosophy and practice
- Align itself with preexisting K–12 certification requirements but protect and reflect the special needs and concerns of the ABE domain (that is, ABE standards would be aligned with but not parallel to K–12 standards)
- Be flexible, accessible, and low cost
- Be voluntary

Though this new system was to be aligned with the existing K–12 certification requirements, the task of SABES was to protect and reflect the special needs of ABE.

Additional stipulations for ABE teacher certification were entered into the state budget for fiscal year 1999. Partners in the movement for change in Massachusetts include the offices of Teacher Certification and Credentialing and of Adult and Community Learning Services, as well as appointed members of the ABE Certification Advisory Committee. In 1999 two new staff positions were created in the Massachusetts Department of Education and SABES. Appointees to the positions (Mary Jane Fay and Carey Reid) were asked to conduct research, produce draft documents for working group and advisory committees, and establish links with delivery agencies (Fay & Reid, 2000).

ACTION PLAN. Originally, the advisory committee to the Massachusetts Department of Education proposed a three-track system for ABE certification that would accommodate teachers with K–12 certification and one year's experience teaching in ABE, teachers with no K–12 certification and at least five years of ABE teaching experience, and teachers with K–12 certification and at least five years of teaching experience in either K–12 or ABE. Certification in Massachusetts, as in other states, was to be built on a foundation of required "competencies," with the added provision that in establishing the competencies the state will be "flexible and creative" (Department of Education, Mass., 1999, p. 5) so as to ensure that this certification reflects the unique characteristics of ABE. On January 26, 2001, the state Board of Education approved a draft set of regulations for providing a voluntary license for teachers of adult basic education. The Department hopes to accommodate the needs of the field by proposing four "routes" to licensure, ranging from prospective and novice ABE teachers to those with five years of ABE teaching experience. To obtain a license, even the most experienced teachers must indicate proficiency in at least eight "standards." The standards listed in the new regulations are basically the same as the recommended list of competencies for Massachusetts listed in the 1999 report, but the term *standards* is now used for them.

Establishing these standards was a result of intensive in-state and out-of-state research review and consensus building. The proposed list adopted virtually all the teaching competencies already required in Massachusetts for K–12 teachers, with "minor revisions to make them more age appropriate." Additional competencies are those that have been cited by practitioners as particularly relevant to teachers of adult literacy, adult secondary, and ESOL teaching, including knowledge in core areas such as adult learning theory and in areas of specialization such as reading or ESOL.

The Massachusetts Department of Education has stipulated that the standards to be established for ABE certification should focus on mastery of what adult educators need to know and be able to do to ensure the success of their students. While the department does state that certification will be voluntary and that it is committed to facilitating access to certification for all ABE teachers, it has acknowledged the difficulties that part-time workers will encounter in pursuing certification (Department of Education, Mass., 1999, p. 6). The department suggests that the proposed regulations present a proficiency-based license, and notes that if accepted, "this will be the first stand-alone ABE teacher's license in the nation" (Department of Education, Mass., 2001).

Though the routes to professionalization are both diverse and flexible, the state's primary commitment appears to be the certification of full-time professionals. According to the 1999 report, the state believes that "to achieve high levels of performance, we must foster a core of full time career adult educators within each [ABE] program. We will continue to promote policies that support an increase in the number of the full time staff in the [ABE] programs we fund" (Department of Education, Mass., 1999, p. 6). It is clear from this statement that program funding will be affected by the number of "full-time" professionals employed.

MEASUREMENT OF SUCCESS. It is not clear how teacher competencies and standards, once established, will be documented. Several different methods have been proposed that might provide evidence of proficiency. Among these are résumés, summaries of staff development, self-directed learning projects with demonstrable outcomes, collaborative projects that met stated goals, case studies illustrating the development of strategies or materials, annotated bibliographies, videotapes of classes, presentations, and awards. While it is not clear how this will be done, it appears that these various kinds of evidence of proficiency will be evaluated, perhaps by alignment with competency standards established by the state. However, it is clear that at least some coursework or some combination of courses and "clusters of competencies" (meaning sets of related competencies that work together in a particular area) will be a core requirement. There is also some evidence that proficiency can be demonstrated by passing Part 1 of the Massachusetts Teacher's Test. Issues still to be resolved include the title of certification, practicum requirements, options for demonstrating proficiency, recertification, requirements, and piloting of the certification process. Perhaps more important, however, is assessing the impact of increased demand for evidence of teacher certification on program outcomes and student learning. As yet, no tools are in place to measure these.

STATUS REPORT. The system is not yet in place, and the state continues to solicit input to try to arrive at a consensus for a certification process that will both ensure a professional workforce and be flexible enough to accommodate nontraditional evidence of teaching proficiency. A note in the proposed regulations document, which states,

"The department may not require the licensure of teachers of ABE, but it may be required by individual employers or other agencies that sponsor ABE programs" (Department of Education, Commonwealth of Massachusetts, 2001, p. 21), may cause some initial problems and confusion because of conflicting requirements. The state's shift away from a top-down mandate and toward bottom-up consensus building may indicate that Massachusetts fits our definition of a hybrid model of change, since efforts have been driven by a number of different forces, including pressure from federal or state legislation and the perception of unmet student needs within the existing system. However, it is clear from the reports on the process of developing competencies that it was both controlled and directed from the state level. While input from the field was sought, the traditional methods of coursework (either alone or in combination with "competencies"), testing, and in-service training to ensure competency remain firmly in place. Though the state has invested considerable resources in developing indicators of competency, not much visible effort has been expended on measurement or evaluation. Nor has any systematic research been conducted on the process and progress of teachers as they try to find ways to meet these requirements.

Texas

In the early 1990s, the Texas Association for Literacy and Adult Education (TALAE), a professional organization of ABE practitioners and administrators, made initial attempts to raise interest in credentialing and moving toward standardization of professional development for adult educators. They got as far as having a bill brought before the state legislature, but funding for the process was not forthcoming. The effort was then abandoned. As this effort was going on, the K–12 system initiated a statewide teacher certification examination requirement as part of an effort to justify state funding and to ensure that qualified teachers were being hired.

DIRECTION OF CHANGE. During the late 1990s, the TALAE perceived that if state appropriations for ABE were to be increased, the field would have to express its needs and priorities to the legislature more clearly and make it apparent that the ABE system is staffed with a professional cadre of educators who provide high-quality services. TALAE members felt that the development of an ABE credential would provide this assurance. They saw that another beneficial outcome of a movement toward credentialing adult educators might be that high-quality educators would be attracted to working in the field, thereby improving ABE provision and programs. The rationale, as articulated by acting state director Deborah Stedman, was that credentialing would lead to better teachers, which in turn would lead to better outcomes, outcomes that would both demonstrate accountability and impress legislators. This process, once completed, would ultimately lead to better funding.

Under the 1998 Adult Education and Family Literacy Act, Title II of the Workforce Investment Act, the Division of Adult and Community Education of the Texas Education Agency developed the Texas State Plan for Adult and Family Education to guide ABE provision for the next five years. The state established fifty-five geographic areas to manage ABE and held a competitive application process to establish the fiscal agents to oversee ABE in each area. Approximately half of the fifty-five fiscal agents are school districts, about a quarter are regional educational service centers that are state-funded and generally provide technical support to K–12 systems, and another quarter are public colleges, mostly community and junior colleges. Two fiscal agents are community-based organizations.

The fiscal agents oversee approximately 3,500 teachers, of whom 200–250 teach full time; more than 90 percent of the ABE teaching force work part time. The minimum qualification established by the State Department of Education for adult educators is attainment of a bachelor's degree. State teacher certification in any discipline is rewarded with a higher salary and fewer required professional development hours. Most ABE teachers are active or retired schoolteachers who have certification.

An initial credentialing system has been designed to function within the structures of the fifty-five fiscal agents. Additional input was sought from all stakeholders through focus groups, organization and project online discussion groups, and conference sessions. The credentialing process is being pilot tested during 2001 with a limited number of educators from across the state.

ACTION PLAN. The TALAE petitioned the State Board of Education Task Force to set aside money for an effort to professionalize the field. This resulted in the establishment of Section 29.252 of the Education Code, mandating that the Texas Education Agency "prescribe and administer standards and accrediting policies for ABE; prescribe and administer rules for teacher certification for adult education." Funding was granted and a three-pronged process was undertaken to achieve this goal.

First, the Adult Education Professional Development Consortium, in place since 1992, was charged with primary responsibility for providing the state's ABE teachers with high-quality professional development. The consortium is composed of four major centers, two of which focus on ABE and two on ESL provision, plus other smaller professional development providers. While professional development requirements for teachers are still being fulfilled by seat-time requirements rather than by professional outcomes or products, the consortium is in a position to provide or monitor the quality of professional development activities to ensure high standards.

Second, to inform the priorities and design of professional development provision, the consortium was also charged with developing a list of teacher proficiencies. Input from all stakeholders was encouraged, and focus groups were held around the state. The initial draft of proficiencies was disseminated widely and, following additional input from teachers, administrators, and consortium members, underwent significant revision.

Third, and at the same time, Southwest Texas State University was contracted to develop a workable model for a voluntary ABE credential and credentialing system that would have the support of the field. It has not yet been decided which state department will monitor the system. The Adult Education Credential Project has at this point proposed a credential model for new educators as well as those with more than three years of ABE teaching experience. The model addresses proposed content areas, a proposed delivery system, and a proposed documentation system.

The proposed Texas credentialing system is designed to achieve a number of worthy goals. Primarily, the system is to build local capacity by supporting the development of a cadre of master teachers to share their knowledge and skills and to serve as mentors. The system also builds on and will enhance the existing professional development structure rather than create a parallel system. Many of the courses, workshops, conferences, and institutes already exist, and demand from the field and consistent monitoring by the credential project staff and the Texas Education Agency should increase availability and accountability.

An attempt has been made to strike a balance between a seat-time requirement (time spent taking a course, participating in a workshop, or attending conference sessions) and content proficiency demonstration (being observed, presenting at a conference, mentoring another teacher, or conducting action research). In addition, to receive credit for any seat-time activity, participants must submit a culminating reflection and response report that includes a summary of what was learned, a reflection on the relevance of the content to them and to their classes, and an explanation of how they will implement what they have learned—with evidence of that implementation, if appropriate. The system is flexible enough to meet the varying needs of teachers—such as those living in rural areas, working full-time during the day, or caring for family members—so that their participation is not prohibited.

The system relies on the current professional development system already in place in Texas but contributes a structure and standardization to the system. The range of delivery options is intentionally wide, and each option is assigned a number of points that will count toward achieving the credential. Alternatives include

- University course (3 semester hours; 30 points)
- Online course (3 semester hours; 30 points)
- Intensive institute (25 points)
- Standard institute (15 points)
- Instructor observation (15 points)
- Mentorship (15 points)
- Study group (15 points)
- Two-day workshop (10 points)
- One-day workshop (5 points)
- Five conference sessions (5 points)
- Presentation at conference (5 points)
- Web page development (5 points)

The particular content of the professional development activity will determine the assignment of points to core content areas; each activity type requires a particular form of documentation.

The proposed system varies slightly for those just entering the field and for those who are already working as full- or part-time teachers with more than three years of experience. Each teacher is required to complete 115 points (125 for new teachers) that are spread across six core content areas:

- Principles of adult learning (25 points)

- Teaching-learning transaction with adult students (30 points)

- Diverse learning styles, abilities, and cultures (20 points)

- Integrating technology into adult learning (20 points)

- Accountability systems (15 points)

- Field participation (15 points)

Once the core credential has been completed, an optional subject area specialization (70 additional points) is available for those interested.

New and experienced full-time teachers will be given three years to complete their credential; part-timers will have six years. The final year for all will be devoted to a structured, formal teacher action research project with required products, using the Project IDEA model of El Paso Community College and monitored by the Credential Project. Before the final year, a Credential-Project-approved team member will conduct an on-site instructional evaluation of the candidate. Experienced teachers will have an opportunity to receive credit for professional development activities in which they participated over the last five years and for graduate coursework they completed over the last seven years.

MEASUREMENT OF SUCCESS. The strength of the model resides in the congruence it attempts to establish between the Texas Adult Education Instructor Proficiencies and the core content areas of the Adult Education Credential Model. The extent to which stakeholders perceive that the credential reflects attainment of meaningful skills and competencies will determine its legitimacy.

Measuring the success of the Texas credentialing system is difficult, especially since participation has been envisioned as voluntary, although the new state director, Sheila Rosenberg, anticipates that participation will become required. It is hoped that a practitioner who attains the credential will have a better chance of being given one of the limited number of full-time positions that provide benefits. Such a commitment by hiring organizations would certainly encourage participation. An additional measure of success will be if the system is legitimized and supported by a state education agency. Alternatively, perhaps a professional association will adopt the system and encourage participation.

One particular bright spot in the Texas plan is its commitment to documenting the development of the credentialing system. This will help others understand, appreciate, and learn from the pitfalls, false starts, ongoing concerns, and necessary compromises that were made. Insight into the development process allows those both inside and outside of the system to understand it better.

STATUS REPORT. Project personnel believe that the system will be fully functional by 2005 or 2006. In the course of the development process, the system is continually being reviewed by all stakeholders, with numerous scheduled forums providing opportunities for input as well as an open call for comments from Texans and any other interested parties.

During 2001, the project is undertaking a year-long pilot test of the system. Ten practitioners will work toward their certification and will receive stipends to contribute to a qualitative and quantitative evaluation of their experience. An additional hundred volunteer practitioners will also participate. If the project is refunded, the pilot testing will be extended.

The documentation process for the credentialing system will be electronic and work continues in the development of the software to manage the data. Participating teachers will have electronic portfolios in which to keep their documentation from professional development providers, individual professional development plans, transcripts, attendance records, instructor observation reports, reflections, and so on.

Summary

The plans for professionalization of the ABE workforce in both Massachusetts and Texas demonstrate that each state is very much aware of the debate in K–12 education on the reform of teacher preparation and development. Each state has adopted performance evaluation methods that combine some seat-time requirements (coursework, workshops) with alternative, performance-based measures (port-folios). Texas has also pledged to support a "core" of professional teachers whom the state will look to for leadership as they work to create an infrastructure on which to build. The approach to building the systems is different: Texas will try to create a system that builds on the one in place, while Massachusetts has set up a system that is separate from but parallel to the K–12 system.

One interesting aspect of both efforts is the decision to make participation in these systems voluntary. No state has a voluntary K–12 system. All K–12 teachers are required to have at least some credentials for both hiring and continued employment. Nor, to our knowledge, is the achievement of basic credentials voluntary in any other profession. Built into K–12 systems are incentives for teachers to increase their expertise well beyond these basic requirements. While Texas has included some incentives (like salary increases) for teachers who voluntarily increase their professional expertise, Massachusetts has not (to date) done so. This raises a number of questions: What kind of results can be expected from a completely voluntary system of professionalization? Will teachers in fact choose to participate? Although some might do so for altruistic reasons or for personal enrichment and interest, for many, participation may depend on external incentives for gaining the credential. What can teachers expect in return for investing their time and energy in becoming certified in a field where there are few full-time, stable positions that include benefits?

It may be, of course, that the states see the voluntary option as temporary, to be used only as they try to create viable systems and increase funding. That both states are committed to the certification of full-time professionals and are establishing rather detailed requirements indicates that they may be moving in that direction. Their success in professionalizing the ABE field will depend on where they end up. If the credential eventually required is perceived as imposed and arbitrary—a top-down mandate—there may be great resistance to it on the part of those to be certified. If, however, the credential is perceived as an expression of the profession's own standards (a bottom-up movement), then, as the experience of Massachusetts demonstrates, more support will be forthcoming. If, in addition, the credential is supported at the policy level, conferring benefits such as status, salary increases, and stability it is still more likely to succeed. Teachers must see some advantage in being credentialed.

OBSTACLES TO CHANGE

Even with the many promising initiatives now under way, a number of major obstacles remain in the path of professionalization for adult educators.

- *Overzealous accountability demands from the top down.* The positive atmosphere in which certification is now being considered was built on the efforts of states and programs committed to providing and supporting professional development in a flexible manner with the goal of improving program effectiveness and student outcomes. If certification is perceived by practitioners and programs as merely a means of punitive evaluation and bureaucratic intrusion, then field resistance will block change. Grassroots buy-in is essential to continued progress.

- *Accountability anxiety from the bottom up.* The increased accountability demand of the WIA and the phasing in of state and national reporting systems have increased anxiety at the program level and raised suspicions that the demands on programs are exceeding the resources and support provided. Part-timers, volunteers, and other support staff may perceive any professionalization initiative as an effort to push them out.

- *Credibility of adult basic education within the administering organizations in the state.* Adult literacy is still administered by state departments of education, community college systems, departments of labor, and combinations of these and other governmental agencies. The stature and influence of adult literacy vary greatly from state to state. Progress may require negotiating or collaborating with these organizations, forging new alliances, or advocating directly to state legislatures. Progress may rest entirely on the leadership and experience of the adult literacy state director, a position with a high turnover rate.

- *One-size-fits-all solutions.* Rapid changes in student populations and demographics, a growing field with a changing infrastructure, and a changing legislative and policy environment are all factors in favor of flexible, multileveled systems.

- *Supply and demand of the K–12 system.* The shortage of K–12 teachers is a problem nationwide, and the infrastructure that would make ABE an economically attractive choice is not in place. Given such dynamics, competing with school systems for qualified adult professionals is a reality.

IMPLICATIONS FOR POLICY, PRACTICE, AND RESEARCH

Much as it is important to document obstacles to the development of professionalization and certification in the field of adult basic education, it is important to note the many opportunities for change that present themselves. This section recommends positive actions for change in policy, practice, and research.

Policy

A number of policies recommend themselves to successful efforts at increasing professionalization, and several of these have been adopted in Massachusetts and Texas—for example,

- State commitment to the value of professionalization for full-time adult educators, which encourages increased professionalization for other practitioners
- An established track record of supporting professional development at multiple levels
- Providing incentives at the teacher and program levels
- Fostering coalition building among stakeholders
- Grassroots involvement in the setting of teaching and learning standards that will become the foundation of requirements
- Constructing flexible systems with multiple options that suggest a willingness to adapt and revise

A number of other policies can also be recommended to states seeking to establish a professional ABE workforce. These include a long-term vision that recognizes that professionalization is not an end in itself but rather a tool for building capacity and a comprehensive ABE service system for learners. States also should establish processes for aligning competencies and professional development activities to teacher needs and changing learner demographics and for aligning certification and professional development to learner standards and outcomes. Evaluation and monitoring systems that provide programs and policymakers with feedback for improvement are not much in evidence, and are sorely needed. Finally, states should support research and evaluation that links certification and competency processes to program improvement and learner outcomes.

Practice

Practitioners need to reflect on the knowledge, skills, practices, and proficiencies that define competence in teaching in general and that are specific to the adult literacy educator. To what extent are the teaching standards and competencies embodied in the PRO-NET and various NBPTS frameworks applicable to the adult educator? What accountability mechanisms can the field of practitioners accept and embrace as legitimately reflecting the standards of performance teachers expect of their peers?

Practitioners also need to reflect on the learning needs of adults and how they are embodied in content standards. How relevant are the specific K–12 content standards to adult educators? The K–12 curriculum standards represent a societal judgment regarding the outcome of education expected for all citizens. One could conclude that the expectations for adult learners would be to achieve and even exceed the standards set for K–12 students. On the other hand, the needs of adult literacy learners as expressed in the EFF framework put greater emphasis on adult roles and responsibilities than on the subject matter content that is the curricular focus of K–12 education. Preparing to teach as if both approaches are of equal weight would only increase the burden on adult educators. Resolving this apparent conflict is critical to better defining an adult literacy teaching profession.

Practitioners should also consider the extent to which they wish to form a stronger alliance with the K–12 professional community in general. The benefits of a stronger alliance could include greater prestige and status in the educational community, stronger support and advocacy on the part of teacher unions, and the potential for increased salary and job stability. At the same time, the concerns cited by Perin (1998–99) and others about the disadvantages of alliance with K–12 continue to be valid. Vigilance is necessary to guard against the implementation of systems that

- Discriminate against ABE in favor of K–12
- Restrict the entry of or eliminate valuable staff members with less formal preparation, such as staff with close ties to the community, part-time staff, and volunteers (which does not mean these staff should not be required to demonstrate teaching competence)
- Increase bureaucratic control or government intrusion into teacher preparation and program activities
- Favor seat-time over teaching standards and competence-based approaches

In sum, the disadvantages include loss of a "valid and distinct" identity as an adult literacy educator. A goal of professionalization may be to better define a collection of persons as representing a field of endeavor, but the difficulty is that decisions regarding who is included and excluded in that professional community must be faced. Finally, practitioners must be active participants and advocates for their profession through active membership in state coalitions and professional organizations. As noted, progressive policy-level initiatives look to the grass roots to be informed of how best to implement change. In this way, practitioners can continue to provide leadership in advocating for legislative change, developing teaching and learning standards or competencies, and organizing, communicating, or gathering input from the field to inform policy that helps build the capacity and infrastructure to support an adult literacy teaching profession.

Research

A research agenda to support and inform the movement toward professionalization would address a number of issues. Foremost are studies linking the impact of competencies and certification processes to learner outcomes and program improvement. Such studies must be longitudinal and may be difficult and expensive to conduct. However, they are helpful in understanding and evaluating the foundational knowledge and competencies upon which credentialing systems are built. Case studies focused on innovative state programs such as those described in this chapter and in the National Institute for Literacy (2000) report are also needed to better understand the impact of policy on the recruitment, retention, and morale of adult educators. Similarly, more needs analyses and surveys of adult educators should be conducted (full- and part-time teachers across the variety of programs and contexts serving adults) to better gauge and understand their interest in certification and their views as to whether such certification would have positive or negative impacts on job stability, salary, status, and self-improvement.

Another line of research would address the relationship between K–12 teacher preparation and ABE teaching competence, with special attention to how reforms of the K–12 system can inform a more progressive ABE teacher system. Questions to address might include the following: How would programs specifically targeted to adult educators differ from the typical teacher preparation program? Would a specialization consisting of a set of courses specifically on ABE theory and practice suffice? Are courses aligned to specific K–12 certification types (for example, early childhood education) relevant to ABE, or would such courses foster misconceptions about adult learning?

In general, the body of research that looks at teaching and teacher education in K–12 is quite rich and elaborated. The unique and valid characteristics of adult literacy educators may best be articulated and documented by conducting research comparing and contrasting their perspectives, experiences, and contexts against this body of work.

Notes

1. One goal of standardizing the profession would be to provide the public at large with the assurance that adult education practitioners maintain a high level of competence that is consistent throughout the profession (Galbraith & Gilley, 1986). The notion of standardized professional responses does not mean that all professional adult educators would act with unanimity—for example, all applying the same instructional methods. However, the range of instructional methods would be more limited, and all would be consistent with high standards of competence serving as guidelines for the profession.

2. K–12 accountability is a complex issue of its own and we have not addressed here the many ethical and operational ramifications that different approaches to accountability entail. Two such fundamental issues

are the nature and types of assessment one uses to measure student outcome and who should or can be accountable for results. Regarding the latter issue, John Tibbetts (personal communication, Feb. 21, 2001) commented, "Teachers should not (cannot) be held accountable for student learning any more than we would make a rehabilitation counselor responsible for a client's failure to stop drinking. *Teachers should be held accountable for teaching in the best way that we know how to teach.* They can do no more than that. Students, in the best constructivist tradition, must be accountable for their own learning. And management must be accountable for providing structure, guidance and support to programs and instructors."

We are concerned, as are many in the educational community, of the misuse of testing and accountability in education. Our point is that accountability is a political and operational reality. Our goal and hope is that it be implemented sensibly and responsibly, serving the ends of a continuous improvement program evaluation model. To illustrate using the reviewer's example, given the same population and counseling program for clientele with alcohol addictions, a measure of outcomes could show that one counselor had a considerably higher rate of success than a colleague in preventing the recurrence of alcohol abuse in clients. If that information were validly and reliably collected, and the sources of those difference in performance can be identified and used to improve training or support for other counselors or the program, then the accountability mechanisms are justifiable.

3. The GED program has provided an alternative pathway to attaining a high school equivalency diploma for adults for many years. Its credibility as a credential for higher education institutions and business is built upon, in part, its correspondence to the standards of the academic curriculum of secondary education (reading, writing, mathematics, science, and social studies) and its normative reference to graduating high school seniors, which establishes validity of the test as demonstrating that adults who pass the test have skills comparable to those of this target group.

Whether and to what extent the content of the high school curriculum or the approaches to teaching it are adapted to the functional needs of adults is a somewhat different content standards issue. The GED tests are given to high school seniors in the norm-referencing validation studies, so the content and skills necessary to achieve high scores on the tests cannot be highly related to different or unique adult learning principles or contexts in contrast to those that are part of secondary school education. Our point here is that, as sensible as it may be to have established the validity of an adult credential by benchmarking "tests" against the curriculum standards of a secondary education diploma, it still leaves open the question of what the most appropriate and best curriculum standards for adults may be. Thanks to a reviewer for recommending this expanded discussion.

4. Sherman et al. (1999) cite using as resources guidelines published in Minnesota (Teaching Principles and Competencies for the Minnesota Adult Educator), Kentucky (Competency Profile of an Adult Basic Skills Instructor), Texas (Adult Education Instructor), several from California (including ESL Handbook for Adult Education Instructors, Model Standards for Adult Education, and the Adult Education Programs of Excellence), and Pennsylvania's ABLE Practitioners of Excellence Project. As noted by a reviewer, the foundational work done by Mocker (1974) was an oft-used resource in state development projects.

5. A full description of the National Board Assessment system can be found at http://www.nbpts.org.

References

American Federation of Teachers K–16 Teacher Education Task Force. (2000). *Building a profession: Strengthening teacher preparation and induction.* Washington, DC: Author.

Belzer, A., Drennon, C., & Smith, C. (2001). Building professional development systems in adult basic education. In J. Comings, B. Garner, & C. Smith (Eds.), *Annual review of adult learning and literacy* (Vol. 2). San Francisco: Jossey-Bass.

Condelli, L. (2000). *Measures and methods for the National Reporting System for adult education: Implementation guidelines.* Washington, DC: Council of Chief State School Officers, Pelavin Research Institute.

Department of Education, Commonwealth of Massachusetts. (1999). *Interim report on the development of ABE certification.* Malden, MA: Author.

Department of Education, Commonwealth of Massachusetts. (2001, January 26). Memorandum: Draft regulations for adult basic education teacher license. Malden, MA: Author.

ERIC Digest. (1986). Teacher certification. *ERIC Digest 11*. Washington, DC: ERIC Clearinghouse on Teacher Education.

Evans, A., & Sherman, R. (1999). *Guide to ABE in graduate programs.* Washington, DC: Pelavin Research Institute.

Fay, M. J., & Reid, C. (2000, March). Developing an Adult Basic Education Teacher Certification in Massachusetts. Paper presented at the Adult Education Research Conference, Penn State University, State College, PA.

Galbraith, M. W., & Gilley, J. W. (1985). An examination of professional certification. *Lifelong learning: An omnibus of practice and research, 9*(2), 12–15.

Galbraith, M. W., & Gilley, J. W. (1986). *Professional certification: Implications for adult education and HRD.* Washington, DC: Office of Educational Research and Improvement, U.S. Department of Education.

Kutner, M., Herman, R., Stephenson, E., Webb, L., Tibbetts, J., & Klein, M. (1991). *Study of ABE/ESL instructor training approaches: State profiles report.* Washington, DC: Pelavin Research Institute.

Kutner, M., Webb, L., & Matheson, N. (1996). *A review of statewide learner competency and assessment systems.* Washington, DC: Pelavin Research Institute.

McAninch, A. M. (1993). *Teacher thinking and the case method: Theory and future directions.* New York: Teachers College Press.

Merrifield, J. (1998). *Contested ground: Performance accountability in adult education* (NCSALL Reports 1). Cambridge, MA: National Center for the Study of Adult Learning and Literacy.

Mocker, D. W. (1974). *Report on the identification, classification, and ranking of competencies.* Washington, DC: ERIC Clearinghouse on Adult, Career, and Vocational Education.

National Adult Education Professional Development Consortium. (1998). *State organizational survey 1996–1997.* Washington, DC: Author.

National Adult Education Professional Development Consortium. (forthcoming). *State organizational survey.* Washington, DC: Author.

National Board for Professional Teaching Standards. (2000). Available online: http://www.nbpts.org/. Access date: August 4, 2001.

National Council for the Social Studies. (1994). *Expectations of excellence: Curriculum standards for social studies.* Washington, DC: Author.

National Council of Teachers of Mathematics. (2000). *Principles and standards for school mathematics.* Reston, VA: Author.

National Institute for Literacy. (1995). *Equipped for the future: A customer-driven vision for adult literacy and lifelong learning.* Washington, DC: Author.

National Institute for Literacy. (2000). *The professionalization of adult education: Can state certification of adult educators contribute to a more professional workforce?* Washington, DC: Author.

National Literacy Summit. (2000). *From the margins to the mainstream: An action agenda for literacy.* Washington, DC: Author.

National Research Council. (1996). *National science education standards.* Washington, DC: National Academy Press.

Office of Vocational and Adult Education. (1992, July). *Model indicators of program quality for adult education programs, U.S. Department of Education.* Washington, DC: Author. (ERIC Document Reproduction Service No. ED 352 499).

Perin, D. (1998–99). Professionalizing adult literacy: Would a credential help? *Journal of Adolescent and Adult Literacy, 42,* 610–627.

Sabatini, J. P., Daniels, M., Limeul, K., Russell, M., Ginsburg, L., & Stites, R. (2000). *Profiles of an emergent profession: Findings from a national survey of adult literacy professionals.* (Technical Report 00–01). Philadelphia: National Center on Adult Literacy.

Secretary's Commission on Achieving Necessary Skills (SCANS). (1991). *What work requires of schools: A SCANS report for America 2000.* Washington, DC: U.S. Department of Labor.

Shanahan, T., Meehan, M., & Mogge, S. (1994). *The professionalization of the teacher in adult literacy education.* Philadelphia: National Center on Adult Literacy.

Sherman, R., Tibbetts, J., Woodruff, D., & Wiedler, D. (1999). *Instructor competencies and performance indicators for the improvement of adult education programs.* Washington, DC: Pelavin Research Institute.

U.S. Department of Education. (2000). *Eliminating the barriers to improving teaching.* Washington, DC: Author.

Webb, L. (1997). *Adult education instructor competencies: Soliciting input from the field.* Washington, DC: Pelavin Research Institute.

CHAPTER SEVEN

Current Areas of Interest in Family Literacy

Vivian L. Gadsden

F amily literacy has developed over the past decade into an increasingly significant—and often contested—area of research, practice, and policymaking in the fields of literacy and family studies as well as in the broader arenas of education and schooling. The purpose of this chapter is to give the reader a better understanding of the general state of family literacy today—a snapshot—with an eye toward strengthening the relationship between family literacy and adult literacy and learning. The chapter is divided into three sections. The first section provides a brief background of, or context for, the research, practice, and policy that have led to current efforts. The second presents areas that have emerged as critical domains of interest to the field: parent-child interactions, including emergent literacy; intergenerational literacy; ESOL and language differences; assessment and evaluation; and culture and context. The third section summarizes persistent challenges to the field as well as possibilities for implementing meaningful linkages between research and practice. Following this chapter is an annotated bibliography recommending a number of resources readers can turn to for more information about each of these areas.

Definitions of family literacy are rarely clear-cut. Arguably, no one definition can capture the full range of issues or the complexity of the field. However, most definitions tend to describe family literacy in relation to the ways parents, children, and extended family members use literacy at home and in their community (Morrow, Paratore, & Tracey, 1994). Within these definitions, family literacy may include parents' and children's relationships around reading, writing, and problem solving prior to and during school years as well as children's acquisition of knowledge about the conventions and purposes of print and the uses of language in culturally organized activities (Wasik, 2001). Such definitions reflect the thrust of most family literacy programs, which typically address one or more of the following: reduction of children's difficulties and subsequent failure in school; involvement of parents and families in programs for young children; improvement of parents' reading and literacy when parents have low levels of literacy and schooling; and the relationship between parents' literacy levels and schooling and their children's school achievement. In federal legislation such as the Reading Excellence Act of 1998, these definitions are collapsed into a single description of "family literacy services" and are described as integrating "(a) interactive literacy activities between parents and their children, (b) training for parents regarding how to be the primary teacher for their children and full partners in the education of their children, (c) parent literacy training that leads to economic self-sufficiency, and (d) an age-appropriate education to prepare children for success in school and life experiences." Expansive definitions of family literacy focus not only on children's literacy development in families but also on adult literacy and learning in the home as well as on the intersections of child and adult literacy, communication patterns in the family, and family practices that enhance the literacy knowledge and skills of family members. This chapter has been developed with these expansive definitions in mind.

BRIEF BACKGROUND OF THE FIELD

Before looking at the field of family literacy as it exists today, it is useful to look back briefly to see how it arrived at this juncture. Current conceptions of family literacy are drawn from two primary sources. One is the variety of studies in reading and literacy undertaken as early as the 1960s and 1970s, an example being Durkin's (1966) work with low-income African American children and parents in inner-city Chicago. Many of these studies focused on the influence of verbal language—that is, nonstandard dialects such as black or African American Vernacular English (AAVE)—on the reading development of children, specifically the reading of poor, urban minority children. In many of these studies, reading failure was attributed to "deficits" in the linguistic and literacy experiences of children resulting from their "disadvantaged" families and low-income communities (Bereiter & Engelmann, 1966; Deutsch, 1965). Other studies (for example, Baratz, 1969; Labov, 1965, 1972; Ruddell, 1965) challenged these theories by proposing "difference" theory, in which AAVE was viewed simply as one dialect among many spoken dialects and was examined to determine the degree to which it interfered—if at all—with reading development. Still others (for example, Goodman & Buck, 1973) argued that the reading failure of African American children was largely due to their teachers' problematic attitudes toward the dialect.

All these debates centered on the origins of reading problems and the barriers to reading development. They were part of the growing emphasis on understanding how reading is learned and what are the most effective approaches to teaching it, with some advocating phonics or skills-based approaches and others advocating sight and word recognition approaches. These debates also sowed the seeds for greater attention paid during the early 1980s to the sociolinguistic, cultural, and contextual factors that influence children's literacy, including home and school, and the specific role of parents' literacy in shaping home environments that lead to children's literacy success and school achievement.

By the mid to late 1980s, reading research was beginning to acknowledge a range of social and cultural factors that influence both children's early literacy productions and parents' involvement, opening up the way for a serious discussion of families as an important context for understanding literacy development and of family literacy as a potentially viable field (Strickland, 1979; Strickland & Morrow, 1989). This shift was most evident in research such as William Teale and Elizabeth Sulzby's (1986) study of emergent literacy and the effects of parent involvement and home environment on children's early reading. Denny Taylor's volume *Family Literacy* (1983) made the connections between classroom, home, and literacy that had surfaced in the 1960s and 1970s more explicit by identifying some of the functions of literacy for both children and adults in diverse families. The combination of this increasing interest by researchers in the role of parents and families in reading development and school achievement with emerging activities in practice led to a second source of current conceptions of family literacy—the formalization of applied family literacy efforts and programs. Sharon Darling's work in Kentucky's Parent and Child Education Program, supported by the William R. Kenan Charitable Trusts, is an example of leading efforts through the 1980s. By 1989, she had established the National Center for Family Literacy (NCFL), which helped to increase the visibility of family literacy nationally and contributed to the integration of family literacy into federal initiatives in education (such as Even Start) and social services (such as Head Start).

At the same time, publications such as *Becoming a Nation of Readers* (Anderson, Hiebert, Scott, & Wilkinson, 1985) argued that reading aloud to children was the most significant factor in preparing them to read and to learn in school, while *A Nation at Risk* (National Commission on Excellence in Education, 1983) raised awareness about the persistence of children's poor literacy performance, particularly in impoverished, isolated, and vulnerable communities. Simultaneously, adult literacy was gaining increased momentum, and programmatic efforts in family literacy were expanding—attaching problems of low literacy to a range of negative life outcomes and focusing on improving the literacy of children subject to the intergenerational problems of low literacy in poor and often minority families.

Research

In the 1990s, family literacy both prospered and struggled as a field. It began to develop an identity within early childhood education, K–12 education, and adult literacy efforts, coming to be associated with four conceptual themes: children's acquisition of basic cognitive and linguistic skills within the context of the family; the occurrence of substantial literacy learning by children in the years prior to receiving formal literacy instruction; parental education and literacy practices in the home and their relationship to children's school achievement and test performance; and the limitations of parents with lower-level literacy skills to help their children with literacy learning (Purcell-Gates, 1993). In addition, as a sign of its initiation into the field of literacy, family literacy became embroiled in the reading debates that divided the field on issues such as the use of "deficit models" that appeared to minimize, if not ignore, the prior knowledge of child and adult learners (Taylor, 1995).

At least two theoretical stances have dominated family literacy research. One suggests that parents in family literacy programs have little of the formal literacy knowledge to assist their children to achieve in school and that they need to be taught specific literacy skills to ensure their children's cognitive development. Because proponents of this stance often do not indicate whether and how they will use the prior knowledge and existing skills of parents, families, and community members as a context for supporting the literacy development of children and families, and because they appear to rely heavily on school-like or skills-based models, the stance is sometimes associated with deficit approaches. The second stance is linked theoretically to a social-contextual approach that begins by seeking information from the family (typically parent—usually mother—and child) about family practices and interactions in order to better understand the functions, uses, and purposes of literacy within families—by children and adults—and to then build literacy support based on this knowledge. Because this stance is based on the idea that teachers and learners co-construct knowledge over the course of learning, proponents tend to focus on the processes of interaction and to draw from a range of approaches and assessments rather than from a single skills-based approach.

Although the two stances are associated with distinctive research camps, they do not represent all-or-nothing commitments in actual practice. In short, it is more likely that most family literacy services are developed with some combination of the two stances and use approaches that draw upon both. However, it is also possible that in articulating and promoting their individual positions, proponents of the two stances appear either to minimize the abilities and contextual strengths of the families or to stress the skills and cognitive domains of learning at the exclusion of social, cultural, or contextual factors.

Studies derived from the two stances reflect, and in some cases share, two dominant, sometimes overlapping, views on literacy learning in the home. The first suggests that parents' literacy has a significant influence on children's motivation to acquire, develop, and use literacy. From this view, the physical environment, such as whether books and other reading materials are readily available, is considered to have a sizable impact on children's efficacy with print (Mason & Allen, 1986; Strickland, Morrow, Taylor, & Walls, 1990). A second view is that literacy can serve as a liberating and empowering force for all members of the family. Specifically, the argument is that adults who gain a sense of personal control as a result of improved literacy and who are given opportunities to accept or reject alternatives to their current practices are able to model for their children the importance of literacy to personal success and power (Auerbach, 1990; Street, 1992; Taylor, 1983; Shockley, Michalove, & Allen, 1995).

Research related to both of these positions suggests that the ability of programs to foster the development of literacy in many homes may be constrained by social distance (created as a result of misunderstanding or lack of information) between family and program. This distance may be perpetuated by literacy providers who lack knowledge of or fail to pay attention to the cultural beliefs and practices in the home and community, the literacy needs of family members, and the expectations of literacy learning on the part of children and parents. This distance may be exacerbated by a perception in families that literacy is inaccessible to them—both children and adults—because of social or cultural differences, institutional barriers in society, or learners' own past negative experiences with literacy learning and instruction (Coles, 1985; Johnston, 1985). Family members may come to see the price of literacy as being too high or may associate literacy with real or perceived tradeoffs between the demands of home and culture and the requirements of literacy and schooling (Gadsden, 1991).

A prominent feature of the growing impetus around family literacy research is that it focuses primarily on children's literacy development in relation to their parents and the environment their parents create to enhance their literacy development. Few family literacy research discussions explore its implications for adult learning and literacy. As a result, approaches that build solid foundations for adult-related practice are missing. To understand the full range of issues in family literacy requires that researchers, while addressing children's literacy, help practitioners cast family literacy's net widely to include adult literacy and learning, highlighting the need for family and adult researchers and practitioners to become co-constructors in (re)defining the field, identifying critical questions and conducting meaningful research that recognizes the significance of both the cognitive abilities and the social processes that are associated with developing literacy, whether in school, at home, or in community settings.

Practice

Unlike other areas of literacy research, in which theory and practice tend to develop in tandem, family literacy has traditionally been seen as practice-oriented and drawn together by a loosely connected set of activities pulled from early childhood or prekindergarten efforts to K–12 and adult literacy. While there is still a distance to go, more sophisticated information is now available to practitioners on the potential for literacy outcomes to be realized by children with parents who participate in family literacy programs such as Even Start (St. Pierre & Layzer, 1999). In addition, publications such as the National Institute for Literacy's *Equipped for the Future: A New Framework for Adult Learning* (1999) have been essential in supporting programs and practice to create conceptual frameworks for providing, assessing, and reorganizing services that increase adults' and families' abilities to plan for their own well-being and for achieving their life goals.

The past decade's expansion of family literacy is due, in part, to the visibility the field has gained from increasingly prominent independent nonprofit organizations and programs focused on literacy, early childhood education, and parent and family involvement. The establishment of the National Center for Family Literacy (NCFL) in 1989 with private funding contributed to a significant shift in attention to family literacy. A nonprofit educational organization, NCFL supports a four-component national family literacy program model, referred to as the Kenan model. It serves families through adult education typically focused on basic education and life skills, English for speakers of other languages (ESOL), and workplace literacy; children's education, usually for preschool children; parent and child learning together (PACT) time, during which children and parents engage in a shared literacy activity; and parent time, during which parents are given information about children's development and an opportunity to discuss their development. Another program designed to improve children's literacy by involving parents is the Parents as Teachers (PAT) program, which began as a pilot program in Missouri in 1981. The goal of the PAT program is to foster an early partnership between home and school so that parents take a far more active role during their children's formal years of schooling. In addition, children and families in the Home Instruction Program for Preschool Youth (HIPPY) are exposed to a home-based early intervention that helps parents provide their preschool children with educational and literacy enrichment.

All of the models—PACT, PAT, HIPPY, and others—share the strengths of engaging children and adults in literacy and attending to many limitations in the literacy experiences of family learners; there is much to be learned from using them. However, each has inherent limitations when used alone. No single model can capture the full range of knowledge needs of family literacy practitioners or provide a systematic or foolproof approach. Practice based on these or any other models should reflect a rigorous investigation of the approaches and their uses within the context of what has been learned over the past twenty years from research on how children learn, how adults learn, how families function and support learning in different educational and literacy settings, and how the effects of program engagement on child and adult learning can best be assessed.

Policy

Independent efforts such as those discussed in the above section on practice have spawned numerous programs, estimated to number in the hundreds. However, it is the federally funded Even Start/Family Literacy initiative that has been most successful in institutionalizing the concept of family literacy in discussions of education and policy. With the purpose of improving the educational opportunities of low-income families by integrating early childhood education, adult basic education, and parenting education into a unified family literacy program, Even Start has been developed around three interrelated goals: to help parents become full partners in the education of their children; to assist children in reaching their full potential as learners; and to provide literacy training for the parents of children (McKee & Rhett, 1995).

Despite varying degrees of government support over time, family literacy has been integrated into many federal and state policy initiatives in reading, adult literacy, and welfare reform. Goals 2000 identified parental involvement (Goal 8) and children's school readiness (Goal 1) as focal areas of a national educational agenda and noted their importance to improving children's literacy and level of achievement in school. The 1999 reauthorization of Title I of the Elementary and Secondary Education Act (ESEA) included a focus on family literacy.

National programs such as the Office of Educational Research and Improvement's Reading Excellence Program require that states receiving awards demonstrate their capacity and plans to develop and implement a family literacy component or to integrate family literacy fully into statewide reading improvement efforts. Early education programs, such as Head Start, which were built around parental involvement, concentrate more than ever before on children's early and emergent literacy in relationship to parent-child interactions and the role of family members other than parents in young children's learning.

In the past five years, the legislation with the most potential impact on family literacy has been welfare reform. It requires family members to assume new responsibilities and practice new behaviors in relationship to work and family maintenance, and this has inadvertently limited the availability of parents and other family members who typically participate in family literacy programs. In addition, labor-related initiatives around Temporary Assistance to Needy Families (TANF) and other legislation, as well as the residuals of welfare reform, either mention the significance of family literacy or include a family literacy component.

Last, federal policy over the past decade has supported family literacy through the establishment of several federally funded centers that address children's achievement and adult learning inside and outside of school and traditional learning settings. Among these centers are the National Center for the Study of Adult Literacy and Learning at Harvard University, the Center for Research on the Education of Students Placed At-Risk at Johns Hopkins University, the Center for the Improvement of Early Reading Achievement at the University of Michigan, the Goodling Center for Family Literacy at Penn State University, the National Center on Adult Literacy at the University of Pennsylvania, and the Center for Research in Education, Diversity, and Excellence at the University of California–Santa Cruz. Research studies in these centers typically focus on parent-child literacy, on families and literacy, or on adult literacy and have helped to influence or shape the current areas of interest in family literacy.

CURRENT AREAS OF INTEREST

Family literacy is a variegated field of endeavor in that it focuses on both children and adults as well as on the cognitive, educational, and social factors that affect their ability to develop literacy. It also must recognize the diversity of families—ethnic background, family form (two-parent, single-parent, grandparent, guardian), income level, learning strengths and weaknesses, intergenerational history, and resources. Thus, I have tried to determine broad categories that are currently at the forefront of discussions on family literacy research and practice and have used them to organize the resources that follow this chapter. Three areas that I initially thought to include in this chapter and in the bibliography were technology; issues of class, poverty, and gender; and professional development. Ultimately, I decided to exclude all three, in large part because of the limited work that has been done in each area. However, these issues are critical to the continued development of the field. For example, although information about the use and effects of technology in family literacy programs is limited, the implications of technology for school-age students and for adults in the workplace are severe for families who have little access to technology; the real and perceived dimensions of the "digital divide" separating the poor from the middle class attests to the significance of the problem. More research and practice in this area are needed.

The same scarcity of published information is also a problem when trying to assess the influence of class, poverty, and gender in family literacy. Most work in family literacy addresses the needs of and issues faced by low-income families, and most work attends disproportionately to issues facing mothers and children. Few studies focus on the dynamics of poverty in relation to its role as a barrier to literacy learning or to the ways in which literacy development is constructed within economic poverty (Whitehurst, Epstein, Angell, Payne, Crone, & Fischel, 1994). In other words, several studies and most programs draw from low-income populations, but few provide a critical discussion of the meaning and impact of poverty or gender on the development of literacy. Several studies and descriptions of programs focus on the intergenerational poverty of families served and on women (mostly mothers and grandmothers); however, few studies examine how these issues are addressed or what role they play in program activities and research efforts.

Similarly, little work has been done on professional development and instructional methods in family literacy. The dearth of empirical and programmatic work in this area can be attributed in part to ongoing efforts to develop the field and to formulate frameworks that can respond to the diversity of participants in family literacy programs. In addition, the field has relied heavily on structured or commercial models that provide program strategies but are unable to provide a systematic body of support that emanates from an organized field of study in a recognized area of research or practice.

Parent-Child Literacy

Parents' role in supporting children's literacy development and appropriate approaches to helping parents help their children learn to read and write continue to be the focus of most family literacy research and practice. A significant subset of the work on interactions between parents and children involves emergent literacy and is based on the notion that the first years of a child's life represent a period when legitimate reading and writing development takes place and when the literacy of parents counts most. Children's engagement with literacy is seen as a continuum. Thus, at this early stage, their literacy is considered to be in the process of *becoming;* it is not a period of *pre*learning or *pre*reading. Children build on early knowledge and experience, changing and refining their motives and strategies, developing new ones, and learning through processes of assimilation and accommodation. Work in emergent literacy assumes that growth in reading and writing originates within the child but is equally affected by environmental stimulation. Rather than representing a new area to explore, current research on emergent literacy, like that on parent-child literacy, reflects deepened analysis and effort. The area of greatest growth in research concerns the effects of early interventions on later literacy performance in school and into adulthood (Jordan, Snow, & Porche, 2000). Indeed, the more recent work of Kaderavek and Sulzby (1999), Edwards (1996), Wasik (2001), and others suggests that to achieve success, children must be engaged early and that parents and other adults engaged in children's lives can facilitate children's learning if they are aware of the meaning-making demonstrated in children's invented spelling and early manipulation of print.

The research on parent-child interactions also points to other potential directions that have been only modestly explored: the different ways that parents and other family members transfer literacy knowledge to children; the kinds of literacies other than reading (such as writing and math) that family members use; the relationship between children's motivations to read and their parents' beliefs about the value and utility of literacy; the nature and content of literacy in homes that are diverse in cultural history and language; and parents' reasons for engaging in their children's literacy development.

A limitation of the work being done in parent-child literacy is the failure to address the role of adult literacy and of both parents—fathers as well as mothers. When research and practice focus on parent-child interactions, they tend to address the needs of children primarily or only, with little attention to the reciprocal nature of children's literacy and adult literacy. When research and practice do focus on parents, it is generally on mothers rather than fathers, in large part because mothers have traditionally been children's primary or sole caregivers. In some cases, fathers are unavailable because they are the family's primary breadwinner; in others, fathers live outside the home and are not considered to play an important role in their children's lives; in still other cases they may be difficult or even impossible to reach. As a result, few fathers participate in family literacy programs, and little information is available about those who do attend (see Gadsden, Brooks, & Jackson, 1997).

Intergenerational Literacy

The term *intergenerational literacy* is often used interchangeably with family literacy, but it is actually a subset of family literacy—a specific strand of inquiry that focuses on the transmission of knowledge and behavior from one generation to the next. As such, parent-child literacy is actually a subset of intergenerational literacy. Intergenerational literacy bears special consideration not only because of the profound influence that each generation has on subsequent generations but also because it attempts to examine the influences of earlier generations on the patterns, beliefs, and learning that guide family practices in literacy. Most descriptions of intergenerational literacy focus on adult modeling of literate behaviors, through which adults demonstrate the value and importance of certain beliefs, attitudes, and practices and help the child understand the often unspoken rules of the environment in which literacy is used (Gadsden, 1998).

A less studied, but equally important, area of interest is the bi-directionality of literacy—that is, how children assist adults as well as how adults teach children. When both parent and child are non-native speakers of English, children may assist parents in activities such as responding to written requests and paying bills. The balance of authority between parent and child is often tested in such cases and is determined in large part by the cultural frames of reference of family and community (Weinstein, 1998). This leads to another category of interest, the development of literacy in families who are nonnative speakers of English.

ESOL and Language Differences

Efforts in ESOL have typically been attached to K–12 settings or adult literacy programs (see Paratore, Melzi, & Krol-Sinclair, 1999; Quintero & Huerta-Macias, 1995). Snow and Strucker (2000) point to the need to investigate the instructional strategies that work to promote comprehension, analysis, word learning, inference, and critical thinking among children and adults. In addition to the instructional and contextual factors affecting ESOL learning are the related issues of role changes and reversals in English-learning families—the reciprocal relationship between child and parent or other adult family member, particularly when the fluent speaker is the child but the breadwinner is the parent. This relationship is most evident in Weinstein-Shr's (1991; Weinstein, 1998) research on older Southeast Asians with limited English proficiency, in which the author describes the complex relationships, compromises, and negotiations that take place when the English-language facility of the child challenges the authority of the parent.

Most studies of ESOL learning and teaching in family literacy and most family literacy ESOL programs (both within and external to Even Start) focus on two generations of Spanish-speaking learners (see, for example, Shanahan & Rodriguez-Brown, 1995). The studies highlight the complexity of attempting to separate language and cultural issues in the family literacy development of immigrant groups (Delgado-Gaitan, 1996; Duran, Duran, Perry-Romero, & Sanchez, 2001). More work needs to be done on the increasing numbers of non-Spanish-speaking groups, such as Asians and Eastern Europeans. Three critical issues—language, literacy, and culture—tend to be combined and to act as barriers to many immigrant groups as well as indigenous minority groups. They are deeply intertwined and must be addressed together if researchers and practitioners are to support the social, cultural, and linguistic transitions that family literacy development requires (Duran, Duran, Perry-Romero, & Sanchez, 2001).

Assessment and Evaluation

In their summary of family literacy efforts in Michigan, Parecki, Paris, and Seidenberg (1997) called attention to the absence of a discussion of assessment and evaluation measures. The current state of assessment and evaluation is significantly improved yet still considerably lacking (Holt, 1994). National evaluations of programs such as Even Start (St. Pierre & Swartz, 1995) provide sound evidence as to whether and how programs are working. How programs implement, assess, monitor, and revise their practices in the normal course of their daily work is more difficult to determine, however. Not even in the national evaluation studies are there specific outcome data on changes in participants' lives. What do exist are wonderful vignettes of individual children and families that tend to focus on the result of change but offer little information on the process of change or the ways in which that process is influenced by the nature and quality of teaching and curricula. The 1998 Reading Excellence Act requires that each state receiving funds develop indicators of program quality "based on the best available research and evaluation data." Although focused on the larger state evaluation, these indicators will provide a framework on which programs can build while encouraging the development of sound assessment measures that will help the field determine specific outcomes for children and adults in a family and better understand the nature and process of family literacy learning and teaching.

Culture and Context

Family literacy specialists—researchers, practitioners, and others with expertise in the field—often have limited knowledge of the experiences of minority groups as well as vastly different definitions of culture and the approaches that should be used to integrate culture with research and practice. The term *culture* actually has much in common with the term *family* in that both imply cohesiveness and solidarity—that is, traditions, expectations, and practices that ostensibly serve the common purpose of the healthy development of children and the welfare of the family (Gadsden, 1996, 2001). The terms *context* and *culture* are used widely in literacy research and practice—for instance, sociocultural and sociocontextual bases for literacy learning—with context referring to the settings or sites in which learning occurs and to the kinds of interpersonal approaches to learning, beliefs, and practices that are influenced by, and that have influenced, an individual's literacy experiences. Context thus includes the knowledge and uses of literacy that stem from national, ethnic, and family traditions. In a field where large numbers of participants represent diverse ethnic and racial histories and experiences, it is important that practitioners both learn more about these histories and experiences and raise questions about what it would mean for a family literacy program to address issues of culture, race, and diversity.

CLOSING CONSIDERATIONS

Family literacy has expanded in meaningful ways as a field during the past decade. Connections are slowly but increasingly being made between family literacy and parent involvement and children's early literacy development and between family literacy and other areas of early childhood and family studies. Researchers and practitioners in family and social services are focusing more directly on family literacy, and family literacy researchers and practitioners are examining more carefully issues of family health and welfare in relationship to literacy learning. As models are refined, they are attending to broad issues about how families function and the specific needs of family members as learners.

Despite these modest though notable advances, several prominent problems persist. The first is the need to deepen our understanding of how children's literacy is affected by their interactions with parents and other caregivers. A second concerns the absence of critical discussion about adult learning and literacy within the context of family literacy and reciprocity between the two areas, adult literacy and family literacy. A focus on "parent time" in which parents address only children's developmental issues may well miss the opportunity to understand what adults learn through family literacy efforts and what implications this has for teaching and research in adult basic education.

Unlike other areas of literacy, family literacy has the potential to study and serve individuals over the life-course, from early childhood to old age, and to contribute to our understanding of the nature and quality of literacy used and developed over time and the intersections of learning by multiple family members. Some models, such as the Kenan model, attempt to address ABE and parent issues while emphasizing children's literacy. Others, such as PAT, attempt to help through specific exercises in home visiting. Still other models, such as those developed by Edwards (1996), attend to the low literacy of adults as a precursor to parents' helping children. Despite the value of these and other approaches, most of the discussion of family literacy takes place within one sphere—that is, how one parent helps one child as opposed to how the literacy of both child and adult learner is stimulated and developed. Thus, family literacy must be primed to respond to questions about the approaches from adult literacy research and practice that can be infused into family literacy, and adult literacy research must address comparable issues from family literacy.

A second fundamental problem in family literacy is the divide between research and practice, a problem not unique to family literacy. As with other fields, family literacy continues to be guided by a philosophy in which theory and research flow to practice rather than more progressive and reflexive approaches in which practice informs research and research informs practice. In family literacy, the two worlds of researchers and practitioners rarely, if ever, meet. The only exception occurs during evaluations—the most awkward moments for building a core of collaborative effort between these two parties. In related work on fathers and families (Gadsden, Kane, & Armorer, 1996), my colleagues and I have focused exclusively on practice-derived research and research-informed practice as a point of entry for more critical, rigorous, and inclusive discourses and action. The practical issues of forging a relationship in which the voices of practitioners are not simply privileged along with those of researchers but also represent a sound body of knowledge, resources, and analyses are difficult to parse. When a nexus between the goals and work of researchers and practitioners is achieved and each group maintains an identity, entrée into and participation in the world of the other in response to problems and possibilities in the field can be realized.

As with other areas of educational research and practice, efforts in family literacy starkly remind us of the promise that can be realized by threading together critical components of inquiry: known reading, writing, and problem-solving literacy issues of students at different points in their schooling; the potential of homes and schools as sites for learning; and the inherent complexities of goals that involve not only the improvement of children's literacy but also an improvement of the range and scope of literacy learning among their parents and other adults. While we know more about family literacy than we did a decade ago, there is much more to learn and many complexities to disentangle regarding the problems that interfere with literacy learning of children and adults.

References

Anderson, R. C., Hiebert, E. H., Scott, J. A., & Wilkinson, I.A.G. (1985). *Becoming a nation of readers: The report of the commission on reading.* Washington, DC: National Institute of Education, U.S. Department of Education.

Auerbach, E. (1990). *Making meaning, making change: A guide to participatory curriculum development for adult ESL and family literacy.* Boston: University of Massachusetts. (ERIC Document Reproduction No. ED3 21 593).

Baratz, J. C. (1969). Teaching reading in an urban Negro school system. In J. C. Baratz & J. C. Shuy (Eds.), *Teaching Black Children to Read* (pp. 92–116). Washington, DC: Center for Applied Linguistics.

Bereiter, C., & Engelmann, S. (1966). *Teaching disadvantaged children in preschool.* Upper Saddle River, NJ: Prentice Hall.

Brizius, J. A., & Foster, S. A. (1993). Generation to generation: Realizing the promise of family literacy. Ypsilanti, MI: High/Scope Press.

Coles, R. (1985). The moral life of children. *Educational Leadership, 43*(4), 19–25.

Delgado-Gaitan, C. (1996). *Protean literacy: Extending the discourse of empowerment.* Bristol, PA: Falmer Press.

Deutsch, M. (1965). *The disadvantaged child.* New York: Basic Books.

Dickinson, D. K., & DeTemple, J. (1998). Putting parents in the picture: Maternal reports of preschool literacy as a prediction of early reading. *Early Childhood Research Quarterly, 13*(2), 241–261.

Dickinson, D., & Tabors, P. (1991). Early literacy: Linkages between home, school, and literacy achievement at age five. *Journal of Research in Childhood Education, 6,* 30–46.

Duran, R. P., Duran, J., Perry-Romero, D., & Sanchez, E. (2001). Latino immigrant parents and children learning and publishing together in an after school setting. *Journal of Education for Students Placed at Risk, 6*(1–2), 95–113.

Durkin, D. (1966). *Reading and the kindergarten: An annotated bibliography.* Newark, DE: International Reading Association.

Edwards, P. A. (1996). Creating sharing time conversations: Parents and teachers work together. *Language Arts, 73*(5), 344–349.

Gadsden, V. L. (1991). Trying one more time! Gaining access to literacy. In M. Foster (Ed.), *Readings in equal education.* Vol. 11: *Qualitative investigations into schools and schooling* (pp. 189–201). New York: AMS Press.

Gadsden, V. L. (1996). How do we account for racial, ethnic, religious, and other cultural differences when designing and conducting family literacy programs? In R. LeGrand (Ed.), *Family literacy: Directions in research and implications for practice.* Washington, DC: Office of Educational Research and Improvement, U.S. Department of Education.

Gadsden, V. L. (1998). Family culture and literacy learning. In F. Lehr, J. Osborn, & P. D. Pearson (Eds.), *Learning to read.* New York: Garland.

Gadsden, V. L. (2001). Family literacy and culture. In B. Wasik (Ed.), *Summary of research on Even Start.* Washington, DC: U.S. Department of Education.

Gadsden, V. L., Brooks, W., & Jackson, J. (1997, March). African American fathers, poverty, and learning: Issues in supporting children in and out of school. Paper presented at the annual meeting of the American Educational Research Association, Chicago.

Gadsden, V. L., Kane, D. C., & Armorer, K. R. (1996). *The Fathers and Families core learnings: An update from the field.* Philadelphia: National Center on Fathers and Families.

Goodman, K., & Buck, C. (1973). Dialect barriers to reading comprehension revisited. *Reading Teacher, 27,* 6–12.

Holt, D. D. (Ed.). (1994). *Assessing success in family literacy projects: Alternative approaches to assessment and evaluation.* McHenry, IL: Delta Systems.

Johnston, P. H. (1985). Understanding reading disability: A case study approach. *Harvard Educational Review, 55*(2), 153–177.

Jordan, G. E., Snow, C. E., & Porche, M. V. (2000). Project EASE: The effect of a family literacy project on kindergarten students' early literacy skills. *Reading Research Quarterly, 35,* 524–546.

Kaderavek, J. N., & Sulzby, E. (1999). *Issues in emergent literacy for children with language impairments.* Washington, DC: National Institute on Early Childhood Development and Education (ED/OERI).

Labov, W. A. (1965). Linguistic research on nonstandard English of Negro children. Paper presented to the New York Society for the Experimental Study of Education, New York.

Labov, W. (1972). Language in the inner city: Studies in the black English vernacular. Philadelphia, PA: University of Pennsylvania Press.

Mason, J. M., & Allen, J. (1986). A review of emergent literacy with implications for research and practice in reading (Technical Report No.
379, Center for the Study of Reading, Illinois U., Urbana, and Bolt,
Beranek and Newman, Cambridge, MA.) Washington, DC: National
Institute of Education.

McKee, P., & Rhett, N. (1995). Even Start family literacy. In L. M. Morrow
(Ed.), *Family literacy: Connections in schools and communities*
(pp. 155–166). Newark, DE: International Reading Association.

Morrow, L. M., Paratore, J. R., & Tracey, D. H. (1994). *Family literacy: New
perspectives, new opportunities.* Newark, DE: International Reading
Association.

National Commission on Excellence in Education. (1983). A *nation at
risk: The imperative for educational reform.* A report to the nation
and the Secretary of Education. Washington, DC: U.S. Department
of Education.

National Institute for Literacy. (1999). *Equipped for the future: A new
framework for adult learning.* Washington, DC: Author.

Paratore, J. R., Melzi, G., & Krol-Sinclair, B. (1999). What should we
expect of family literacy? Experiences of Latino children whose
parents participate in an intergenerational literacy project. Newark,
DE: International Reading Association.

Parecki, A. D., Paris, S. G., & Seidenberg, J. L. (1997). *Characteristics of
effective family literacy programs in Michigan.* Philadelphia: National
Center on Adult Literacy.

Purcell-Gates, V. (1993). Issues for family literacy research: Voices from
the trenches (focus on research). *Language Arts, 70*(8), 670–677.

Quintero, E., & Huerta-Macias, A. (1995). Bilingual children's writing:
Evidence of active learning in social context. *Journal of Research in
Childhood Education, 9,* 157–165.

Ruddell, R. B. (1965). The effect of oral and written patterns of language
structure on reading comprehension. *Reading Teacher, 18,* 270–275.

Shanahan, T., & Rodriguez-Brown, F. (1995). Project FLAME: Lessons
learned from a family literacy program for linguistic minority families. *Reading Teacher, 48,* 586–593.

Shockley, B., Michalove, B., & Allen, J. (1995). *Engaging families: Connecting
home and school literacy communities.* Portsmouth, NH: Heinemann.

Snow, C. E., & Strucker, J. (2000). Lessons from *Preventing Reading Difficulties in Young Children for Adult Learning and Literacy.* In *Annual review of adult learning and literacy* (Vol. 1, pp. 25–73). San Francisco:
Jossey-Bass.

St. Pierre, R. G., & Layzer, J. I. (1999). Using home visits for multiple purposes: The comprehensive child development program. *Future of Children, 9*(1), 134–151.

St. Pierre, R., & Swartz, J. (1995). The Even Start Family Literacy Program. In S. Smith (Ed.), *Two generation programs for families in poverty: A new intervention strategy. Advances in applied developmental psychology* (p. 9). Norwood, NJ: Ablex.

Street, B. (1992). *Cross-cultural approaches to literacy.* New York: Cambridge University Press.

Strickland, D. S. (1979). On reading (an ACEI position paper). *Childhood Education, 56*(2), 67–74.

Strickland, D. S., & Morrow, L. M. (1989). Oral language development: Children as storytellers (Emerging readers and writers). *Reading Teacher, 43*(3), 260–261.

Strickland, D., Morrow, L., Taylor, D., & Walls, L. (1990). Educating parents about their children's early literacy development (Emerging readers and writers). *Reading Teacher, 44,* 72–74.

Taylor, D. (1983). *Family literacy: Young children learning to read and write.* Portsmouth, NH: Heinemann.

Taylor, R. L. (1995). Functional uses of reading and shared literacy activities in Icelandic homes: A monograph in family literacy. *Reading Research Quarterly, 30,* 194–219.

Teale, W. H., & Sulzby, E. (Eds.). (1986). *Emergent literacy: Writing and reading.* Norwood, NJ: Ablex.

Wasik, B. (Ed.). (2001). *Summary of research on Even Start.* Washington, DC: U.S. Department of Education.

Weinstein, G. (1998, June). *Family and intergenerational literacy in multilingual communities.* Washington, DC: Office of Educational Research and Improvement, U.S. Department of Education.

Weinstein-Shr, G. (1991). Literacy and second language learners: A family agenda. Paper presented at the annual meeting of the American Educational Research Association, San Francisco, CA.

Whitehurst, G. J., Epstein, J. N., Angell, A. L., Payne, A. C., Crone, D. A., & Fischel, J. E. (1994). Outcomes of an emergent literacy intervention in Head Start. *Journal of Educational Psychology, 86,* 542–555.

Resources on
Family Literacy

Vivian L. Gadsden

～～～ T he resources listed here represent a small core of available materials on family literacy, intended to provide the reader with a short profile of the kinds of issues discussed in the field. The materials have been drawn primarily from research studies, reports and reviews of programs, and analyses of federally and state-funded programs and initiatives designed to enhance family literacy activities. These resources, however, do not constitute an exhaustive annotated bibliography. There are several other fine articles, reports, and books that would have been included if this were a comprehensive rather than a selected listing of materials on family literacy.

Resources that are cited were identified through the Education Resources Information Center (ERIC), the Psychological Literature database, the sociology database, and the social work resource database, using keywords such as *family literacy, family learning, parent-*

The author is grateful for assistance provided by Dana Jones-Robinson, Jeanine Staples (University of Pennsylvania), and Jennifer Turri Wofford (University of Pennsylvania).

child literacy, emergent reading, intergenerational literacy, adult literacy, and *family support.* A separate search of the literature on English for speakers of other languages (ESOL) *outside* family literacy was not conducted. Books were located by means of a Library of Congress search using the same keywords as those used to search the databases, and bibliographies in those books were reviewed to identify additional citations. Also consulted were materials from Even Start, Head Start, and the National Center for Family Literacy, as well as federally contracted studies written by a variety of researchers.

There are two other points of information that should guide the reader. First, the headings used to group materials reflect the existing and dominant areas in the field and were chosen by me based upon my review of bibliographies, reports, and discussions with specialists. A resource was assigned one heading versus another if its primary focus appeared to fall under that heading. However, some features of the resource may be equally appropriate for other headings and some may well have been placed under another heading (for example, parent-child interaction and emergent literacy) and cross-listed, had that format been used for this publication. Second, several terms related to family literacy are used throughout this annotated bibliography to refer to relevant concepts and programs. Distinctions between these terms are often minimal, but two bear clarification: *family literacy program* and *family literacy intervention.* A *family literacy program* as defined here is a program that has been designed and implemented to respond to identified reading, writing, and other literacy problems facing children, their parents, and other family members. Family literacy programs and related activities may be located in schools, community-based programs, and similar learning settings. They may be supported through state funding or may be part of national initiatives such as Even Start. *Family literacy interventions* are typically part of a research study designed to focus on a particular literacy issue or to determine whether specific approaches or frameworks result in change for program participants. Interventions are often intended to test a new strategy or approach to literacy instruction or program development.

OVERVIEWS AND SUMMARIES

The scope of family literacy research and practice is broad, and background issues in the field are often overlooked or superficially addressed in research and program reports. The selections in this section are intended to highlight many of the debates and resulting themes evident in discussions of family literacy over the past ten years that have led to the educational approaches now in use. The articles, reports, and reviews here will provide readers with a critical perspective on past and present tensions in the field.

Auerbach, E. (1995). Deconstructing the discourse of strengths in family literacy. *Journal of Reading Behavior, 27,* 643–661.

Focus: Program development

Recommended audience: Practitioners, program developers, researchers

Auerbach puts family literacy programs into three broad categories based on their theoretical underpinnings. The first category, intervention/prevention, draws from the theory that America's literacy problems are the result of "uneducated parents" who do not value literacy and do not promote it in interactions with their children at home. Programs based on this approach are geared toward changing parental beliefs about literacy and parents' interactions with their children regarding literacy activities. The second category, multiple literacies, is derived from the idea that the literacy problems of children and parents stem from a cultural "mismatch" between literacy practices at home and at school. The curricula in these programs draw from students' cultural experiences at home. The third category, social change, is based on the theory that the literacy problems of "marginalized" individuals are a by-product of social, political, and economic issues operating in the larger society. Programs developed from this perspective focus on helping students to change the forces that contribute to the marginalization of certain groups and to reduce their own marginalization.

Gadsden, V. L. (1994). Understanding family literacy: Conceptual issues facing the field. *Teachers College Record, 96,* 58–86.

Focus: Conceptual issues in the research and practice of family literacy

Recommended audience: Policymakers, practitioners, researchers

Although the relative absence of universally accepted theoretical frameworks in the field of family literacy makes it difficult to develop long-term agendas for change, it does give literacy educators the opportunity to participate in the construction of these frameworks. This article reviews the status of work in family literacy and suggests pathways that family literacy research and practice should take to build a framework and set of goals that link relevant areas of literacy education and family services. The author argues that because theory and practice in family literacy are relatively new, both existing and emerging assumptions as to what works and what does not must be tested as program developers determine programs' missions, implement curricula and instruction, and assess progress. Such assessment would involve the following: (1) exploring the idea of the family as the mediator of learning—as likely to support as to obstruct literacy development; (2) focusing on program goals in relationship to family expectations, that is, practitioners examining their goals for learners vis à vis learners' and families' goals; (3) understanding the family as a developing and changing unit, changing as individual family members develop and as they come to (re)shape family practices; (4) utilizing knowledge about the cultural and social practices within families and determining how such knowledge can be applied to curricula, instructional content, and classroom interactions; and (5) finding a midpoint between the perspective that casts learners as lacking in literacy and creating obstacles to children's school success and the perspective that casts them as possessing literacy knowledge that can serve as a basis for teaching. The article draws from research in family literacy, literacy, and family studies and provides recommendations for research, practice, and policy.

Hendrix, S. (2000). Family literacy education: Panacea or false promise? *Journal of Adolescent and Adult Literacy, 43*, 338–346.

Focus: Program development

Recommended audience: Practitioners, program developers, researchers

The author offers a critique of family literacy programs on four fronts, starting with the compensatory program model, which is described as an effort "to make up" for some lack of knowledge in the family. This model assumes that family literacy programs help children and parents overcome their limited, or inadequate, literacy and does not seek to understand the literacy knowledge that the family does possess and on which programs can build. Next is the one-child/one-parent model, in which one parent and one child, usually a preschooler, are the focus and older children and other family members who contribute to the child's literacy development are largely excluded from the learning process. Another area of discussion concerns the difficulty of integrating different areas of literacy (such as adult literacy and ESOL) into a coherent framework for family literacy programming. The fourth area of discussion concerns the instability of funding for family literacy programs and the ways in which this prohibits the future growth of the field. Hendrix asserts that the instability of funding is due in large part to the "adjunct" status of family literacy programs as compared with K–12 and adult literacy initiatives.

Morrow, L. M., Tracey, D. H., & Maxwell, C. M. (Eds.). (1995). *A survey of family literacy in the United States.* Newark, DE: International Reading Association.

Focus: Historical overview of family literacy

Recommended audience: Practitioners, researchers

In addition to tracing the historical development of family literacy, the authors provide an overview of the field in the United States. More than one hundred sources on family literacy are discussed, with information provided on particular existing family literacy programs as well as new initiatives. Sections include "Intergenerational Programs," "Research on Naturally Occurring Literacy in Families," and "Agencies and Associations that Deal with Family Literacy."

National Center for Family Literacy. (1993). *The future of family literacy.* Louisville, KY: Author.

Focus: Conceptual overview

Recommended audience: Policymakers, program directors

This book traces the history of family literacy as a concept, as a beginning program, and as a public policy movement. The authors show state policymakers and program managers how to anticipate and grapple with issues surrounding family literacy. They suggest how individuals can begin new family literacy programs tailored to their communities.

Wasik, B. (Ed.). (2001). *Summary of research on Even Start.* Washington, DC: U.S. Department of Education.

Focus: Summary of issues in family literacy programming

Recommended audience: Practitioners, researchers

This report was prepared to examine and synthesize research pertaining to family literacy programs, particularly those supported by Even Start initiatives. Ten chapters are included in the book, the first of which provides an overview of family literacy programs. Subsequent chapters focus on program content (for example, emergent literacy culture and family literacy, English as a second language), programmatic issues (for example, the role of family literacy programs in service integration and local and state evaluation efforts), and recommendations for program improvement and future research.

PARENT-CHILD LITERACY

Work on parent-child literacy has for more than a decade aimed to uncover the specific interactions that parents and children experience as children learn to read, write, and develop other types of literacy. Federally funded centers such as the Center for the Improvement of Early Reading and Achievement at the University of Michigan reinforce the significance of early readiness and the role of parents and other family members in the development of literacy in children. The resources in this section concern the effect of home practices on children's reading, ways to help young parents participate in the selection and use of children's literature to teach their children to read, and activities that program developers might use to engage parents and children in reading and other literacy activities. These selections reflect the diversity of issues in early and emergent literacy and parent-child interaction, from implementation of programs to research findings.

Journal Articles

Baker, L., Scher, D., & Mackler, K. (1997). Home and family influences on motivations for reading. *Educational Psychologist, 32,* 69–82.

Focus: Influences of home environment on children's literacy

Recommended audience: Parents, practitioners, researchers

The authors review the growing literature on home and family influences on children's motivation to read. Topics covered include the nature of children's early encounters with literacy, their self-initiated interactions with print at home, shared storybook reading, and parental attitudes toward reading.

Doneson, S. G. (1991). Reading as a second chance: Teen mothers and children's books. *Journal of Reading, 35,* 220–223.

Focus: Use of reading materials relative to teen mothers' life situations

Recommended audience: Practitioners, program directors

Doneson describes a literacy program for pregnant and parenting high school students. The program's goals were to encourage reading by providing teens with books and magazines on parenting as well as with books they could read to their children. The program also provided the teens with an outlet for discussion of their personal issues and problems. By the end of the program, the class had formed a cohesive unit in which students could discuss both parenting and personal issues.

Primavera, J. (2000). Enhancing family competence through literacy activities. *Journal of Prevention and Intervention in the Community, 20,* 85–101.

Focus: Program efficacy

Recommended audience: Practitioners, program developers, program directors, researchers

Primavera reports on the positive benefits for parents and their young children of parental participation in family literacy activities. The participants were one hundred parent attendees at several family literacy workshops designed to teach them literacy skills to improve their children's school readiness and emergent literacy skills. The positive outcomes for children included increased reading time spent with parents, improved language skills, increased interest in books, and increased enjoyment in reading. Benefits for parents included increased self-esteem, confidence, literacy competence, parental efficacy, and interest in their own education as well as a better understanding of the important role parents play in their children's education.

Books and Parts of Books

National Center for Family Literacy. (1996). *Frontiers in family learning: A showcase of exemplary family literacy programs.* Louisville, KY: Author.

Focus: Successful family literacy programs

Recommended audience: Practitioners, program developers, program directors

This report identifies four programs nationally recognized as leaders in family literacy by the National Diffusion Network, an agency within the U.S. Department of Education: (1) Literacy Volunteers of America—Chippewa Valley, Eau Claire, Wisconsin; (2) Even Start Project, Manhattan/Ogden and Junction City/Fort Riley, Kansas; (3) Webster Groves Even Start, Rock Hill, Missouri; and (4) Family Intergenerational Literacy Model (FILM), Oklahoma City, Oklahoma. The report discusses the funding, organization, and activities of the programs, and is divided into eight sections: (1) introduction to family literacy; (2) two routes to program validation; (3) program profiles; (4) essential components of family literacy; (5) community involvement; (6) special features of the programs; (7) meeting learners' needs; and (8) resources for family literacy.

Rodriguez-Brown, F. V., & Meehan, M. A. (1998). Family literacy and adult education: Project FLAME. In M. C. Smith (Ed.), *Literacy for the twenty-first century: Research, policy, practices, and the National Adult Literacy Survey.* Westport, CT: Praeger.

Focus: Adult literacy and its relationship to family literacy

Recommended audience: Practitioners, policymakers, researchers

In this chapter, the authors argue that family literacy is a component of parent involvement in which parents model problem solving for their children and establish literacy practices in the family. They examine parental involvement and family literacy by focusing on Hispanic communities and the ways that the cultural history and background of family literacy participants should be allowed to shape the nature and content of instruction, curricula, and classroom interactions between practitioners and learners.

INTERGENERATIONAL LITERACY

Intergenerational literacy research and practice focus on the ways in which parents and other adult family members influence children's literacy development and the ways in which children assist their parents in learning to read. The studies and reports included here focus on programs designed for two or more generations within a family, adult literacy programs that focus on families, and research that has implications for developing approaches that increase the strength of knowledge transfer from one generation to another.

Journal Articles

Baker, A.J.L., Piotrkowski, C. S., & Brooks-Gunn, J. (1998). The effects of the Home Instruction Program for Preschool Youngsters (HIPPY) on children's school performance at the end of the program and one year later. *Early Childhood Research Quarterly, 13,* 571–588.

Focus: Efficacy of the HIPPY program

Recommended audience: Practitioners and program directors, especially those who use the HIPPY program

The Home Instruction Program for Preschool Youngsters is a two-year home-based early childhood education intervention program intended to help parents with limited formal education prepare their children for school. The participants in this longitudinal study, which is part of a larger evaluation study of the program, were 182 low-income families (84 in the intervention, 98 in the control group). There were two cohorts of pre-kindergartners: one entering the program in winter 1990 and the other entering in fall 1991. The outcomes assessed were children's cognitive skills, adaptation to the classroom, and standardized achievement at the end of the first year (kindergarten) and during first grade. The findings showed that there were significant differences between the HIPPY participants and the control group children (for example, children in the HIPPY program had higher scores on the cognitive measure; at the one-year follow-up, children in the HIPPY program had higher standardized reading scores) at both assessment times. However, the positive results for children in Cohort 1 were not found for children in Cohort 2 who were exposed to the same program. The authors are cautious about the reasons that children in Cohort 2 did not have the same positive results as those in Cohort 1 but suggest that outside of program features, we should examine the nature of parental involvement and the way parents are prepared to participate in such programs.

Goldsmith, E. (1995). Deepening the conversations. *Journal of Adolescent and Adult Literacy, 38*(7), 558–563.

Focus: Program development

Recommended audience: Practitioners, program developers, researchers

Goldsmith discusses how children's literature can be used in family literacy programs to help adults reflect on their educational experiences and relationships with their children and to stimulate discussion between parents and teachers. The author draws from her experiences conducting workshops with participants in the Parent Readers Program (New York City) as well as her work with day care and Head Start teachers from Reading Starts with Us (NYC) and with adult literacy teachers and students from across the United States. She uses two children's books to frame her discussion.

Hill, M. H. (1998). Teen fathers learn the power of literacy for their children. *Journal of Adolescent and Adult Literacy, 42*, 196–202.

Focus: The significance of literacy for adolescent fathers and their children

Recommended audience: Practitioners, program developers, program directors, researchers

This article describes a case study of a practitioner in a juvenile residential facility who worked to engage young fathers in a literacy classroom of peers, using literature from a range of genres. The author argues the importance of stimulating an interest in reading and literature in young fathers if they are to identify with being readers, writers, and storytellers and to pass along literacy to their children. The article describes three themes of the program discussion and readings—the bully (meanness); embarrassing moments; and anxiety, competition, and fear—each taken from the participants' experiences as boys, each covered in relevant literature, and each having relevance to the messages of survival and caring that the young fathers convey when reading to their children and encouraging their children to read.

Moulton, M., & Holmes, V. L. (1995). An adult learns to read: A family affair. *Journal of Adolescent and Adult Literacy, 38*, 542–549.

Focus: Family involvement and the development of adult literacy

Recommended audience: Practitioners, researchers

The authors use a case study approach to explore the influence of a family's literacy interactions on all family members. The focus is Len, a forty-seven-year-old father and grandfather who is learning to read. After he invited his family to participate in his reading activities, his reading improved and the frequency and nature of the family's interactions changed: some family members cut out relevant newspaper articles; Len participated more actively in oral reading during the family's religious evenings; Len's expectations for his son's reading increased; and Len and his children helped each other with their homework. The authors remind family literacy specialists that family literacy both strengthens and challenges relationships in families. For example, despite the success that Len experienced, the changes in Len's literacy and motivations to read affected the family, with the family sometimes interfering with and other times facilitating the process.

Quintero, E., & Cristina-Velarde, M. (1990). Intergenerational literacy: A developmental, bilingual approach. *Young Children, 45*, 10–15.

Focus: Program development

Recommended audience: Practitioners, program developers, researchers

This study describes the development and implementation of the El Paso Community College's Intergenerational Literacy Project. The project brings Spanish-speaking parents and their children together in the classroom in an effort to improve the two groups' literacy skills in both English and Spanish. The authors describe the curriculum as well as the nature of teacher and parent involvement, the questions they posed, and the knowledge they brought to the program. The results of the study suggest that the parents' English reading level increased and that their attitudes and behaviors toward assisting their children with reading improved after participating in the program.

Reutzel, D., & Fawson, P. (1990). "Traveling Tales": Connecting parents and children through writing. *Reading Teacher, 44*, 222–227.

Focus: Program development for parents and children

Recommended audience: Practitioners, program developers, researchers

The authors report on a program they created in which children bring home a "Traveling Tales" backpack filled with materials for the children to use while writing stories at home with their parents. A list of basic guidelines for parents is included in the backpack to help children to generate story ideas and drafts. Parents are telephoned before children take the backpacks home, and there is a resident "grandmother" in the class who works with those children whose parents do not want to participate. The authors found that the program elicited involvement not only from parents but also from children's siblings and neighbors.

Smith, S. (1991). Two-generation program models: A new intervention strategy. *Social Policy Report: Society for Research in Child Development, 5,* 1–15.

Focus: Effects of five intervention models on welfare-dependent women with young children

Recommended audience: Policymakers, practitioners, program developers, researchers

The author describes five programs intended to help welfare-dependent women with young children attain economic self-sufficiency through education and job training while also providing services that foster the healthy development of their children, such as parenting education and high-quality childcare. Two of the models were linked with the Job Opportunities and Basic Skills program, one with the Comprehensive Child Development Program, one with New Chance, and one with Even Start. Related research efforts assessed the effects of participation on parent employment and child development. The author makes recommendations on how to evaluate the effectiveness of two-generation interventions based on systematic variation of family types, interdisciplinary collaboration, assessment of component services, and federal provision of policy guidance, standards, and resources.

Wagner, M., & Clayton, S. (1999). The Parents as Teachers program: Results from two demonstrations. *Future of Children, 9,* 91–115.

Focus: Description and evaluation of the Parents as Teachers program

Recommended audience: Practitioners, program developers, researchers

The authors describe Parents as Teachers (PAT), a parent education program that includes home visits from PAT-trained parenting and literacy practitioners. The authors report the results of an evaluation of two demonstration projects, one with a largely adult, Latino population and a second with teen mothers with two randomized trials of PAT participants. Results from the study suggest that home visits produced about a one-month developmental advantage per ten visits for participating children.

Books and Parts of Books

Gadsden, V. L. (2000). Intergenerational literacy within families. In M. L. Kamil, P. B. Mosenthal, P. D. Pearson, & R. Barr (Eds.), *Handbook of reading research* (Vol. 4, pp. 871–887). Mahwah, NJ: Erlbaum.

Focus: Theories of intergenerational learning

Recommended audience: Researchers, practitioners

The author uses an interdisciplinary approach to explore conceptual and theoretical issues in intergenerational literacy, including (1) the degree to which reading research deepens our understanding of the social, cultural, and gender factors that influence literacy within and across different generations; (2) the extent to which reading research utilizes interdisciplinary knowledge about intergenerational learning within families; and (3) the ways in which reading research can advance the construction of integrative frameworks that capture the nature and mode of transmission of literacy in diverse populations. Although the focus of this chapter is on families, the author works from the assumption that intergenerational literacy is not exclusive to families but may involve a variety of individuals other than biological family members and a variety of contexts other than the family or home.

Neuman, S. B. (2000). Social contexts for literacy development: A family literacy program. In K. A. Roskos & J. F. Christie (Eds.), *Play and literacy in early childhood: Research from multiple perspectives* (pp. 153–168). Mahwah, NJ: Erlbaum.

Focus: Practices of adult and family literacy programs

Recommended audience: Practitioners, program developers, program directors

The author describes an intervention program designed to improve guided participation and coaching among adolescent, urban, low-income mothers and their children. The thirty mothers were participants in an adult basic education and graduate equivalency program that offered day care for their children. The program focused on four basic components: (1) getting set, in which caregivers adjust their level of involvement to the level of perceived competence of the child; (2) giving meaning, in which caregivers share with children the importance of the literacy activities and interaction; (3) building bridges through real and imaginary play; and (4) stepping back, in which the parent or other adult teacher provides encouragement while allowing the child to demonstrate mastery of the recently learned materials. Data on mothers' ability to engage children throughout the four components were collected and analyzed. Findings demonstrate the significance of interpersonal communication and instructional setting in engaging young children and helping them transfer knowledge from one point in time to another.

Papers and Reports

Connors-Tadros, L. (1995, October). *Participation in adult education and its effects on home literacy.* [Report No. 32]. Baltimore: Center on Families, Communities, Schools, and Children's Learning, Johns Hopkins University.

Focus: Adult literacy education

Recommended audience: Practitioners, program developers and directors, researchers

The author describes parent participation in and completion of adult basic education courses and the importance of determining the impact of such participation on selected indicators of home support for children's learning. For this purpose, the researcher completed multiple analyses on data from a subsample of 815 families surveyed in the 1991 National Household Education Survey. The findings showed that parents participate in adult education programs primarily for job-related skill improvement (for their current job or future jobs). Other predictors included prior education, minority status, and experiences related to their children's childcare. Children's daily television viewing was also predicted by parents' participation in adult education.

Matthias, M., & Gulley, B. (Eds.). (1995). *Celebrating family literacy through intergenerational programming.* Wheaton, MD: Association for Childhood Education International.

Focus: How to facilitate improvement in intergenerational literacy

Recommended audience: Practitioners, program developers, program directors

The authors examine ways in which parents can increase their involvement in their children's literacy development, focusing on the parental role as a child's first teacher. The paper is divided into four parts. Part 1 gives background information on intergenerational family literacy programs, Part 2 describes three family literacy programs that emphasize parents' and children's interactions around literacy, Part 3 explores family literacy in multicultural communities, and Part 4 focuses on methods practitioners can use to encourage parent-child interactions around literacy.

ESOL AND LANGUAGE DIFFERENCES

Issues related to language and linguistic differences, particularly English for speakers of other languages (ESOL), are slowly being integrated into family literacy discussions. However, to date, there are relatively few written analyses and even fewer empirical studies in this area. The articles and reports in this section represent a small collection of curricular resources and empirical and evaluation research. They focus both on the social and cognitive processes of family literacy and on the importance of these processes in developing and providing instructional support for learners representing diverse non-English language histories and linguistic experiences.

Journal Article

Shanahan, T., Mulhern, M., & Rodriguez-Brown, F. (1995). Project FLAME: Lessons learned from a family literacy program for linguistic minority families. *Reading Teacher, 48,* 586–593.

Focus: Multilingual program development

Recommended audience: Practitioners, program developers, researchers

Project FLAME is a Chicago-based family literacy program designed to provide simultaneous education for Latino parents and their children. The authors describe how the "parents as teachers" and ESOL components of the program are connected, how to construct a family literacy curriculum, what language should be used for literacy instruction, and what happens in the community when the program ends. Although the study was reported prior to the end of the program, data from the program showed that parents, after two years of participation, were taking part in parent-school organizations and activities. The parents reported reading stories to their children, and many came to lead Parents as Teachers seminars in local schools. The authors suggest that family literacy programs can be carried out at lower cost when parents are prepared to become trainers. In this way, they ensure the stability of the program while increasing the self-sufficiency of their families and communities.

Papers and Reports

Nash, A., Caston, A., Rhum, M., McGrail, L., & Gomez-Sanford, R. (1992). *Talking shop: A curriculum sourcebook for participatory adult ESL.* Washington, DC: Center for Applied Linguistics

Focus: Curriculum for participatory ESOL programs.

Recommended audience: ESOL practitioners and program directors; family literacy programs that operate in a bilingual or multilingual environment.

This is a collection of narratives by five teachers who worked in community-based adult education programs in the Boston area. The curriculum for the programs was based on a participatory approach that stressed the daily concerns and learning needs of the students. Topics covered include immigrant experiences, mother-child relationships in terms of ESOL curriculum and parental involvement in children's learning, and pedagogical techniques and approaches to literacy.

Weinstein, G. (1998, June). *Family and intergenerational literacy in multilingual communities.* Washington, DC: National Center for ESL Literacy Education.

Focus: Family literacy models and approaches

Recommended audience: Practitioners, program developers, program directors, researchers

Weinstein reviews selected research in the field of family and intergenerational literacy, beginning with the early findings of emergent literacy research that led to the creation of many family literacy programs (for example, that parents' literacy skills and practices influence their children's performance in school) and concluding with language and literacy research with nonnative speakers of English. The author also includes brief discussions of policy initiatives that have had an effect on the field, family literacy program models, and curriculum approaches. Weinstein offers several suggestions for future work in the area of family and intergenerational literacy research for nonnative speakers of English.

ASSESSMENT AND EVALUATION

Much of the work in family literacy has focused on curriculum and instruction, with relatively less attention to assessment and evaluation. The selections here focus on approaches to assessment and the content of measures to assess learning in family literacy programs. Because as yet, little has been written about family literacy assessment, these selections omit an issue that has received considerable attention in K–12 education: linking curricular content to appropriate assessment.

Books and Parts of Books

Holt, D. D. (Ed.). (1994). *Assessing success in family literacy projects: Alternative approaches to assessment and evaluation.* McHenry, IL: Delta Systems.

Focus: Program assessment and evaluation

Recommended audience: Practitioners and researchers

Holt discusses alternatives to traditional methods of evaluating family literacy programs. The author clarifies the difference between standardized and alternative assessments and highlights special considerations for the evaluation of family literacy projects. Each of the five chapters covers a different aspect of assessment and evaluation to help program personnel design and implement appropriate alternative approaches to assessment.

Ryan, K., Geissler, B., & Knell, S. (1994). Evaluating family literacy programs: Tales from the field. In D. K. Dickinson (Ed.), *Bridges to literacy: Children, families, and schools* (pp. 236–264). Cambridge, MA: Blackwell.

Focus: Program assessment and evaluation

Recommended audience: Practitioners, program developers, researchers

The authors discuss an ongoing assessment of family literacy programs in Illinois, using a five-tiered approach to program evaluation and case studies to illustrate how evaluation can occur at each of these tiers. They suggest that programs should base their evaluations on the literacy and learning needs identified by both parents and service providers. The authors note the recurrent finding that men's viewpoints are grossly underrepresented in most evaluations of literacy programs, even when they are active participants, and that male participation in adult literacy programs is extremely low.

Paper

Debruin-Parecki, A. (1998). The identification of effective practices and the development of authentic assessments for family literacy programs. Doctoral dissertation, University of Michigan. *Dissertation Abstracts International, 58,* 10-A.

Focus: Program assessment

Recommended audience: Researchers, practitioners

The research for this dissertation was conducted at a family literacy program site in Michigan. Two studies were conducted. In the first, the Adult/Child Interactive Reading Inventory was used to evaluate parent-child interaction during storybook reading. In the second, a family portfolio assessment system was used to evaluate aspects of the program that might not be captured by standardized tests.

CULTURE AND CONTEXT

Until recently, writings in family literacy rarely accounted for the significance of culture and race in family literacy other than by making reference to the ethnic background of learners. As the terms are used here, *culture* refers to the traditions, beliefs, and practices that groups develop over time, and *context* refers to the settings in which people live and learn—settings that represent the individual and combined influences of people's ethnicity, culture, and race as well as the value they assign to them. Family literacy programs are populated disproportionately by low-income, ethnic minority, or immigrant children and families. The selections here represent a few of the writings to have emerged over the past few years.

Journal Articles

Elish-Piper, L. (1997). Literacy and their lives: Four low-income families enrolled in a summer family literacy program. *Journal of Adolescent and Adult Literacy, 40,* 256–268.

Focus: Case studies demonstrating the effects of an intensive enrichment program

Recommended audience: Practitioners, program developers, researchers

This article reports the activities of four families participating in a summer family literacy program. The author details the families' uses for and degrees of literacy, which "is viewed as a social and cultural phenomenon that develops and is practiced in the context of social interactions for social purposes" (p. 257). Program activities included weekly sessions with families and the "exploration of literacy through environmental print materials including newspapers, coupons, telephone books, and television guides" (p. 258). The author found that the participating families used literacy for meaningful purposes and that the social-contextual factors of the families "greatly influenced how and why they used literacy in their lives" (p. 264). The author recommends that such programs be expanded to cover the academic school year.

Tippeconnic, J. W., III, & Jones, P. (1995). A description of Family and Child Education (FACE): A comprehensive approach to family literacy. *Journal of American Indian Education, 35,* 6–9.

Focus: Culture-specific program development

Recommended audience: Practitioners, researchers, program developers

Family and Child Education (FACE) is a program specially designed to help American Indian parents and their children. Supported by the U.S. Bureau of Indian Affairs, the program provides home-based or center-based early childhood education for infants and children up to the age of five. The program teaches parents about child development and shows them how to promote active learning in their children. Additionally, it addresses parents' educational needs. In 1994–95, twenty-two FACE programs served 951 families.

Books and Parts of Books

Gadsden, V. L. (2001). Family literacy and culture. In B. Wasik (Ed.), *Synthesis of research on family literacy programs.* Washington, DC: U.S. Department of Education.

Focus: Culture and race

Recommended audience: Policymakers, practitioners, program developers, researchers

In this chapter, the author focuses on family literacy and culture as a way to understand, study, and work with diverse families. The chapter includes sections on historical contexts of reading that led to greater attention to the diversity, culture, and families of students and on definitions of culture and race and their relationship to family literacy. The author highlights programmatic approaches to instruction and curricular development, drawing on case studies with two Even Start literacy programs located in the Midwest and the South.

Weinstein-Shr, G., & Quintero, E. (Eds.). (1995). *Immigrant learners and their families.* McHenry, IL: Center for Applied Linguistics and Delta Systems Co.

Focus: Cultural differences in the nature of intergenerational learning and literacy

Recommended audience: Practitioners, program developers, researchers

This resource is a collection of teachers' and developers' descriptions of intergenerational literacy programs for immigrants. Intergenerational learning is strongly emphasized. The topics addressed include student journals, traditional and personal storytelling as an approach to developing literacy, improving educational options, and the experiences of learners who are refugees.

Name Index

⟞⟍⟍⟋⟍⟋ Subject Index